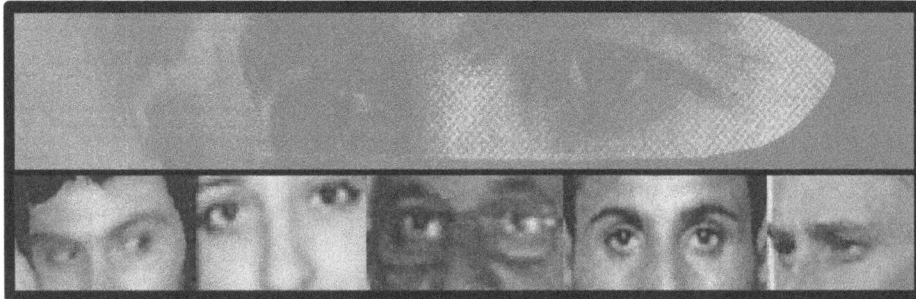

A Military Guide

to

Terrorism

in the Twenty-First Century

US Army Training and Doctrine Command
TRADOC G2
TRADOC Intelligence Support Activity (TRISA) – Threats

15 August 2007

Published by Books Express Publishing
Copyright © Books Express, 2011
ISBN 978-1-780390-41-3

Books Express publications are available from all good retail and online booksellers. For
publishing proposals and direct ordering please contact us at: info@books-express.com

Summary of Change

U.S. Army TRADOC G2 Handbook No. 1 (Version 5.0)
A Military Guide to Terrorism in the Twenty-First Century

Specifically, this handbook dated 15 August 2007

- Provides an information update since the DCSINT Handbook No. 1, *A Military Guide to Terrorism in the Twenty-First Century,* publication dated 10 August 2006 (Version 4.0).

- References the U.S. Department of State, Office of the Coordinator for Counterterrorism, *Country Reports on Terrorism 2006* dated April 2007.

- References the National Counterterrorism Center (NCTC), *Reports on Terrorist Incidents - 2006,* dated 30 April 2007.

- Deletes Appendix A, *Terrorist Threat to Combatant Commands.* By country assessments are available in U.S. Department of State, Office of the Coordinator for Counterterrorism, *Country Reports on Terrorism 2006* dated April 2007.

- Deletes Appendix C, *Terrorist Operations and Tactics.* These topics are covered in chapter 4 of the 2007 handbook. Emerging patterns and trends are addressed in chapter 5 of the 2007 handbook.

- Deletes Appendix F, *Weapons of Mass Destruction.* See TRADOC G2 Handbook No.1.04.

- Refers to updated 2007 Supplemental TRADOC G2 Handbook No.1.01, *Terror Operations: Case Studies in Terror,* dated 25 July 2007.

- Refers to Supplemental DCSINT Handbook No. 1.02, *Critical Infrastructure Threats and Terrorism,* dated 10 August 2006.

- Refers to Supplemental DCSINT Handbook No. 1.03, *Suicide Bombing in the COE,* dated 10 August 2006.

- Refers to new 2007 Supplemental TRADOC G2 Handbook No. 1.04, *Terrorism and WMD in the Contemporary Operational Environment*, dated 20 August 2007.

- Refers to For Official Use Only (FOUO) Supplemental DCSINT Handbook No. 1.05, *A Military Primer to Terrorism in the Contemporary Operational Environment*, dated 10 August 2006.

- This 2007 Version 5.0 supersedes DCSINT G2 Handbook No. 1, *A Military Guide to Terrorism in the Twenty-First Century,* publication dated 10 August 2006 (Version 4.0).

Contents

Preface... v

Introduction.. 1

   The Problem.. 2

   Purpose.. 4

   Scope of the Issue 6

   WOT and the Contemporary Operational Environment.. 8

   Targeting Vulnerabilities 8

   Approach to Understanding Terrorism 10

   Conclusion 12

Chapter 1 The Face of Terrroism Today 1-1

   Section I: What is Terrorism... 1-2

      Defining Terrorism 1-2

      Vectors of Action... 1-3

   Section II: Objectives... 1-4

   Section III: Terrorism and Insurgency 1-5

   Section IV: State Sponsored Terror 1-9

   Section V: Other Forms of Terrorism... 1-11

   Conclusion 1-12

Chapter 2 Terrorist Motivations and Behaviors... 2-1

   Section I: Goals.. 2-2

      Operational Intent of Terrorism 2-4

   Section II: Motivation... 2-5

      Ideology Influences.. 2-6

      Ideological Categories 2-7

      Location or Geographic Categories 2-9

   Section III: Behavior... 2-11

      Individual Behaviors.. 2-11

      Organizational Behavior 2-14

   Conclusion 2-16

Chapter 3 Terrorist Organizational Models 3-1

   Section I: Organizational Commitment 3-3

      Levels of Commitment 3-3

Section II: Organizational Structure 3-5
  Cellular Foundation 3-5
  Hierarchical Structure 3-6
  Networked Structure 3-7
  Types of Structure... 3-8
  Ideological Affiliation... 3-9

Section III: Organizational Categories.. 3-9
  Terrorist Affiliation... 3-9
  Support... 3-11
  Weapons and Equipment 3-13

Conclusion 3-14

Chapter 4 Terrorist Targeting of U.S. Military Forces............................... 4-1

Section I: Operational Environments and U.S. Military Forces 4-2
  Deployed Forces 4-3
  In-Transit Forces.. 4-3
  Institutional Forces.. 4-3

Section II: Circumstances and Influences.. 4-3
  Reasons for Targeting 4-4

Section III: Terrorist Attack Threats to U.S. Forces 4-13
  General.. 4-13
  Contemporary Setting 4-13

Forms of Terrorism 4-14
  Arson... 4-15
  Sabotage.. 4-15
  Bombing.. 4-16
  Kidnapping.. 4-18
  Hostage Taking 4-20
  Hijack-Seizure.. 4-21
  Raid or Ambush 4-22
  Assassination.. 4-23

Aircraft Threats.. 4-25

Maritime Threats.. 4-27

Suicide Tactics 4-28

Conclusion 4-30

Chapter 5 Terrorism of the Foreseebale Future... 5-1

Section I: Future Trends in Terrorism 5-2

Section II: Assessing the Trends.. 5-3

Section III: Enablers to Terror 5-17

Conclusion 5-21

Appendix A Terrorist Planning Cycle A-1

    Phase I: Broad Target Selection A-2

    Phase II: Intelligence Gathering and Surveillance A-2

    Phase III: Specific Target Selection A-3

    Phase IV: Pre-attack Surveillance and Planning A-4

    Phase V: Rehearsals A-4

    Phase VI: Actions on the Objective A-5

    Phase VII: Escape and Exploitation A-5

Appendix B Firearms B-1

    General B-1

    Handguns B-2

    Submachine Guns B-6

    Assault Rifles B-9

    Sniper Rifles B-12

    Shotguns B-15

Appendix C Conventional Military Munitions C-1

    General C-1

    Fragmentation Grenades C-1

    Rocket Propelled Grenade C-3

    Air Defense Weapons C-4

    Bombs and Artillery C-5

    Mines C-8

Glossary Glossary-1

Selected Bibliography Bibliography-1

This Page Intentionally Blank

Preface

A Military Guide to Terrorism in the Twenty-First Century is a reference guide prepared under the direction of the U.S. Army Training and Doctrine Command (TRADOC), TRADOC G2 as a capstone reference guide on terrorism. TRADOC G2 Handbook No. 1, *A Military Guide to Terrorism in the Twenty-First Century* is prepared by the TRADOC Intelligence Support Activity (TRISA)-Threats. Understanding terrorism spans foreign and domestic threats of nation-states, rogue states with international or transnational agents, and other actors with specific strategies, tactics, and targets. This terrorism guide addresses foreign and domestic threats against the United States of America in a contemporary operational environment (COE).

Purpose. This informational handbook supports institutional training, professional military education, and operational missions for U.S. military forces in the War on Terrorism (WOT). This document provides an introduction to the nature of terrorism and recognition of terrorist threats to U.S. military forces. A common situational awareness by U.S. military forces considers three principal venues for armed forces: forces that are deployed, forces that are in transit to or from an operational mission, and forces that are primarily installation or institution support. Compiled from open source materials, this handbook promotes a "Threats" perspective and enemy situational awareness of U.S. strategies and operations in combating terrorism. Neither a counterterrorism directive nor antiterrorism manual, this handbook complements but does not replace Army training and intelligence products on terrorism.

Intended Audience. This handbook exists primarily for U.S. military forces; however, other applicable groups include interdepartmental, interagency, intergovernmental, civilian contractor, nongovernmental, private volunteer, and humanitarian relief organizations, and the general citizenry.

Handbook Use. Study of contemporary terrorist motivations and behavior, terrorist goals and objectives, and knowledge of terrorist tactics, techniques, and procedures (TTP) improve training and readiness of U.S. military forces. This handbook will be updated as necessary to enhance a current and relevant resource. A selected bibliography presents citations for detailed study of specific terrorism topics. Unless stated otherwise, masculine nouns or pronouns do not refer exclusively to men.

Proponent Statement. Headquarters, U.S. Army Training and Doctrine Command (TRADOC) is the proponent for this publication. Periodic updates will accommodate emergent user requirements on terrorism. Send comments and recommendations on DA Form 2028 directly to Director, U.S. Army TRADOC Intelligence Support Activity (TRISA)-Threats, ATTN: ATIN-T, Threats Terrorism Team, Bldg 53, 700 Scott Avenue, Fort Leavenworth, Kansas 66027-1323.

This handbook is available at https://dcsint-threats.leavenworth.army.mil. and requires an Army Knowledge Online (AKO) login for access.

This Page Intentionally Blank

Introduction

Introduction

Violent extremist networks and ideologies will continue to be a threat to the United States and our allies for many years. The ambition of these networks to acquire chemical, biological, and nuclear weapons is real, as is their desire to launch more attacks on our country and on our interests around the world.

**Honorable Robert Gates
U.S. Secretary of Defense
May 2007**

A Military Guide to Terrorism in the Twenty-First Century is a capstone reference guide that describes terrorism[1] and highlights the nature of terrorism present in a full spectrum contemporary operational environment (COE),[2] and the likely impacts on U.S. military operations.

Figure 1. **Vectors of Domestic and Foreign Terrorism**

Despite the consistent menace of terrorism, threats can be misunderstood and frequently confused due to widely divergent views on how to define terrorism. Terrorism as discussed in this handbook centers on known principal terrorist "Threats" to the United States of America. The United States confronts terrorism in daily circumstances, both foreign and domestic, and adapts the security environment and force protection against

---

[1] Joint Publication 1-02. *Department of Defense Dictionary of Military Terms and Associated Terms,* 12 April 2001, as amended through 13 June 2007. See also, U.S. Army Training and Doctrine Command, TRADOC G2, TRADOC Intelligence Support Activity (TRISA) White Paper, *The Contemporary Operational Environment*, July 2007.
[2] U.S. Army Field Manual FM 7-100, *Opposing Force Doctrinal Framework and Strategy,* May 2003, iv to xvi.

terrorism. The most significant U.S. concerns are terrorist organizations with demonstrated global reach capabilities and those terrorist organizations that seek to acquire and use weapons of mass destruction (WMD).

The Problem

What is the "Threat" of terrorism? How does terrorism impact on U.S. military forces in the conduct of operations and institutional support? What measures exist to minimize terrorist action in the contemporary operational environment?

The threat of terrorism to the U.S. is present across the entire spectrum of conflict. The use of terrorism ranges from individual acts of wanton damage or destruction to property or person, to highly sophisticated operations conducted by organized extremist groups with social, environmental, religious, economic, or political agendas. Any of these terrorist activities can have significant negative impact on the conduct of missions by U.S. military forces.

> **Terrorism**
>
> The calculated use of unlawful violence or threat of unlawful violence to inculcate fear; intended to coerce or to intimidate governments or societies in the pursuit of goals that are generally political, religious, or ideological.
>
> Joint Pub 1-02

The U.S. Department of Defense (DOD) defines operational environment (OE) as a composite of the conditions, circumstances, and influences that affect the employment of capabilities and bear on the decisions of the commander.[3] The U.S. Army builds on this DOD definition and further defines a mission setting for the current or the near-term future circumstances – the Contemporary Operational Environment.[4]

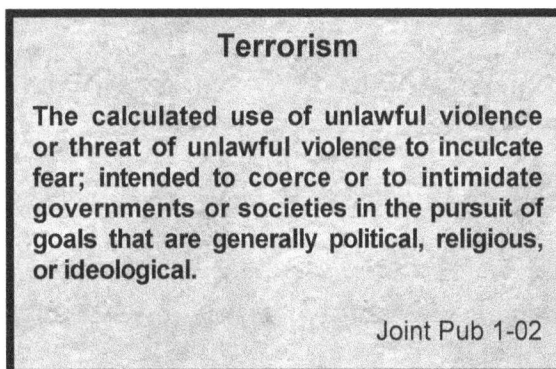

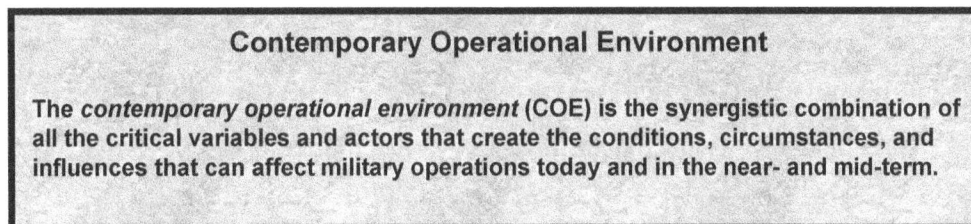

> **Contemporary Operational Environment**
>
> The *contemporary operational environment* (COE) is the synergistic combination of all the critical variables and actors that create the conditions, circumstances, and influences that can affect military operations today and in the near- and mid-term.

The *Contemporary Operational Environment* (COE) has several common threads or constants for defining the environment. The U.S. will not experience a peer competitor until 2020 or beyond. Armed forces will continue to be used as a tool to pursue national interests. The United States of America may direct military action within the context of

---

[3] Joint Publication 1-02, *Department of Defense Dictionary of Military and Associated Terms*, 12 April 2001, as amended through 13 June 2007.
[4] Army Field Manual 7-100, *Opposing Force Doctrinal Framework and Strategy,* May 2003, Foreword and iv.

an alliance, a coalition, or even as unilateral action, with or without United Nations sanctions. Military actions will be waged in a larger environment of diplomatic, information, and economic operations. Modernization of capabilities by potential or known adversaries could negate U.S. overmatch for select periods of time or specific capabilities. Similarly, advanced technologies will be readily available on a world market for nation states and non-state actors. Non-state actors can cause significant impacts on a military operation as combatants and noncombatants. Adversaries or enemies may use very simple means to counter the sophistication of specific U.S. systems. Of course, factors and their effects will vary depending on a particular situation. One additional constant that must be addressed is the issue of variables.

This contemporary period can be assessed as "…the most dangerous times of our lifetime…not so much because we know precisely what somebody's going to do, when and where, or how they're going to do it; but that we know their intent and we know what the possibilities are and we know what our vulnerabilities are…So terrorism is part of the tactic. In other ways it's [terrorism] an 'ism', much like communism and the others, only so much as it's embodied in whatever movements and for whatever reasons."[5]

A dynamic and adaptive process means being more aware, better prepared, and fully ready to counter any adversary or enemy that could negatively impact on conduct of an assigned U.S. military mission. Action can range from peaceful humanitarian assistance to high-intensity combat operations.

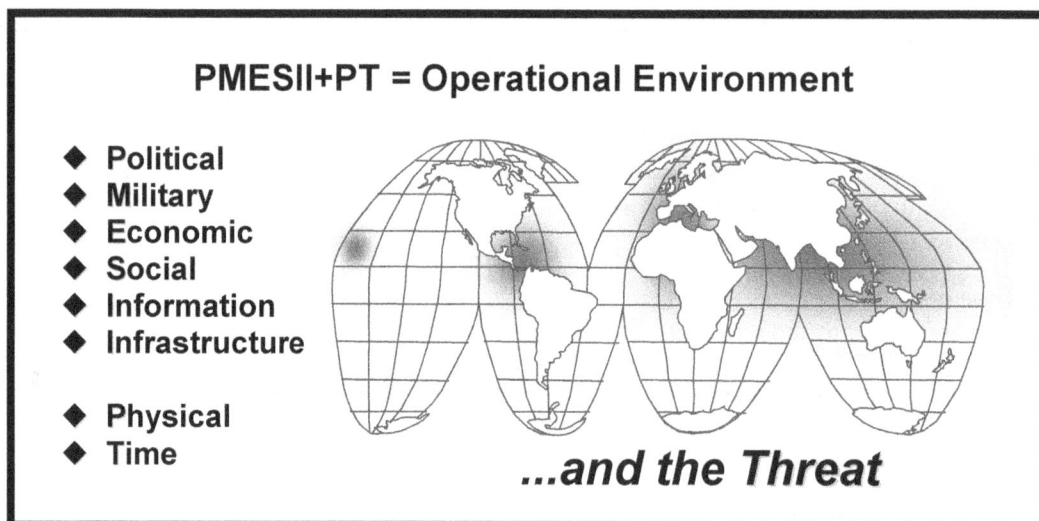

PMESII+PT = Operational Environment

◆ **Political**
◆ **Military**
◆ **Economic**
◆ **Social**
◆ **Information**
◆ **Infrastructure**

◆ **Physical**
◆ **Time**

…and the Threat

Figure 2. **Operational Environment and the Threat**

---

[5] General Peter Schoomaker, U.S. Army Chief of Staff, "Media Roundtable at the Association of the United States Army Annual Convention, Washington, D.C., 4 October 2004; available from http://www.army.mil/leaders/leaders/csa/interviews/04Oct04Roundtable.html; Internet; accessed 11 January 2005.

To understand the complex interactions of the Operational Environment (OE), a framework of "systems" assists in assessing and gaining situational awareness. Joint doctrine uses systems of Political, Military, Economic, Social, Infrastructure, and Information (PMESII) to shape and conduct missions. PMESII and other variables such as physical environment and time (PMESII+PT) affect circumstances and information operations throughout the domains of air, land, sea, and space. This broader perspective, combined with mission, enemy and belligerents, friendly forces and partners, and cultural sensitivities and resolve, are critical to mission success. Defining physical environmental conditions include terrain or urban settings such as (space, super-surface, surface and sub-surface features), weather, topography, and hydrology. The variable of time influences action such as planning, multi-echelon decision cycles, tempo of operations, and projected pacing of popular support or dissatisfaction for operations. Whether a real world threat or an opposing force (OPFOR) created to simulate relevant conditions for training readiness, PMESII and other variables such as physical environment and time describe the OE.

The April 2007 *Country Reports on Terrorism 2006* by the Department of State[6] and a complementary report by the National Counter Terrorism Center (NCTC), *Reports on Terrorism Incidents - 2006*, cite the significance of key terms and definitions applied to terrorism. For example, NCTC statistics and assessment do not contain information specifically concerning combatants. Engagement among actors in the COE affects a broad band of issues from formal nation state interaction to the impact on individual combatants and noncombatants. The NCTC uses the definition of combatant as "…personnel in the military, paramilitary, militia, and police under military command and control, who are in specific areas or regions where war zones or war-like settings exist."[7]

Acts of terrorism are part of this daily reality. Assessing and evaluating terrorism is a collection of ongoing and emerging issues. Comparing statistical data on most terrorism information collected by the State Department and other U.S. Federal activities in previous years is inappropriate based on the different collection and reporting methods currently in use.[8] The Department of State report provides a five year review of progress as well as a focus on calendar year 2006. National Counterterrorism Center data is comparable between the NCTC 2005 assessment and the 2006 report issued in April 2007.[9]

Purpose

This U.S. Army TRADOC G2 handbook serves as an unclassified resource to inform U.S. military members on the nature of terrorism. The intention is to create situational awareness and understanding of current terrorism capabilities and limitations, and

---

[6] Department of State, *Country Reports on terrorism 2006*, April 2007; available from http://www.terrorisminfo.mipt.org/Patterns-of-global-terrorism.asp; Internet; accessed 2 May 2007.
[7] National Counterterrorism Center (NCTC), *Reports on Terrorism Incidents - 2006*, 30 April 2007, 4 and 5; available from http://www.terrorisminfo.mipt.org/Patterns-of-global-terrorism.asp; Internet; accessed 2 May 2007.
[8] Ibid., 5. See also, "NCTC Revises, Raises Terror Incident List From 2004," 6 July 2005; available from http://www.foxnews.com/printer_friendly_story/0,3566,161645,00.html; Internet; accessed 6 July 2005.
[9] Ibid., 2.

complement the deliberate processes of military risk management, protection of the force, mission orders conduct, and leader decision-making. This handbook is a credible awareness tool for real world threats or an opposing force (OPFOR) used as conditions for training readiness.

From a "Threats" perspective, terrorism capabilities and limitations indicate possible or probable types of threat action that may be directed against U.S. military members, organizations, and activities. Factors other than military power may place constraints on both threats ands friendly forces. Commanders, organizational leaders, and other military members must "think like the threat" and can use this handbook to create operational opportunities to:

- Understand the nature of a terrorist threat, methods of planning and action, and organizational structures commonly used by terrorists and terrorist organizations.

- Know terrorist goals and objectives. Acknowledge asymmetric operations available to a terrorist. Study situational patterns and techniques in terrorism over time that can offer insight and possible trends of an adaptive enemy.

- Appreciate threat of terrorism to U.S. military forces, equipment, and infrastructure.

- Relate appropriate levels of force protection (FP), operational security (OPSEC), and terrorism countermeasures based upon unit status and situation.

Threat and Opposing Force
Threat. Any specific foreign nation or organization with intentions and military capabilities that suggest it could become an adversary or challenge the national security interests of the United States or its allies.
U.S. Army Regulation 350-2
Opposing Force. (OPFOR) A plausible, flexible military and/or para-military force representing a composite of varying capabilities of actual worldwide forces, used in lieu of a specific threat force, for training and developing U.S. armed forces.
U.S. Army Regulation 350-2

- Provide relevant terrorism information that
applies to U.S. military forces that are: (1) deployed on an operational mission, (2) in transit to or from an operational mission, or (3) military activities designated as installation or institutional support.

- Complement research, analysis, and contingency techniques within a "red teaming" concept and process.[10]

---

[10] Department of Defense, Defense Science Board, *Defense Science Board Task Force on The Role and Status of DoD Red Teaming Activities,* (Washington, D.C.: Office of the Under Secretary of Defense for Acquisition, Technology, and Logistics, September 2003).

Scope of the Issue

Terrorism is a significant operational condition for U.S. military forces in the twenty-first century. Terrorist violence has changed in recent years from sporadic incidents of the politically disenfranchised to a significant asymmetric form of conflict employed against adversaries and enemies with economic, military, social, and political aims.

While terrorist acts may have appeared to be extraordinary events several decades ago, today terrorism eclipses these former acts and demonstrates a profound impact on populations at the local, regional, national, and international levels. Terrorists do not plan on defeating the U.S. in a purely military sense. As part of a larger listing of threats, "…foes today are not trying to defeat us [U.S.] purely militarily. They're approaching this from a far broader strategic context, and in fact, they're least interested in taking us [U.S.] on head-on. They're interested in tying us down militarily, but they are really working on defeating us informationally, economically, and politically, the other dimensions of National power."[11]

Terrorism is defined by the U.S. Department of Defense (DOD) as: "The calculated use of unlawful violence or threat of unlawful violence to inculcate fear; intended to coerce or to intimidate governments or societies in the pursuit of goals that are generally political, religious, or ideological."[12] This is not a universally accepted definition outside of the Department of Defense. For this handbook, the DOD doctrinal definition will be used unless otherwise noted in the text.

Terrorism is a special type of violence. While terrorist actions may have political or other motives, terrorism is a criminal act. Although terrorism has not yet caused the physical devastation and number of casualties normally associated with conventional warfare, terrorism often produces significant adverse psychological impacts.[13] Examples of this impact on the United States are the 9/11 attacks and the anthrax incidents of 2001. For many people in the U.S., these attacks weakened their sense of safety and security. The experience of catastrophic terrorism was evidence that the United States was not immune to attacks by international or transnational terrorist groups. These attacks caused severe economic impacts on the nation. As Brian Jenkins testified to the 9/11 Commission, "The September 11 attack produced cascading economic effects that directly and indirectly have cost the United States hundreds of billions of dollars."[14] However for many U.S. citizens, these terrorist acts fortified their will and resolve to respond and defeat this enemy. A national determination emerged from these catastrophic incidents to

---

[11] General Peter Schoomaker, Army Chief of Staff, "CSA Interview: Joint and Expeditionary Capabilities," (Washington, D.C.: Pentagon, 4 October, 2004), available from http://www.army.mil/leaders/leaders/csa/interviews/04Oct04.html; Internet; accessed 11 January 2005.

[12] FM 100-20, *Military Operations in Low Intensity Conflict*, 5 December 1990; and Joint Pub 1-02, *Department of Defense Dictionary of Military and Associated Terms*, 12 April 2001, as amended through 13 June 2007.

[13] Bruce Hoffman, *Inside Terrorism* (New York: Columbia University Press, 1998), 33-34.

[14] National Commission on Terrorist Attacks Upon the United States, Statement of Brian Jenkins to the Commission, March 31, 2003; available from http://www.9-11commission.gov/hearings/hearing1/witness_jenkins.htm; Internet; accessed 23 September 2004.

reassert commitment to a democratic way of life and to combat terrorism in the U.S. Homeland and on a global scale.

International concern about terrorism mounts too. Multinational groups such as the Club of Madrid, comprised of former presidents and prime ministers of democratic countries, seek an international cooperation against terrorism. Principles include acknowledging terrorism as a crime against all humanity, recognizing terrorism an attack on democracy and human rights, and rejecting any ideology that guides the actions of terrorists.[15]

Similarly, the Secretary General of the United Nations called for a world treaty on terrorism that would outlaw attacks targeting civilians and establish a framework for a collective response to the global terrorist threat. A complementary agreement might include a universal definition of terrorism, knowing that many different definitions exist for terrorism.[16] However, the UN Member States still have no universal definition. One terrorism expert recommended in a report for the then UN Crime Branch that taking the existing consensus on what constitutes a war crime is a credible point of departure. If the core of war crimes is deliberate attacks on civilians, hostage taking, and the killing of prisoners, and is extended to conditions other than war, a simple definition could describe acts of terrorism as "peacetime equivalents of war crimes."[17]

Terrorists may have their own definitions of terrorism. Notwithstanding, terrorist acts often fail to translate into concrete long-term gains or achieve an ultimate terrorist objective.[18] Escalating acts of terrorism can be self-defeating when the acts become so extreme that public reaction loses attention on the terrorist's intended purpose and focuses on the acts rather than the political issue. The example of Palestinian defiance to Israeli controls in this geographic region of the Middle East illustrates how progressively violent acts of resistance or terrorism can sometimes alienate large sections of public opinion that once may have supported a Palestinian viewpoint.[19] When the threat or use of terrorism is used in coordination with capabilities such as political or military power, strategic impact may be successful. Some people see the struggles for Algerian independence or Israeli independence as strategic outcomes that used terrorism as a major instrument of influence. Other people may see the 2004 Spanish withdrawal from coalition forces in Iraq as an operational outcome of terrorism in Spain, and a means toward terrorist strategic aims to fracture the coalition and eventually cause removal of U.S. presence and prestige in the Middle East.

---

[15] *The Madrid Agenda*, Club de Madrid, available from http://www.clubmadrid.org/cmadrid; Internet; accessed 26 April 2005.

[16] Ed McCullough, "Annan calls for treaty outlawing terrorism," Associated Press, 10 March 2005; available from http://www.kentucky.com/mld/kentucky/news/weird_news/11099663.htm?template; Internet; accessed 26 April 2005.

[17] United Nations, Office on Drugs and Crime, "Definitions of Terrorism," available from http://www.unodc.org/unodc/terrorism_definitions.html; Internet; accessed 11 May 2007.

[18] Caleb Carr, *The Lessons of Terror: A History of Warfare Against Civilians: Why it has Always Failed and Why it will Fail Again* (New York: Random House, 2002), 11.

[19] Caleb Carr, "TIME.com Interview with Calib Carr," 1 February 2002; available at http://www.time.com/time/2002/carr/interview.html; Internet; accessed 31 August 2004.

WOT and the Contemporary Operational Environment

The U.S. *National Defense Strategy* identifies four types of challenging threats. Traditional challenges exist by states that employ recognized military capabilities and forces in the more conventional forms of military competition and conflict. Irregular challenges are the more unconventional ways and means to counter the traditional advantages of stronger opponents. Catastrophic challenges involve the acquisition, possession, and possible use of WMD or methods that produce WMD-like effects. Disruptive challenges may be the use of breakthrough technologies to limit or negate the operational advantage of an opponent.[20]

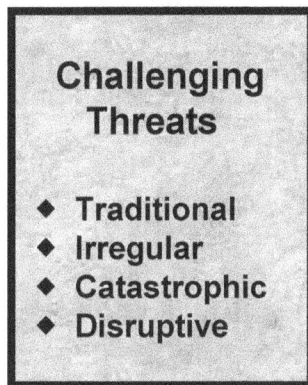

Challenging Threats

- **Traditional**
- **Irregular**
- **Catastrophic**
- **Disruptive**

On a global scale, the U.S. *National Defense Strategy* has four strategic objectives: (1) secure the United States from direct attack, (2) secure strategic access and retain global freedom of action, (3) strengthen alliances and partnerships, and (4) establish favorable security conditions. Four ways that the U.S. accomplishes those objectives are assuring allies and friends, dissuading potential adversaries, deterring aggression and coercion, and when necessary, defeating adversaries.[21] These principles are integral to situational awareness in the War on Terrorism (WOT).

The *National Military Strategic Plan for the War on Terrorism* (NMSP-WOT) addresses the WOT nature of the threat, and states priorities and responsibilities within the U.S. Armed Forces. The nature of this environment is a war against extremists that advocate the use of violence to gain control over others, and in doing so, threaten our [U.S.] way of life. Success will rely heavily on close cooperation and integration of all instruments of national power and the combined efforts of the international community. The overall goal of this war is to preserve and promote the way of life of free and open societies based on rule of law, defeat terrorist extremism as a threat to that way of life, and create a global environment inhospitable to terrorist extremists.[22]

Targeting Vulnerabilities

Vulnerabilities exist in terrorist plans, operations, and support functions. The United States targets eight major terrorist vulnerabilities. The intent is to maintain the initiative and determine the tempo, timing, and direction of military operations.

For example, denying resources to terrorists and terrorist networks is critical to countering the ideological support of terrorism. These efforts minimize or eliminate state and private support for terrorism as well as make it politically unsustainable for any

---

[20] *The National Defense Strategy of the United States of America,* 1 March 2005, 2.

[21] Ibid., iv.

[22] Joint Chiefs of Staff, J5 War on Terrorism, Strategic Planning Division, Briefing (U) *The National Military Strategic Plan for the War on Terrorism (NMSP-WOT),* Version 18 April 2005.

country to support or condone terrorism. Techniques in coordinating such actions may include a methodology of identifying or mapping key organizational components that affect resources such as technology, key figures, and locations. Identifying the major connections among these components can spotlight weak assailable links of networks and where targeting and action plans may be most effective. Measuring results and adapting operations enable a process for improved U.S. Joint leader education, training, and WOT operations.[23]

Interaction among these elements may range from peaceful humanitarian assistance to high-intensity combat operations. Alliances and coalitions are the expectation in most operations, but U.S. unilateral action is always a consideration. Military operations are considered with other elements of national power such as diplomatic, economic, social-cultural, and information for both the U.S. and an adversary. Advanced technologies are available to almost anyone, yet sophistication of weapon systems may be a liability. Intelligence and operational tools must overlap and integrate complex sensor-surveillance systems and the clarity of human intelligence "eyes on the ground" collection and analysis. Engagement among significant actors in the COE can span formal nation-state representatives to the impact of individual combatants and noncombatants on a farmer's field or city alleyway.

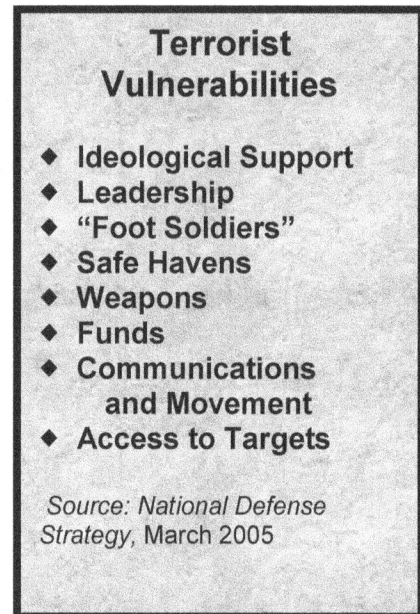

Terrorist Vulnerabilities

- ◆ Ideological Support
- ◆ Leadership
- ◆ "Foot Soldiers"
- ◆ Safe Havens
- ◆ Weapons
- ◆ Funds
- ◆ Communications and Movement
- ◆ Access to Targets

Source: National Defense Strategy, March 2005

Red Teaming

What is "Red Teaming?" Red Teaming is a concept to analyze and appreciate adversary and enemy thinking, planning, and action. This methodology complements and informs intelligence collection and analysis of friendly forces, and enhances predictive estimates of adversary intentions and capabilities. Aggressive red teaming challenges emerging operational concepts, evolving contingency plans, and operational orders of friendly forces. The purpose is to discover weaknesses of friendly forces before an adversary or enemy identifies vulnerabilities and takes advantage of them. The perspective of an adversary may be that of a confirmed threat or a contingency that poses scenarios for friendly forces training and readiness.

A U.S. Defense Science Board task force validated two primary reasons for expanding the role of red teaming in the Department of Defense (DOD): (1) To deepen understanding of the adversaries the U.S. now faces in the war on terrorism and in particular their capabilities and potential responses to U.S. initiatives, and (2) To guard against complacency. Red teaming

---

[23] Joint Chiefs of Staff, J5 War on Terrorism, Strategic Planning Division, Briefing (U) *Countering Ideological Support for Terrorism,* Version 19Jan05, 5 April 2005.

stresses concepts, plans, and systems to identify vulnerabilities and capabilities before direct confrontation with a real world adversary. To best apply red teaming programs, red team members must be able to understand the thinking and motivations of adversaries with different cultural and social backgrounds, assess and analyze acting as independent and adaptive adversaries, and interact and recommend in constructive and creative ways with the supported friendly forces leader and military decisionmaker.[24]

Understanding the rationale of a terrorist involves detailed study of different cultural decisionmaking, societal norms, or theological conviction. Extremism, as is the case of al-Qaida or associated ideological movements, can be a violent and distorted variant of religion and a desire for secular power. Terrorism may be used by groups with a single issue such as environmental or animal protection. Threats differ depending on conditions, circumstances, and influences in the contemporary operational environment.

Assessing the Threat

- ◆ Mapping the Threat
- ◆ Analyzing Networks
- ◆ Planning Actions
- ◆ Determining Metrics
- ◆ Tracking Actions
- ◆ Evaluating Outcomes
- ◆ Adapting Methods
- ◆ Improving Results

Approach to Understanding Terrorism

The 2007 version of *A Military Guide to Terrorism in the Twenty-First Century* builds on a database of open source information and focus topic updates. The purpose and intended audience, although primarily U.S. military forces, provides a useful awareness to other activities in interagency, interdepartmental, intergovernmental, nongovernmental, private volunteer, humanitarian relief, and civilian organizations. The chapters of this handbook address the following topics:

Chapter 1: *The Face of Terrorism Today*, defines the concept of terrorism and provides basic terms of reference for a common vocabulary. Attention focuses on contemporary terrorism. Patterns and trends are addressed further in chapter 5.

Chapter 2: *Terrorist Motivations and Behaviors*, presents an overview of terrorist behavior and examines individual or group declared ideology or philosophy. General descriptions highlight the diversity of mindset, lifestyle, and conduct of a terrorist.

Chapter 3: *Terrorist Organizational Models*, provides examples and diagrams of hierarchical and networked terrorist group organizations, as well as address on the increasing number of loosely affiliated or independent terrorist cells with ideological support to international or transnational terrorist organizations such as al-Qaida. Each type of model has its capabilities and limitations for analysis and intelligence preparation of the battlefield.

---

[24] Department of Defense, Defense Science Board, *Defense Science Board Task Force on The Role and Status of DoD Red Teaming Activities*, (Washington, D.C.: Office of the Under Secretary of Defense for Acquisition, Technology, and Logistics, September 2003), 1, 15, 16, and Appendix 1.

Chapter 4: **Terrorist Targeting of U.S. Military Forces,** assesses potential or probable targeting of U.S. military forces by terrorist organizations. Three operational environments are a situational framework for protection of the force and risk management: (1) friendly forces that are deployed in operational missions, (2) friendly forces in-transit to or from an operational mission, or (3) friendly forces that are primarily static in location such as an installation or other institutional support location.

Chapter 5: **Terrorism of the Foreseeable Future,** examines the future of terrorism with an adaptive enemy. Patterns of current operations and emergent actions offer possible and probable trends for the immediate future. These trends include flexible organizational models, enhanced methods of attack, expanded transnational support structures, increased weapon system lethality, exploited media marketing, escalating ideological extremism, and geographic regions of increased terrorist activity.

Appendices to Army TRADOC G2 Handbook No. 1 provide additional information to understanding terror and the ways and means of conducting terrorism.

A: **Terrorist Planning Cycle.** Description of traditional planning and operations sequence provide a baseline for understanding emergent actions by terrorists. An adaptive enemy demonstrates the ability to abbreviate detailed planning and conduct of operations in a much reduced time period.

B: **Firearms.** Illustrations, photographs, and descriptions present a survey of selected conventional small arms used by terrorists. Open source intelligence summaries and reports provide the basis for this sampling of hand or shoulder fired weapons.

C: **Conventional Military Munitions.** Illustrations, photographs, and descriptions present a survey of selected conventional military munitions used by terrorists including fragmentation grenades, rocket propelled grenades, shoulder-fired surface-to-air missiles, and artillery munitions.

In 2007, five supplemental handbooks to TRADOC G2 Handbook No.1, *A Military Guide to Terrorism in the Twenty-First Century,* focus topics of terrorism:

- TRADOC G2 Handbook 1.01, **Terror Operations: Case Studies in Terrorism.** (2007) v 5.0
- DCSINT Handbook 1.02, **Critical Infrastructure Threats and Terrorism.** (2006)
- DCSINT Handbook 1.03, **Suicide Bombing in the COE.** (2006)
- TRADOC G2 Handbook 1.04, **Terrorism and WMD in the Contemporary Operational Environment.** (2007)
- DCSINT Handbook No. 1.05, **A Military Primer on Terrorism in the Contemporary Operational Environment.** (2006) This handbook is a U.S. Army "For Official Use Only" reference guide on terrorism and is published as a 5 inch by 7 inch, hip-pocket booklet.

Conclusion

This capstone handbook and its supplemental handbooks provide an appreciation of an increasingly common method of conflict – Terrorism. Promoting knowledge and awareness of terrorism enhances the ability of U.S. military forces to assess conditional vulnerabilities, determine enemy threats, dissuade and deter terrorist acts, deny use of particular terrorism means, and defend against terrorist attack.[25] These actions are a combination of defensive and offensive measures to combat terrorism. The *National Strategy for Combating Terrorism* describes campaigning along four simultaneous fronts: (1) defeat terrorist organizations of global reach through relentless action; (2) deny support to terrorism; (3) diminish the conditions that encourage terrorism; and (4) defend the people and interests of the United States of America against terrorism.[26]

The aim of the terrorist, whether terrorism is viewed as a strategy, a campaign, or a tactic, is an attack on resolve. The world today is complex. A significant difference in the War on Terrorism from previous recent wars is the reality of a protracted conflict of uncertain duration.[27] The War will be conducted and assessed in a perspective of decades rather than in weeks, months, or years.

The overarching purpose of this "Threats" handbook is to create situational awareness and understanding of terrorism, and to complement the deliberate processes of military risk management, protection of the force, mission orders conduct, and leader decisionmaking.

---

[25] Moilanen, Jon H. "Engagement and Disarmament: A U.S. National Security Strategy for Biological Weapons of Mass Destruction," *Essays on Strategy XIII.* Mary A. Sommervile ed., Washington, D.C., National Defense University Press, 1996.

[26] The White House, "National Strategy for Combating Terrorism," Washington, D.C. (February 2003): 11, 29-30; available from http://www.state.gov/s/ct/rls/rm/2003/17798.htm; Internet; accessed 8 December 2003.

[27] Cofer Black, "The International Terrorism Threat," Testimony before the House International Relations committee, Subcommittee on International Terrorism, Nonproliferation, and Human Rights, Washington, D.C., 26 March 2003; 6, available from http://www.state.gov/s/ct/rls/rm/2003/19136.htm; Internet; accessed 21 April 2005.

1 Terrorism Today

Chapter 1

The Face of Terrorism Today

America is at War...the grave challenge we face – the rise of terrorism fueled by an aggressive ideology of hatred and murder, fully revealed to the American people on September 11, 2001.

> **President George W. Bush**
> ***The National Security Strategy***
> ***of the United States of America***
> **March 2006**

Terrorist acts or the threat of terrorism have been in existence for thousands of years. Despite a history longer than the modern nation-state, the use of terror by governments and those that contest their power appears poorly understood. When terror is applied to acts and actors in the real world of today, meaning and intent can point in many directions. Part of this dilemma is due to use of terror tactics by actors at all levels of social and political interaction. Is the "Unabomber"[28] with his solo campaign of terror a criminal, terrorist, or revolutionary? How does a Timothy McVeigh[29] differ from a Theodore Kaczynski? Can either of them be compared to a revolutionary government who coined the word terrorism by instituting systematic state terror against its population in the 1790s? What differs in radicalized American-based Islamic terrorists with no direct links to transnational networks such as al-Qaida?[30] How does a domestic or "home grown" terrorist differ from an insurgent in Iraq or Afghanistan or other regions of the world? What is the face of terrorism today?

Figure 1-1. **The Faces of Terrorism Today**

---

[28] "The Unibomber Manifesto," available from http://www.ed.brocku.ca/~rahul/Misc/unibomber.html; Internet; accessed 30 May 2007.
[29] "Murrah Federal Building Bombing," US Army TRADOC, TRADOC G2 Handbook No. 1, *Terror Operations: Case Studies in Terror*, Fort Leavenworth, KS: TRADOC Intelligence Support Activity-Threats, 10 August 2006; available from https://dcsint-threats.leavenworth.army.mil; US Army Battle Command Knowledge System (BCKS); accessed 30 May 2007. US Army Knowledge Online (AKO) password required to access.
[30] "FBI Warns of growing Terrorist Threat from American-Based Islamic Extremists," available from http://news.rgp.com/apps/pbcs.dll/article?AID=/20070513/NEWS18/705130372; Internet; accessed 18 May 2007.

"Terrorism is theatre."[31] Terrorism, like a theatrical play, can be viewed as a deliberate presentation to a large audience in order to gain attention, spotlight a particular message, and seek a response favorable to the actor. The purpose of such actions can have sinister impact on national, regional, and global populations. Global communications provide a stage for near instantaneous media exploitation. Anxiety can increase as random or deliberate acts of terror often target civilians as victims. Similar to a play, the objective of the experience is to affect the feelings and attitudes of the audience.

Section I: What is Terrorism

Terrorism has been described as both a tactic and strategy; a crime and a holy duty; a justified reaction to oppression and an inexcusable action. Definition may depend on whose point of view is being represented. Terrorism has often been an effective tactic for the weaker side in a conflict. As an asymmetric form of conflict, terrorism projects coercive power with many of the advantages of military force at a fraction of the cost to the terrorist. Terrorism is a means -- a method -- to an objective.

Defining Terrorism

The U.S. Department of Defense (DOD) approved definition of terrorism is: "The calculated use of unlawful violence or threat of unlawful violence to inculcate fear; intended to coerce or to intimidate governments or societies in the pursuit of goals that are generally political, religious, or ideological."[32] For the purposes of this document, this will be the standard definition. However, this is one of many definitions. One researcher did a review of writings on terrorism and found 109 different definitions.[33] A sampling of definitions by the Federal Bureau of Investigation (FBI) and the Department of State (DOS) illustrate the different perspectives of categorizing and analyzing terrorism.

The FBI uses this: "Terrorism is the unlawful use of force and violence against persons or property to intimidate or coerce a government, the civilian population, or any segment thereof, in furtherance of political or social objectives."[34] The U.S. Department of State uses the definition contained in Title 22 U.S.C. Section 2656f(d). According to this section, "terrorism" means "premeditated politically-motivated violence perpetrated against non-combatant targets by sub-national groups or clandestine agents."[35] The National Counterterrorism Center (NCTC) uses this Title 22 definition of terrorism also in its annual reports of

---

[31] Bruce Hoffman, *Inside Terrorism* (New York: Columbia University Press, 1998), 38. This is a statement that is quoted often to spotlight the intention of terror to gain attention, to arouse, and to cause reaction.

[32] FM 100-20, *Military Operations in Low Intensity Conflict*, 5 December 1990; and Joint Publication 1-02, *Department of Defense Dictionary of Military and Associated Terms*, 12 April 2001, as amended through 13 June 2007.

[33] Bruce Hoffman, *Inside Terrorism* (New York: Columbia University Press, 1998), 39.

[34] Title 28, Code of Federal Regulations, Section 0.85, *Judicial Administration*, (Washington, D.C., July 2001).

[35] Department of State, *Patterns of Global Terrorism 2001* (Washington, D.C., May 2002), xvi.

terrorism incidents around the world.[36]   These definitions stress the respective institutional concerns of the organizations using them. The FBI concentrates on the unlawful aspect in keeping with its law enforcement mission. The Department of State concerns itself with politically motivated actions by sub-national or clandestine actors as functions affect international relations and diplomacy. Terrorism is "...fundamentally political so the political significance of major events is vital to determining meaningful responses."[37]

Outside the United States Government, there are greater variations in what features of terrorism are emphasized in definitions. One comment used often is, "One state's terrorist is another state's freedom fighter."[38] There is clearly a wide array of definitions for terrorism. Despite this, several common elements may assist in defining terrorism: political, psychological, violent, dynamic, and deliberate. The United Nations produced this description in 1992; "An anxiety inspiring method of repeated violent action, employed by semi-clandestine individual, group or state actors, for idiosyncratic, criminal or political reasons, whereby - in contrast to assassination - the direct targets of violence are not the main targets." The UN has no internationally-agreed definition of terrorism. Yet in September 2006, the United Nations and its Member States demonstrated signs of collective progress in agreement to a global strategy to counter terrorism.[39]   .

Vectors of Action

A way to frame terrorism in the context of a contemporary operational environment is to consider vectors of political, psychological, violent, and deliberate action.

Political. A U.S. State Department official summarized, "The ultimate goals of terrorism are political...Politically motivated terrorism invariably involves a deeply held grievance over some form of injustice. The injustice may be social or economic, but it is nonetheless blamed on a political authority." [40]

---

[36] National Counterterrorism Center (NCTC), *Reports on Terrorism Incidents - 2006*, 30 April 2007, 2; available from http://www.terrorisminfo.mipt.org/Patterns-of-global-terrorism.asp; Internet; accessed 2 May 2007.

[37] Department of State, *Country Reports on terrorism 2006*, April 2007, 11; available from http://www.terrorisminfo.mipt.org/Patterns-of-global-terrorism.asp; Internet; accessed 2 May 2007.

[38] United Nations, Office on Drugs and Crime, "Definitions of Terrorism," available from http://www.unodc.org/unodc/terrorism_definitions.html; Internet; accessed 31 May 2007.

[39] United Nations, "United Nations General Assembly Adopts Global Counter-Terrorism Strategy," available from http://www.un.org/terrorism/strategy-counter-terrorism.html; Internet; accessed 31 May 2007. This citation provides the full text resolution and UN plan of action.

[40] David E. Long, *The Anatomy of Terrorism* (New York: THE FREE PRESS, A Division of Macmillan, Inc., 1990), 4 and 5.

Psychological. Terrorist acts intend to cause a negative psychological effect on a target. Acts may be aimed at a target audience other than the actual victims of the terrorism. The intended target audience of terrorism may be a population as a whole or some selected portion of a society such as an ethnic minority or decisionmakers in a society's political, social, or military population.

Violent. Violence intends to produce a desired physical effect and can contribute to a psychological effect of fear or anxiety. Threats may be effective for a period of time, but usually require complementary physical terrorism action to achieve the degree of desired psychological effect.

Deliberate. Terrorism is purposeful. Victim or target selection can appear random or unprovoked, but analysis of events will usually identify that a target and the impact from attacking a target was premeditated in conjunction with a terrorist objective.

Section II: Objectives

Objective: A standard military definition of *objective* is – "The clearly defined, decisive, and attainable aims which every military operation should be directed towards."[41]

Terrorist objectives refer to the intended result of individual acts or groups and series of actions at the tactical or operational levels of war. Terrorist networks may apply tactical and operational outcomes to enhance achievement of strategic terrorist aims. U.S. military forces will always have some degree of vulnerability to terrorist operations. Terrorism is a specific and pervasive risk for U.S. military forces. For example, al-Qaida has specifically identified military targets as one of its major priorities.[42] Factors contributing to a danger of attack on military forces are:

- Exposure increases as units and individuals are forward deployed and internationally based. Increases in the operations tempo, the number of overseas deployments, and periodic surge requirements into an operational area raise the opportunity that U.S. forces will operate in areas that are more accessible to terrorist groups than the U.S. Homeland or other established overseas bases.

- Symbolic value of successful attacks against military targets has often been a consideration in terrorist planning. Terrorist groups recognize that even relatively small losses of military forces from terrorist attacks receive extensive international media coverage and can diminish popular and political support for military operations and sponsoring governments.[43]

---

[41] Joint Publication 1-02, *Department of Defense Dictionary of Military and Associated Terms*, 12 April 2001, as amended through 13 June 2007.
[42] Ben Venzke and Aimee Ibrahim, *The al-Qaeda Threat: An Analytical Guide to al-Qaeda's Tactics and Targets* (Alexandria: Tempest Publishing, LLC, 2003), 76.
[43] Ibid., 77.

- Extremist Islamic dogma fuels turmoil in many regions of the world. This turmoil incites disenfranchised groups of a population to provide recruits and followers that have been desensitized to violence, who seek purpose and meaning in their lives, and want to escape from a despairing environment. After reading or hearing the works of people such as Mawdudi, Qutb, and Faraj, and other theological interpretations of various schools and Muslin clerics, concepts of violence and religion as a supposed support of terror should not appear surprising.[44] As noted in *Jihad: The Trail of Political Islam*, "The dispersion all over the world, after 1992, of the jihadist-salafists formerly concentrated in Kabul [Afghanistan] and Peshawar [Pakistan], more than anything else, explains the sudden, lightning expansion of radical Islamism in Muslim countries and the West."[45]

Section III: Terrorism and Insurgency

Terrorism is a violent act outside the normal bounds of civil law and conventional military conduct. Terrorism is often linked to an insurgency or guerrilla warfare, but is not necessarily a tactic or technique required of an insurgency or guerrilla campaign. Insurgency and guerilla warfare can overlap in execution. Although these forms of conflict may often have similar goals,[46] differences exist among insurgency, guerilla warfare, and terrorism. An insurgency is a political effort with a specific aim to overthrow a constituted government. Guerrilla warfare is military and paramilitary operations conducted in enemy-held or hostile territory by irregular, predominantly indigenous forces. An insurgency and guerrilla warfare can use terrorism as a means to shape an environment.[47] Adapting to counter superior military forces or technological capabilities, an insurgent or guerrilla can create conditions that persuade or coerce a target audience to directly or indirectly support an insurgent or guerrilla agenda.

Insurgency:
(JP 1-02) (NATO)
An organized movement aimed at the overthrow of a constituted government through the use of subversion and armed conflict.

Guerrilla Warfare:
(JP1-02) (NATO)
Military and paramilitary operations conducted in enemy-held or hostile territory by irregular, predominantly indigenous forces.

While some insurgencies and guerilla campaigns use terror and some conflicts have displayed a predominant use of terrorism against a target population, other examples of conflict renounced the use of terror. The deliberate choice to use terrorism considers its

---

[44] Mark Juergensmeyer, *Terror in the Mind of God* (Berkeley and Los Angeles: University of California Press, 2000), 81-82.

[45] Gilles Kepel, *Jihad: The Trail of Political Islam* (Cambridge: The Belknap Press of Harvard University Press): 299.

[46] *International Encyclopedia of Terrorism*, 1997 ed., s.v. "Theories of Insurgency and Terrorism: Introduction."

[47] Army Field Manual 3-24, *Counterinsurgency*, (Washington, D.C.: Headquarters, Department of the Army, December 2006), 1-3.

effectiveness in inspiring further resistance, destroying government efficiency, and mobilizing support.[48] These objectives usually relate directly to a form of political power.

> **Related Definitions**
>
> **Terrorist:** (JP 1-02)
> An individual who uses violence, terror, and intimidation to achieve a result.
>
> **Counterterrorism:** (JP 1-02)
> Offensive measures taken to prevent, deter, and respond to terrorism.
>
> **Antiterrorism:** (JP 1-02)
> Defensive measures used to reduce the vulnerability of individuals and property to terrorist acts, to include limited response and containment by local military forces.

The goal of an insurgency is to challenge the existing government for control of all or a portion of its territory, or force political concessions in sharing political power. The key element in insurgent strategy is effective control or influence over a relevant population. A supportive population provides security, intelligence, logistical support, and a recruiting base for each side in an insurgency and counter-insurgency struggle. If the insurgency gains control over an increasing percentage of the population, the government will correspondingly lose effective control over a larger percentage of the population. Without a focus on the relevant population, insurgent objectives are nil.[49]

Terrorism normally does not contend for actual control of territory. Actors in an operational environment intend for violent acts to force their will on their targets. Insurgencies require the active or tacit support of some portion of the involved population. A terror group does not require[50] and rarely has the active support of a large percentage of the population. While insurgents may describe themselves as insurgents or guerrillas, terrorists will not usually refer to themselves as terrorists. They may describe themselves using military or political terminology such as freedom fighters, soldiers, or activists. Terrorism relies on public impact, and is therefore conscious of the advantage of avoiding the negative connotations of the term terrorist in identifying themselves.[51]

Other differences relate to the unit size, types of arms, and types of operations. Guerrillas usually fight in small organized formations such as platoon, company, or larger size units, whereas terrorists normally operate in small cells.[52] An example of tenuous distinctions between terrorism and guerrilla warfare is the *Montoneros* of Argentina during the 1970s. Incidents of kidnapping high profile businessmen for ransom or assassination of government officials blurred a widening array of terrorist actions that developed into organized military-type operations. Cellular and compartmented groups gave way to organized unit-type structure for sophisticated attacks against military forces. One attack against an infantry regiment included *Montoneros* marshalling their force over 800

---

[48] Walter Reich, ed., *Origins of Terrorism: Psychologies, Ideologies, Theologies, States of Mind*, rev. ed. (Washington: Woodrow Wilson Center Press, 1998), 16-20.
[49] Ariel Merari, "Terrorism as a Strategy of Insurgency," *Terrorism and Political Violence*, Vol 5, No. 4 (Winter 1993): 224.
[50] Reich, *Origins of Terrorism*, 17.
[51] Hoffman, *Inside Terrorism*, 29-33.
[52] Merari, "Terrorism as a Strategy of Insurgency," 224.

kilometers from previous urban enclaves, forming assault and support elements, conducting the attack, evacuating the force with a hijacked airplane, providing medical treatment enroute to the dispersal landing field, and vanishing among the population after landing.[53]

Table 1-1 provides a simplified comparison of differences among guerilla warfare, terrorism, and conventional war.

Table 1-1.	Simple Comparison of Conflict		
	Conventional War	**Guerilla**	**Terrorism**
Unit Size in Battle	Large (army, corps, division)	Medium (platoon, company, battalion)	Small (usually less than 10 persons)
Weapons	Full range of military weapon systems (air force, armor, artillery, etc)	Mostly infantry-type light weapons but sometimes artillery as well)	Hand guns, hand grenades, assault rifles and specialized weapons, e.g., car bombs; remote-control bombs
Tactics	Usually joint operations involving several military branches	Commando-type tactics	Specialized tactics: kidnap, assassination, car bomb, hijack, barricade-hostage
Targets	Mostly military units, industrial and transportation infrastructure	Mostly military, police and administration staff, as well as political opponents	State symbols, political opponents and the public at large
Intended Impact	Physical destruction of declared enemy	Mainly physical attrition of the enemy	Psychological fear, coercion and anxiety
Control of Territory	Yes	Yes	No
Uniform	Wear uniform	Often wear uniform	Do not wear uniform
Recognition of War Zones	War limited to recognized geographical area	War limited to the region-country in strife	No recognized war zones. Missions can be worldwide
International Legality	Yes, if conducted by international rules	Assessed in accordance with international rules	No
Domestic Legality	Yes	No	No

Terrorists do not usually attempt to challenge government military forces directly, but act to create public perceptions of an ineffectiveness or illegitimate government. This is done by ensuring the widest possible knowledge of the acts of terrorist violence among the target audience. An insurgent or guerilla force may clash with a government combat force to demonstrate that they can effectively challenge the military effectiveness of the government or to acquire military weapons and equipment. Terrorists use methods that

---

[53] Alan C. Lowe, "Todo o Nada: Montonerosa Versus the Army: Urban Terrorism in Argentina," ed. William G. Robertson and Lawrence A. Yates, in *Block by Block: The Challenges of Urban Operations* (Fort Leavenworth, KS: U.S. Army Command and General Staff College Press, 2003), 392-396.

attempt to neutralize the strengths of conventional forces. Bombings and mortar attacks on civilian targets where military or security personnel spend off-duty time, ambushes of convoys, and assassinations of government individuals are common tactics.

Insurgency and guerrilla warfare may actively target noncombatants. Some insurgencies and guerrilla campaigns consider police and security personnel, in addition to military forces, as targets in an expanded definition of combatants. Examples exist of insurgents or guerillas deliberately placing civilians on a target list. A Vietcong directive in 1965 detailed the types of people who must be "repressed," and stated, "The targets of repression are counterrevolutionary elements who seek to impede the revolution and work actively for the enemy and for the destruction of the revolution...Elements who actively fight against the revolution in reactionary parties such as the Vietnamese Nationalist Party, Party for a Greater Viet Nam, Personality and Labor Party, and key reactionaries in organizations and associations founded by the reactionary parties and the U.S. imperialists and the puppet government."[54] Deliberate dehumanization and criminalization of an enemy by a terrorist is a perspective of attempting to justify terrorism.

Insurgents may use more than one form of violence to obtain their objective with a combination of terrorism and insurgent or guerilla warfare as common.[55] Situations in Iraq illustrate the difficulty in identifying a terrorist from a guerilla or an insurgent. One assessment of contemporary threats in Iraq qualified four groups with different tactics and goals.[56] These include: (1) Iraqi nationalists, known as Former Regime Elements, fighting to reclaim secular power lost when Saddam Hussein was deposed, (2) hardcore fighters, many of which are foreign, aligned with terrorist groups who want to turn Iraq into another Afghanistan to be used as an anti-Western stronghold to export Islamic revolution to other countries, (3) conservative Iraqis who want to install an Islamic theocracy, but not use terror tactics, and (4) ordinary criminals that are paid to conduct attacks or who kidnap westerners and sell them to the terrorists.

Real-world events can also present situations that are vague and open to multiple interpretations for the same group. Al-Qaida is a transnational terrorist group. Correspondingly, al-Qaida could be defined as a global insurgency with the intent to overthrow the current world order. Al-Qaida does have political objectives of removing the U.S. from the Middle East to enhance their ability to overthrow their definition of apostate regimes. A long term vision seeks to reconstitute a caliphate across major portions of the Middle East, Northern Africa and areas of the Trans-Sahara, and Indo-South Asia-Southeast Asia regions. Using this secular base of power and the wealth of oil reserves and production, the new caliphate could serve as a means of further spreading a form of fascist ideology throughout the world.

---

[54] Merari, "Terrorism as a Strategy of Insurgency," 216.

[55] Bard E. O'Neill, *Insurgency & Terrorism: Inside Modern Revolutionary Warfare* (Dulles: Brassey's, Inc, 1990), 26.

[56] Jim Krane, "U.S. Faces Complex Insurgency in Iraq," *Duluth News Tribune.com*, (4 October 2004); available from http://www.duluthsuperior.com/mld/duluthsuperior/news/world/9833731.htm; Internet; accessed 16 November 2004; and Bruce Hoffman, *Insurgency and Counterinsurgency in Iraq* (Arlington: RAND Corporation, 2004), 12-13.

Section IV: State Sponsored Terror

Some nations and states often resort to violence to influence segments of their population, or rely on coercive aspects of state institutions. National governments can become involved in terrorism or utilize terror to accomplish the objectives of governments or individual rulers. Most often, terrorism is equated with non-state actors or groups that are not responsible to a sovereign government. However, internal security forces can use terror to aid in repressing dissent, and intelligence or military organizations can perform acts of terror designed to further a state's policy or diplomatic efforts abroad.

The U.S. Department of State lists five state sponsors of terror in its 2006 assessment of terrorism. These state sponsors of terror are; Cuba, Iran, North Korea, Sudan, and Syria. Venezuela is listed in a special category of not fully cooperating with U.S. counterterrorism efforts. Libya's inclusion on the list of state sponsors of terrorism was rescinded in 2003 after Libya officially renounced terrorism and abandoned its WMD programs.[57]

State Terror. This form of terror is sometimes referred to as "terror from above" where a government terrorizes its own population to control and repress them. These actions are acknowledged policy of the government and apply official institutions such as the judiciary, police, military, and other government agencies. Changes to legal codes can permit or encourage torture, killing, or property destruction in pursuit of government policy.

Examples in recent decades include Stalin's purges of the 1930s that terrorized an entire Soviets population. Nazi Germany during the 1930s-1940s aimed at the deliberate destruction of state enemies and intimidation of nations and regional states. Methods included demonstration trials with predetermined verdicts on political opponents, punishing family or friends of suspected enemies of the regime, and extralegal use of police or military force against the population.[58] More recent examples are Amin's policies of mayhem and murder in Uganda, and Saddam Hussein's use of chemical weapons on his own Kurdish population in Iraq.

Other types of state terror can include death squads as unofficial actions taken by officials or functionaries of a regime to repress or intimidate their own population. While these officials will not claim responsibility for such activities, information often indicates that these acts are sponsored by the state. Several programs in South and Central American regimes during the 1970s terrorized their populations with death squads.

States may employ terrorist networks with no formal recognition. Terror activities may be directed against the governmental interests of other nations or private groups or individuals viewed as dangerous to the state. Examples include Soviet and Iranian

---

[57] Department of State, *Country Reports on terrorism 2006*, April 2007, 145; available from http://www.terrorisminfo.mipt.org/Patterns-of-global-terrorism.asp; Internet; accessed 2 May 2007.
[57] United Nations, Office on Drugs and Crime, "Definitions of Terrorism," available from http://www.unodc.org/unodc/terrorism_definitions.html; Internet; accessed 31 May 2007.
[58] *International Encyclopedia of Terrorism*, 1997 ed., s.v. "Stalin's Great Terror."

assassination campaigns against dissidents who had fled abroad, or Libyan and North Korean intelligence operatives destroying airliners on international flights.[59]

State Sponsors of Terror. Some governments provide supplies, training, and other forms of support to non-state terrorist organizations. This support can be provided without intending any specified governing authority by the state. Provision can be safe haven or physical basing for a terrorist network. Another crucial service a state sponsor can provide is false documentation for personal identification such as passports or internal identity documents. Other means of support can include access to training facilities and expertise not readily available to terrorists, extension of diplomatic protections and services such as immunity from extradition, use of embassies and other protected grounds, or diplomatic pouches to transport weapons or explosives.

Iran is the most active state sponsor of terrorism. Official support includes extensive funding, training, and weapons to terrorist networks such as HAMAS, Palestinian Islamic Jihad (PIJ), al-Aqsa Martyrs Brigades, and the popular Front for the Liberation of Palestine-General Command (PLFP-GC). Irrefutable evidence exists that Iran provides guidance, training, and weapons to Shia factions in Iraq. Similarly, Iran provides technology and training to insurgents and terrorists in Iraq for constructing explosively formed projectiles (EFP) as improvised explosive devices (IED).[60] EFP-IEDs are one of the most effective casualty producing weapons in the ongoing coalition presence in Iraq.

Syria's political and material support of Hizballah is another example. Syrian political support includes the physical basing of leadership structure for several terrorist organizations such as Palestinian Islamic Jihad (PIJ), HAMAS, the Popular Front for the Liberation of Palestine (PLFP), and the Popular Front for the Liberation of Palestine-General Command (PLFP-GC). Suspicions remain under investigation on Syrian involvement in the February 2005 assassination of former Lebanese Prime Minister Rafik Hariri.[61]

Other states remain a concern. Sudan has openly supported HAMAS, but has been taking measures to disrupt foreign fighters from using Sudan as a logistics base and transit point fir extremists going to Iraq. North Korea has not been openly supporting terrorist networks for several decades; however, the recent 2006 detonation of a nuclear device by North Korea provides a threat of expanding the possibility of WMD technology being obtained by terrorist networks.

---

[59] Bruce Hoffman, *Inside Terrorism* (New York: Columbia University Press, 1998), 190.
[60] Department of State, *Country Reports on terrorism 2006*, April 2007, 147; available from http://www.terrorisminfo.mipt.org/Patterns-of-global-terrorism.asp; Internet; accessed 2 May 2007.
[61] Ibid., 148.

The U.S. Department of State accents, "A state that directs WMD resources to terrorists, or one from which enabling resources are clandestinely diverted, may pose a potentially grave WMD terrorism threat." [62] Cuba has provided sanctuary to members of the Basque Fatherland and Liberty (ETA), Revolutionary Forces of Columbia (FARC), and National Liberation Army (ELN), and maintained close relationships with other state sponsors of terror such as Iran. [63]

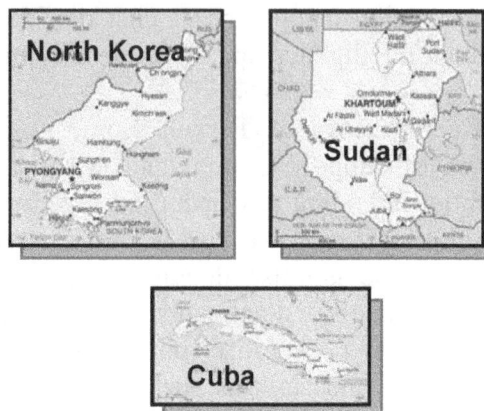

Section V: Other Forms of Terrorism

Forms of terrorism threats range non-state transnational networks with global reach capability such as al-Qaida, terrorist cells affiliated with regional or international aims, or individual self-radicalized and unaffiliated terrorists with single issue agendas. Yet, each type of network or terrorist cell has criminal intentions limited by finite capability. Terrorists exist as a foreign and domestic threat of the United States in the U.S. Homeland and in United States presence throughout the world.

Conflict will continue to be an adaptive and often asymmetric arena. Given the significance of U.S. military power and the effectiveness of other U.S. elements of national power in finance, intelligence, diplomatic, legal, and social domains, a noticeable structural change has occurred in many terrorist activities. Enemy downsizing[64] to reduce physical and cyber visibility already appears as small cells or even individuals acting in a distributed or semi-independent manner. Some terrorists are fully independent and have self-radicalized. Terms such as fifth generation warfare or unrestricted warfare indicate capabilities that globalization provides advanced knowledge and technology, mobile international transportation, and cyber-space communication[65] as expanding means for asymmetric conflict.

The Internet offers a worldwide, near instantaneous communication link to exchange ideas, information, and lessons learned. Indoctrination and training of terrorists can be in a dispersed mode and greatly reduce a need of formal hierarchy or organizational structure. Intent within an ideology can be placed into action by individuals rather than depending on large networks with layers of coordination, control, and logistic support.[66]

---

[62] Ibid., 147 and 153.

[63] Ibid., 146.

[64] Henry Crumpton, "Remarks at Transnational Terrorism Conference, " January 16, 2006; available from http://www.state.gov/s/ct/rls/rm/2006/59987.htm; Internet; accessed 12 May 2007.

[65] "The Architect and Fifth generation Warfare," June 4, 2006; available from http://www.thestrategist.org/archives/2006/06/the_architect_o.html; Internet; accessed 13 March 2007.

[66] Andrew Black, "Al-Suri's Adaptation of fourth Generation Warfare Doctrine," *Global Terrorism Analysis*, the Jamestown Foundation, September 21, 2006; available from http://www.jmaestown.org/terrorism/news/article.php?articleid=2370137; Internet; accessed 1 November 2006.

The descriptor of "homegrown threat" to the United States is indicative of individuals or small groups of individuals resident in the United States that are intent on harming the U.S. citizenry. These terrorists may be U.S. citizens or citizens from other nations. Examples range terrorists who have quietly embedded themselves in our society from international locations to U.S. citizens with special agendas that may result in terrorist attacks. Either type of group or individual may incorporate established criminal links to enhance capabilities. One homegrown Sunni Islamic extremist group self-titled as Assembly of Authentic Islam, operated primarily in state prisons in California and committed armed robberies to finance attacks on perceived enemies of Islam, including the U.S. Government.[67] Incidents in 2007 include a plan to attack U.S. military members on Fort Dix, New Jersey by a small group of Islamic extremists resident in the U.S. for several years. This group appears to have had put an ideological concept into action with no coordinating links to larger terrorist networks.

Figure 1-2. **Foreign, Domestic, or Home Grown Faces of Terrorism?**

Conclusion

Terrorism is foremost a political problem. Common terms and definitions assist in focusing situational awareness of the Threat. Actions consider aspects of terrorist activity that may include political demonstration, criminal conduct, and possible links to paramilitary operations or low intensity conflict.[68]

The psychological impact of terror on a target audience must be viewed as a means to an end. Threats can be evaluated by knowing terrorist intent and functional capabilities. Each threat should be examined in the context of its particular operational environment. Individual terrorist cell or group associations and affiliations, current or projected levels of training, decisionmaking authority within a cell or group to plan and act, and the sophistication of emergent tactics, techniques, and procedures are examples of critical variables with which to assess intent and capability to act.

---

[67] Robert Mueller, Statement Before the Senate Select Committee on Intelligence," January 11, 2007; available from http://www.fbi.gov/congress/congress07/mueller011107.htm; Internet; accessed 14 March 2007.
[68] Long, *The Anatomy of Terrorism,* 11 and 13.

2 Terrorist Motivations and Behaviors

Chapter 2

Terrorist Motivations and Behaviors

Al-Qaida and its loose confederation of affiliated movements remain the most immediate national security threat to the United States and a significant security challenge to the international community…intent to mount large-scale spectacular attacks …current approach focuses on propaganda warfare – using a combination of terrorist attacks, insurgency, media broadcasts, Internet-based propaganda, and subversion to undermine confidence and unity in Western populations and generate a false perception of a powerful worldwide movement.

U.S. Department of State
Country Reports on Terrorism 2006
April 2007

Terrorists are the enemy in the War on Terrorism. The nature of terrorists and their behaviors are a wide ranging set of data. Terrorism in general has many motivations depending on the special interests of the individual or cells. Common characteristics or clearly defined traits may be indicated in simple comparisons, but any detailed study will identify that significant contrasts are more often the norm. Nonetheless, benefits exist in studying varied terrorist motivations and behaviors at the individual and organizational level. Observations on human nature and group dynamics under the conditions of stress, anxiety, and extremist values can provide insight into the causes of particular behaviors.

Figure 2-1. **Terrorism and Propaganda Warfare**

This chapter examines the goals and motivation to use terror. Behavior of a terrorist may vary greatly depending on ideological commitment, individual intelligence and education, geographical setting, and organizational reach. The degrees of intent and capability hold the key of how serious each threat actually is as an enemy.

Section I: Goals

Understanding the goals of the enemy promotes an active approach to analyzing the transfer of goals to objectives, and objectives into operational plans and actions. While prediction is conditional, a terrorist will consider target value and cost required of the terrorist organization to successfully attack. A terrorist will evaluate what force protection measures are in effect in the vicinity of a target and determine a cost benefit analysis. From these analyses and forms of study and surveillance, a terrorist will isolate weaknesses of a target and exploit these weaknesses.

Goals and objectives of terrorist organizations differ throughout the world and range from regional single-issue terrorists to the aims of transnational radicalism and terrorism. As the most prominent democracy and significant economic, military, and political power in the world, the U.S. is a convenient and appealing target for extremists.

A sample statement by an al-Qaida spokesperson focuses on a primary strategic aim of al-Qaida. By causing the United States to commit significant wealth to protect its economy and associated infrastructure and to employ a fully engaged U.S. Armed Forces, al-Qaida intends to stress and degrade U.S. global presence and prestige.[69]

Al-Qaida and its affiliated terrorist networks configure a major terrorist threat with global reach. Attacks on high value economic targets are likely to be targeted within the U.S. Homeland and U.S. presence abroad.

How can comparatively small terrorist groups believe they can successfully confront the United

> **...But our war with America is fundamentally different, for the first time priority is defeating it economically. For that, anything that negatively affects its economy is considered for us a step in the right direction on the path to victory. Military defeats do not greatly effect how we measure total victory, but these defeats indirectly affect the economy which can be demonstrated by the breaching of the confidence of capitalists and investors in this nation's ability to safeguard their various trade and dealings.'**
>
> **Abu Mus'ab al-Najadi**
> **October 2005**

States? For Islamic extremists, part of the answer reflects on jihad fighters in Afghanistan and their success against the Soviet Union in the 1980s. Many of these Islamic fighters were persuaded through their propaganda that they alone had defeated the

---

[69] "Unraveling Al-Qaeda's Target Selection Calculus," April 17, 2007, available from http://cns.miis.edu/pubs/week/070417.htm; Internet; accessed 15 May 2007.

Soviet Union in Afghanistan, even though the U.S. provided substantial support to the Islamic fighters.[70]

Another reason to expect greater use of terrorism against the U.S. is regional or global competitors may feel that they cannot openly challenge, constrain, or defeat the U.S. with any other technique. Nations have employed state sponsored or state directed terrorism to produce results that could not have otherwise been achieved against U.S. opposition. Non-state actors can span the wanton attack of an individual terrorist to apocalyptic or theological extremist groups that seek to acquire and use weapons of mass destruction.

> **"Those youths are different from your soldiers. Your problem will be how to convince your troops to fight, while our problem will be how to restrain our youths to wait for their turn in fighting and in operations."**
>
> **Usama bin Laden, "Declaration of War Against The Americans Occupying the Land of the Two Holy Places" August 26, 1996**

In addition to many potential adversaries, enemies view the U.S. as particularly vulnerable to the psychological impact and uncertainties generated by terror tactics in support of other activities.[71] Consequently, terrorist groups are likely to try capitalizing on what they may perceive as vulnerabilities. They include beliefs that:

- The United States of America is extremely casualty averse. Any loss of life takes on significance out of proportion to the circumstances.

- The U.S. Government policies and policy makers are overly influenced by public opinion, which in turn is particularly susceptible to the adverse psychological impact of terrorism.

- The U.S. economic performance is perception driven, and very vulnerable to the adverse psychological impact of terrorism.

- The U.S. cannot sustain long term efforts or exhibit public sacrifice in pursuit of difficult national goals.

---

[70] Gilles Kepel, *Jihad: The Trail of Political Islam* (Cambridge: The Belknap Press of Harvard University Press, 2002) 10,17.

[71] Qiao Liang and Wang Xiangsui, *Unrestricted Warfare,* trans. Department of State, American Embassy Beijing Staff Translators (Washington, D.C., 1999).

The growing polarization of some domestic political issues means that the U.S. is also likely to see increased terror attacks on its own soil by a variety of domestic or so-called homegrown terrorist groups. These groups may target U.S. forces either as symbols of government oppression, sources of weapons and equipment, or means to gain terrorist organizational prestige through a successful attack.

Operational Intent of Terrorism

Terrorism is primarily a psychological act that communicates through violence or the threat of violence. Terrorist strategies will be aimed at publicly causing damage to symbols or inspiring fear. Timing, location, and method of attacks accommodate mass media dissemination and optimize current news impact.

> **"We have seen in the last decade the decline of the American government and the weakness of the American soldier who is ready to wage Cold Wars and unprepared to fight long wars. This was proven in Beirut when the Marines fled after two explosions. It also proves they can run in less than 24 hours, and this was also repeated in Somalia."**
>
> **Usama bin Laden interview by ABC News' John Miller, May 1998**

A terrorist operation will often have the goal of manipulating popular perceptions, and will achieve this by controlling or dictating media coverage. This control need not be overt, as terrorists analyze and exploit the dynamics of major media outlets and the pressure of the news cycle.[72] A terrorist attack that appears to follow this concept was the bombing of commuter trains in Madrid, Spain in March 2004. There has been much speculation as to the true objective behind these bombings. One view is that Islamic terrorists who conducted the attacks specifically planned to influence the political process in Spain. They believed that a large percentage of the Spanish population opposed the war in Iraq and would feel that the current government was responsible for the bombings, and would vote for the opposition. The attacks occurred during morning rush hour just three days prior to national elections. The timing facilitated maximum casualties on the trains that killed 191 people and injured more than 1800. News coverage was immediate throughout the world and amplified the carnage of the terrorist attack. An antiwar Socialist prime minister was elected and quickly withdrew Spain's military forces from Iraq. Another aspect of the bombings was the terrorist connection to crime and drug dealing in a network that spanned Morocco, Spain, Belgium and the Netherlands.[73]

---

[72] Bruce Hoffman, *Inside Terrorism* (New York: Columbia University Press, 1998), 136-142.

[73] "The Architect and Fifth Generation Warfare," June 4, 2006; available from http://www.thestrategist.org/archives/2006/06/the_architect_o.html; Internet; accessed 13 March 2007.

In considering possible targets, terrorists recognize that a massively destructive attack launched against a target that cannot or will not attract sufficient media coverage is not purposeful. The 1998 bombings of the American embassies in Kenya and Tanzania illustrate how two diplomatic posts created global sensation because of the attacks and resulting media coverage. Modern technology provides immediate broadcast coverage of violence. The September 11, 2001 bombing of the World Trade Center in New York City was observed by millions of people worldwide on live television as the successive attacks occurred and sensational mass destruction followed.

Section II: Motivation

Motivation categories describe terrorist groups in terms of their goals or objectives. Some of common motivational categories are separatist, ethnocentric, nationalistic, and revolutionary.

Motivational Categories

- **Separatist.** Separatist groups reach for a goal of separation from existing entities through independence, political autonomy, or religious freedom or domination. The ideologies that separatists promote include social justice or equity, anti-imperialism, as well as the resistance to conquest or occupation by a foreign power. Categories of ethnicity and nationalism can crossover in support rationale.

Figure 2-2. **Beslan Hostage Crisis**

- **Ethnocentric.** Ethnocentric groups see race as the defining characteristic of a society and a basis of cohesion. Group members promote the attitude that a particular group is superior because of its ethnic or racial characteristics.

- **Nationalistic.** The loyalty and devotion to a nation and the national consciousness place one nation's culture and interests above those of other nations or groups is the motivating factor behind these groups. This can aim to create a new nation or to split away part of an existing state in order to join with another nation that shares the perceived national identity.

- **Revolutionary.** These groups are dedicated to the overthrow of an established order and replacing governance with a new political or social structure. Often associated with communist political ideologies, other political movements can advocate revolutionary methods to achieve their goals.

Ideology Influences

Groups with secular ideologies and nonreligious goals will often attempt highly selective and discriminate acts of violence to achieve a specific political aim. This often requires them to keep casualties at the minimum amount necessary to attain the objective. The intention is to avoid a backlash that might damage the organization's acceptability and maintain the appearance of a rational group that has legitimate grievances. By limiting their attacks they reduce the risk of undermining external political and economic support.

One example of a group that discriminates on target selection is the Revolutionary Organization 17 November. This is a radical leftist organization established in 1975 in Greece that is anti-Greek establishment, anti-United States, anti-Turkey, and anti-NATO. Its operations have included assassinations of senior U.S. officials, Greek public figures, and attacks on and foreign firms investing in Greece. In total, 17 November is believed to have been responsible for over 100 attacks, but just 23 fatalities between 1975 and 2000. [74] In many instances, the group used a .38 caliber pistol or a .45 caliber handgun which came to be regarded as their signature weapon. While face-to-face assassination was their early modus operandi, the group later used rockets and bombs stolen from Greek military facilities. Over 50 rocket attacks were claimed by 17N.[75]

Religiously oriented and millenarian groups may attempt to inflict as many casualties as possible. An apocalyptic or theological extremist frame of reference may determine loss of life as irrelevant and encourage mass casualty producing incidents. In 1995, the Aum Shinrikyo cult in Japan attempted to cause mass casualties by releasing sarin in the Tokyo subway system.

Figure 2-3. **Shoko Asahara and Aum Shinrikyo**

Some terrorists state that killing people labeled as religious nonbelievers is acceptable in an attack. The 1998 bombing of the U.S. Embassy in Kenya inflicted more casualties on the local Kenyan inhabitants than U.S. citizens. The ratio was approximately 20 non-U.S. citizens for every U.S. citizen killed. Wounded people numbered over 5000 Kenyans; 95 percent of the total casualties were non-American.[76] Fear of moral backlash rarely concerns this type of terrorist organization. With numerous dead and maimed Kenyans, terrorists attempted to qualify a rationale for the deaths and appease critics, but overall were unapologetic for the destruction, deaths, or mayhem.

Fig. 2-4. **Nairobi**

---

[74] "Revolutionary Organization 17 November (17N)," CDI Terrorism Project, 5 August 2002; available from http://www.cdi.org/terrorism/17N-pr.cfm; Internet; accessed 24 September 2004.
[75] *Wikipedia*, "Revolutionary Organization November17, " available from
http://en.wikipedia.org/wiki/Revolutionary_Organization_17_November; Internet; accessed 12 May 2007.
[76] Christopher C. Harmon, *Terrorism Today* (London: Frank Cass Publishers, 2000; reprint, Portland: Frank Cass Publishers, 2001), 51.

Muslim Victims of Terrorism 2006

Approximately 58,000 individuals worldwide were either killed or injured by terrorists attacks in 2006...well over 50 percent of the victims were Muslims, and most were victims of attacks in Iraq."

NCTC Reports on Terrorism Incidents - 2006 April 2007

For terrorist groups professing secular political, religious, or social motivations, their targets are often highly symbolic of authority: government offices, banks, national airlines, and multinational corporations with direct relation to the established order. Likewise, they may conduct attacks on representative individuals whom they associate with economic exploitation, social injustice, or political repression. While extremist religious groups also use much of this symbolism, there appears to be a trend to connect attacks to greater physical devastation and suffering. There also is a tendency to add religiously affiliated individuals, such as missionaries, and religious activities such as worship services to the targeting equation.

With much of the global attention on contemporary Islamic extremism and terrorism, the 2007 NCTC *Report on Terrorism Incidents - 2006* cites an interesting statistic. "As in 2005, Muslims in 2006 again bore a substantial share of the victims of terrorist attacks. Approximately 58,000 individuals worldwide were either killed or injured by terrorist attacks in 2006...well over 50 percent of the victims were Muslims, and most were victims of attacks in Iraq."[77]

Symbolism related to ideology may focus terrorist targeting in striking on particular anniversaries or commemorative dates. Nationalist groups may strike to commemorate battles won or lost during a conventional struggle, whereas religious groups may strike to mark particularly appropriate observances. Many groups will attempt to commemorate anniversaries of successful operations, or the executions or deaths of notable individuals related to their particular conflict. For instance, Timothy McVeigh conducted the bombing of the Murrah Federal Building on April 19th, the anniversary of the end of the Branch Davidian siege near Waco, Texas in 1993, as well as a violent incident from the early American Revolution in 1775.

Ideological Categories

Ideological categories describe the political, religious, or social orientation of the group. While some groups will be seriously committed to their avowed ideologies, for others, ideology is poorly understood and primarily a rationale used to provide justification for

---

[77] National Counterterrorism Center (NCTC), *Reports on Terrorism Incidents - 2006*, 30 April 2007, 11; available from http://www.terrorisminfo.mipt.org/Patterns-of-global-terrorism.asp; Internet; accessed 2 May 2007.

their actions to outsiders or sympathizers. Common ideological categories include political, religious, and social.

Political

Political ideologies are concerned with the structure and organization of the forms of government and communities.

- **Right Wing.** These groups are associated with the reactionary or conservative side of the political spectrum, and often are associated with fascism or neo-Nazism. Despite this, right-wing extremists can be every bit as revolutionary in intent as other groups. Their intent is to replace existing forms of government with a particular brand of authoritarian rule.

Fig. 2-5. **Aryan Nation**

- **Left Wing.** These groups are usually associated with revolutionary socialism or variants of communism such as Maoist or Marxist-Leninist. With the demise of many communist regimes and the gradual liberalization of remaining regimes toward capitalism, left-wing rhetoric can often move towards and merge with anarchistic thought.

Fig, 2-6. **Shining Path**

- **Anarchist.** Anarchist groups are anti-authority or anti-government, and strongly support individual liberty and voluntary association of cooperative groups. Often blending anti-capitalism and populist or communist-like messages, modern anarchists tend to neglect the problem of what will replace the current form of government, but generally promote that small communities are the highest form of political organization necessary or desirable.

Religious

Religiously inspired terrorism is on the rise. This is not a new phenomenon. Between 1980 and 1995, international terror groups espousing religious motivation increased by 43 percent.[78] Islamic terrorists and extremist organizations have been the most active and greatest recent threat to the United States. Religious extremism couches terrorism with distorted interpretation of theological dogma and can mask secular objectives as holy writ, infallible guidance, and non-negotiable responsibility. One commentary states, "The literature on terrorism clearly documented a dramatic rise in the religious affiliation

---

[78] Bruce Hoffman, *Inside Terrorism* (New York: Columbia University Press, 1998), 90.

of terrorist organizations. A generation ago none of the eleven international terrorist organizations was religiously oriented. By 2004, nearly half of the world's identifiable and active terrorist groups are classified as motivated by religious. Today, the vast majority of terrorist groups using suicide attacks are Islamic, displacing secular groups like the Tamil Tigers. Furthermore, religiously-oriented organizations account for a disproportionately high percentage of attacks and casualties."[79]

Religious motivations can also be tied to ethnic and nationalist identities, such as Kashmiri separatists combining their desire to break away from India with the religious conflict between Islam and Hinduism. The conflict in Northern Ireland provides an example of the intermingling of religious identity with nationalist motivation. Christian, Jewish, Sikh, Hindu and a host of lesser known religious denominations have seen activists commit terrorism in their name or spawned cults professing adherence to the larger religion while following unique interpretations of that particular religion's dogma.

Figure 2-7. **IRA on City Street**

Social

Often particular social policies or issues will be so contentious among individuals or groups that beliefs incite extremist behavior and terrorism. This form of social terrorism is often referred to as single issue or special interest terrorism. Some issues that have produced terrorist activities in the United States and other countries are: animal rights, abortion, ecology and the environment, anti-government,[80] and ethnic, race, or minority rights.

Location or Geographic Categories

Geographic designation of domestic or foreign terrorism has lost much of its meaning in the evolving membership of terrorist organizations. In the 1990s, domestic terrorism was commonly associated with right-wing or hate groups comprised of U.S. citizens. Concerns about terrorism included the possibility recruiting military personnel into their groups. Terrorist rationales for this recruiting included lending a degree of legitimacy to militant claims, providing trained members to further train other group members in the

---

[79] *Small Wars Journal*, "SWJ Blog: Luttwak's Lament," available from http://smallwarsjournal.com/blog/2007/04/luttwaks-lament/; Internet; accessed 12 May 2007.
[80] "Group Profile, First Mechanical Kansas Militia," available from http://www.tkb.org/Group.jsp?groupID=3418; Internet; accessed 12 May 2007. Some proclaimed groups may be nothing more but individuals with a bizarre concept of the world and conspiracy. Notwithstanding, these type of people can pose a significant threat to military forces when plots develop to attack events such as a 4th of July celebration at a U.S. Army installation.

use of weapons and tactics, and assisting in plans to steal military weapons, munitions, and equipment.[81]

More recent examples of citizens attacking their own country of citizenship blur the description of domestic versus foreign inspired terrorism. Examples include the 2002 Bali, Indonesia bombings that killed over 200 people and wounded over 200 people, and the 2005 London subway and bus bombings that brought a new level of terrorism to the United Kingdom homeland.

- **Domestic or Indigenous.** These terrorists are "home-grown," that is, they can be native born or naturalized citizens of a nation. They operate within and against their own country of residence. They may or may not have direct association with terrorist organizations located external to the United States homeland.

Examples include Timothy McVeigh and his bombing of the Murrah Federal Building, or the six men arrested in May 2007 for conspiring to attack U.S. military people, facilities, and equipment at Fort Dix, New Jersey. The criminal complaint accents that "The philosophy that supports and encourages jihad around the world against Americans came to live here in New Jersey and threaten the lives of our citizens through these defendants."[82] Initial investigation indicates that several of the men entered the U.S. illegally years previous to this incident.

- **International or Transnational.** International can be visualized as terrorist activity that is primarily between two nations and their geographic location. International groups may operate in multiple countries, but retain a geographic focus for their activities. Issues will indicate regional impact as a norm. Transnational is a more expansive realm of operating among multiple national geographic locations, and creating global impact with operational or strategic reach. Capabilities may include use of cyberspace and the Internet, worldwide financial institutions, and satellite headquarters or clandestine cells in multiple hemisphere locales.

For example, Hizballah has several organizational cells worldwide and has conducted operations in multiple countries, but is primarily concerned with political events in the region of Lebanon and Israel. Al-Qaida and its affiliated groups are transnational. Their vision is global and "In general terms...exhibit many characteristics of a globalized insurgency. This insurgency aims to overthrow the existing world order and replace it with a neo-fundamentalist, reactionary, authoritarian,

Fig. 2-8. **Hizballah**

---

[81] Steven Presley, *Rise of Domestic Terrorism and Its Relation to United States Armed Forces*, [Abstract] April 1996, available from http://www.fas.org/irp/eprint/presley.htm; Internet; accessed 12 May 2007.

[82] *CNN.com*, "Official: Radicals wanted to create carnage at Fort Dix," available from http://www.cnn.com/2007/US/05/08/fortdix.plot/index.html; Internet; accessed 12 May 2007.

transnational state. They collect intelligence, engage in denial and deception, use subversion, launch propaganda campaigns, engage in sabotage, and, of course, embrace terror as a defining tactic. Terror, of course, not only serves as a means of destruction, but also garners them visibility and provides them identity."[83]

Section III: Behavior

Individual Behaviors

No one profile exists for terrorists in terms of family background or personal characteristics. Several general observations may assist in understanding the extreme behavior of a terrorist. Notions of a bizarre social misfit or uneducated and unemployed person are a misperception as a norm. An analysis of over 150 al-Qaida terrorists displayed a norm of middle- to upper-class, highly educated, married, middle-aged men.[84] Women are appearing in increasing numbers, and have been significant actors in groups such as the Tamil Tigers in Sri Lanka, but men provide the vast majority of terrorist cadre in actual attacks. Adolescents and children have been used in terrorist attacks too. In some cases, children have been unaware that they were being used as terrorists such as in suicide bombings.[85]

Fig. 2-9. **Children as Suicide Bombs**

Utopian Worldview. Terrorists typically have idealized goals regardless of their aims as political, social, territorial, nationalistic, or religious. This utopianism expresses itself forcefully as an extreme degree of impatience with the rest of the world and convinces the terrorist to validate criminal acts as allowable methods. The terrorist will commonly perceive a crisis too urgent to be solved other than by the most extreme methods. A perception may exist that the government is too corrupt or ineffective to adopt change. This sense of impatience with opposition is central to the terrorist worldview and is a norm of secular and theologically motivated terrorists.

Cost-Benefit Analysis. Terrorist groups require recruitment, preparation, and integration into an operational structure in order to conduct terrorist acts. Recruits require extensive vetting to ensure that they demonstrate the ability to succeed in assigned missions and are

---

[83] Henry Crumpton, Coordinator for Counterterrorism, "Remarks at Transnational Terrorism Conference-12 January 2006," available from http://www.state.gov/s/ct/rls/rm/2006/59987.htm: Internet; accessed 12 May 2007.

[84] Philip G. Wasielewski, "Defining the War on Terror," *Joint Force Quarterly*, 44, 1st Quarter 2007, 16.

[85] "Fatah Tricks 12-year-old Boy into becoming a Suicide Terrorist," 15 March 2004, available from http://www.mfa.gov.il/MFA/Terrorism-+Obstacle+to+Peace/Terrorism+and+Islamic+Fund...; Internet; accessed 8 June 2007.

not infiltrators counter to the group's purpose. Al-Qaida assessed selected volunteers in a number of training camps and screened those individuals with the highest potential and skills. Additional training and testing determined those members who would be chosen for actual terrorist missions. The 9/11 attacks illustrated this type of ideologically indoctrinated, intelligent, and well prepared terrorists committed to a specific terrorist act.[86] Group leaders will consider the relationship between the cost of using, and possibly losing an asset, and the potential benefits to the group's notoriety.[87] Terrorist operational planning focuses on economies of personnel and balances the likelihood of loss against the value of a target and the probability of success. Masked by terms of martyrdom, terrorist propaganda promotes the concept that suicide is an acceptable and sought after means of commitment to an ideal.

For example, suicide bombing has caused significant turmoil in the Middle East region, and in particular, Iraq. Yet, an extremist religious viewpoint accepts suicide as a legitimate act and can be used to encourage this self-destruction and murder. Terrorists in Afghanistan have increased their resistance to the Afghan government and coalition forces in the last year and introduced suicide bombing on a level not experienced in earlier campaigning. Suicide attacks rose 370 percent in 2006 from the previous year. 80 suicide attacks occurred in 2006 compared to 17 in 2005.[88] The pattern in 2007 indicates an increasing number of suicide attacks.

Subordinate to Superior

Unquestioning submission to a group's authority figure may evolve from intensive indoctrination and a personal need to belong to a group and feel a sense of collective purpose. This is true of hierarchical and networked organizations, and in large or small groups. Individual leaders may exhibit great charisma or promote themselves as having a profound understanding of religious or philosophical principles.[89] If an individual feels disenfranchised from society or the ability to influence personal lifestyle and meaning, an authority figure within a terrorist group may be perceived as a role model and can suggest or demand tremendous sacrifices from subordinates. This form of inspirational leader uses persuasion and can also inspire "leaderless resisters" or "lone wolf avengers" to conduct individual acts of terror with no control by a chain of command.[90]

Dehumanization of Non-Members

Dehumanization permits violence to be directed indiscriminately at any target outside of the terrorist group. Assuming that all those outside of the group are either enemies or neutral, terrorists can rationalize in attacking anyone. Dehumanization removes some of

---

[86] Philip G. Wasielewski, "Defining the War on Terror," *Joint Force Quarterly*, 44, 1st Quarter 2007, 17.

[87] Ehud Sprinzak, "Rational Fanatics," *Foreign Policy,* 120 (September/October 2000): 66-73.

[88] National Counterterrorism Center (NCTC), *Reports on Terrorism Incidents - 2006*, 30 April 2007, 76; available from http://www.terrorisminfo.mipt.org/Patterns-of-global-terrorism.asp; Internet; accessed 2 May 2007.

[89] Sabil Frances, "Uniqueness of LTTE's Suicide Bombers," *Institute of Peace and Conflict Studies*, Article no. 321 (4 February 2000): 1; available at http://www.ipcs.org; Internet; accessed 7 September 2002.

[90] Philip G. Wasielewski, "Defining the War on Terror," *Joint Force Quarterly*, 44, 1st Quarter 2007.

the onus of killing innocent people. Some extremist views promote ideas that any compromise with adversaries is impossible. Other extremist views state that particular ethnic groups evolved from animals and are not worthy of any human comparison. Other viewpoints cite a continual struggle between oppressors and oppressed, and that a religious duty exists to fight and defeat inhuman opponents in the name of oppressed people and for the expansion of specific religious beliefs.

A terrorist can be indoctrinated to believe that murder furthers the interests of an unawakened social or ethnic people that are too oppressed or misinformed to realize its own best interests. Whether self-proclaimed as a revolutionary vanguard or a true patriot, a distorted concept assumes that the terrorist acts for the benefit of either a silent or ignorant mass that would approve of their struggle if they were free to choose or if they fully understood.

Terrorists can take this rationale of indiscriminate killing to an extreme. Some extremists promote attacks on civilians. Abu Anas al-Shami states, "Therefore, imams agree that if unbelievers shield themselves with the Muslims, how would it be for the Muslims if they did not fight? Thus it is permissible to fire upon them, and we mean the disbelievers."[91]

Until his death in 2006, Abu Mus'ab al-Zwaqawi actively supported suicide terrorism and rejected any traditional separation of military or government targets from civilians who may be in the same vicinity. In addition to indiscriminate killings, al-Zwaqawi also used very brutal tactics such as videotaped beheadings to create terror.

Fig. 2-10. **Videotaped Murder**

Lifestyle Attractions

The lifestyle of a terrorist, while not particularly appealing for members of stable societies, can provide emotional, physical and sometimes social rewards. Emotional rewards include the feelings of notoriety, power, and belonging. In some societies, there may be a sense of satisfaction in rebellion; in others there may be a perceived increase in social status or power. For some, the intense sense of belonging generated by membership in an illegal group is emotionally satisfying.[92]

---

[91] Brian Fishman, *Zarqawi's Jihad*, Combating Terrorism Center at West Point, U.S. Military Academy, 26 April, 2006, 20.
[92] Ibid., 34-35.

Physical rewards can include such things as money, authority, and adventure.[93] This lure can subvert other motives. Several of the more notorious terrorists of the 1970s and 1980s, such as Abu Nidal,[94] became highly specialized mercenaries, discarding their convictions and working for a variety of causes and sponsors. Abu Nidal is a nom de guerre for Sabri al-Banna and an international terrorist group named after its founder "Abu Nidal" – Abu Nidal Organization (ANO).[95] Sabris al-Banna rose in notoriety in the Palestine Liberation Organization

> "There's something about a good bomb."
>
> **Bill Ayers, Former Weather Underground Leader in his memoir *Fugitive Days***

(PLO) but broke away from the PLO to form his own terror organization in the mid-1970s. The group's goals center on the destruction of the state of Israel, but the group has served as a mercenary terrorist force with connections to several radical regimes including Iraq, Syria, and Libya.[96] ANO activities link to terrorist attacks in 20 countries with killing about 300 people and injuring hundreds of additional people totaling estimates of about 900 victims.[97]

Lifestyle attractions also include a sense of elitism, and a feeling of freedom from societal mores. "Nothing in my life had ever been this exciting!" was a statement by Susan Stern, member of the Weather Underground, describing her involvement with the U.S. domestic terrorist group.[98]

Organizational Behavior

People within groups have different behaviors collectively than they do as individuals. Terrorist organizations have varying motives and reasons for existence, and how the group interprets these guides or determines internal group dynamics. Groups are normally more daring and ruthless than the individual members. No individual wishes to appear less committed than the others, and will not object to proposals within the group they would not consider as an individual.[99] Leaders will not risk being seen as timid, for fear of losing their influence over the group. The end result can be actions not in keeping with individual behavior patterns as far as risk and lethality, but dictated by the pressure of group expectations and suppression of dissent and caution.

---

[93] Ibid., 271.

[94] Bruce Hoffman, *Inside Terrorism* (New York: Columbia University Press, 1998), 187.

[95] "Abu Nidal," *Encyclopedia of the Orient* [database on-line]; available from http://i-cias.com/e.o/abu_nidal.htm; Internet; accessed 24 February 2004.

[96] "Abu Nidal Organization," *Terrorism Questions and Answers* [database on-line]; available from http://cfrterrorism.org/groups/abunidal.html; Internet; accessed 24 February 2004.

[97] "Abu Nidal Organization (ANO)," *FAS Intelligence Resource Program* [database on-line]; available from http://www.fas.org/irp/world/para/ano.htm; Internet, accessed 24Febraury 2004.

[98] Bruce Hoffman, *Inside Terrorism* (New York: Columbia University Press, 1998), 176.

[99] Walter Reich, ed., *Origins of Terrorism: Psychologies, Ideologies, Theologies, States of Mind*, rev. ed. (Washington: Woodrow Wilson Center Press, 1998), 36.

Group commitment stresses secrecy and loyalty to the group. Disagreements are discouraged by the sense of the external threat represented by the outside world, and pressure to conform to the group view. Excommunication from the group adds to the group's loathing and hatred of doubters or deserters.[100] The slightest suspicion of disloyalty can result in torture and murder of the suspect. The ideological intensity that makes terrorists such formidable enemies often turns upon itself, and some groups have purged themselves so effectively that they almost ceased to exist.[101]

Frequently, the existence of the group becomes more important than the goal the members originally embraced. A group may adjust objectives as a reason for continued existence. In some cases, success can mean disbanding the organization. As members reject group direction and methods, individuals or factions may cause factions to develop. The resulting splinter groups or dissenting individual members are extremely volatile and run the risk of compromising the original group's purpose.

In cases where the terrorists are not tied to a particular political or social goal, groups will even adopt a new cause if the original one is resolved. When first formed, many of the Euro-terror groups such as the Red Army Faction (Germany) and Communist Combatant Cells (Belgium) grew out of the 1960s student protest movement. The initial motivations for their actions were supposedly to protest U.S. involvement in Vietnam and support the North Vietnamese government. When American involvement in Vietnam came to an end, some of the radical membership in Europe embraced Palestinian and pro-Arab causes rather than disband. Later, they conducted attacks against research facilities supporting the U.S. Strategic Defense Initiative, and to protest and prevent deployment of the Pershing IRBM (Intermediate Range Ballistic Missile) in Germany.

Organizations that are experiencing difficulties may tend to increase their level of violence. This increase in violence can occur when frustration and low morale develops within the group due to lack of perceived progress or successful counter-terrorism measures that may limit freedom of action within the terrorist group. Members attempt to perform more effectively, but such organizational and cooperative impediments usually result in poor operational performance. The organization hopes that a change to more spectacular tactics or larger casualty lists will overcome the group's internal problems.[102]

After an increase in suicide attacks, the chief military leader of India's northern command in Kashmir stated that militants were launching attacks to lift the morale of their cadres, because continued Indian army operations were killing militants daily and weakening the terrorist group's capabilities.[103]

---

[100] David C. Rapoport, ed., *Inside Terrorist Organizations* (New York: Columbia University Press, 1988), 157.

[101] Christopher C. Harmon, *Terrorism Today* (London: Frank Cass Publishers, 2000; reprint, Portland: Frank Cass Publishers, 2001), 213.

[102] Walter Reich, ed., *Origins of Terrorism: Psychologies, Ideologies, Theologies, States of Mind*, rev. ed. (Washington: Woodrow Wilson Center Press, 1998), 16.

[103] "Kashmir's Army Chief Fears Increased Suicide Attacks by Rebels," *South Asia Monitor*, 6 August 2003, 2; available from http://www.southasiamonitor.org/focus/2003/july/24rebels.html; Internet; accessed 20 April 2004.

Another example is al-Qaida in the Arabian Peninsula. During a 13-month period, this al-Qaida subgroup sustained a number of arrests and killings of their members, including the group's leader being killed and replaced four times. In May and June 2004, the subgroup conducted a wave of hostage taking, beheadings, and gruesome murders. *Sawt Al-Jihad*, an al-Qaida identified journal, interviewed the leader of the Al-Quds Brigade, a subordinate unit of the group that took responsibility for the May 29, 2004 Oasis Compound attack at al-Khobar, Saudi Arabia where 22 people were killed. During this interview, the terrorist commander claimed they had either beheaded or cut the throats of more than twelve of the victims.[104] Al-Qaida in the Arabian Peninsula was also responsible for a number of other murders including Robert Jacobs, an American contract employee, and the beheading of Paul Johnson, an American contract employee. The terrorist group released videotapes of both kidnappings and murders.

Fig. 2-11. **Oasis Compound al-Khobar**

Conclusion

This chapter presented aspects of terrorist motivations and behaviors. Goals and objectives of terrorist organizations differ throughout the world and range from regional single-issue terrorists to the aims of transnational radicalism and terrorism.

Terrorism is primarily a psychological act that communicates through violence or the threat of violence. Common motivational categories include separatism, ethnocentrisms, nationalism, and revolution. Ideological categories can be framed by political, religious, or social purpose.

Domestic or indigenous terrorists are "home-grown," that is, they can be native born or naturalized citizens of a nation. They operate normally within and against their own country of residence. International or transnational terrorists can be visualized as operating primarily between two nations and their geographic region. International groups may operate in multiple countries, but retain a regional geographic focus for their activities. Terrorism is becoming more violent as terrorist organizations realize the value of notoriety due to spectacular attacks and the mass media exploitation that results.

---

[104] *Al-Qaeda in the Arabian Peninsula: Shooting, Hostage Taking, Kidnapping Wave – May/June 2004* (Alexandria: Tempest Publishing, LLC, 2004), 46-60.

The U.S. Depart of State's Coordinator for Counterterrorism states several salient points on how a worldview by democratic nations must address terrorism in a contemporary operational environment.[105]

Combating Transnational Terrrorism

"Our global interdependence makes us stronger, but also in some aspects, more vulnerable. There is also a backlash from those who view globalization as a threat to traditional culture and their vested interests. Some discontented, illiberal non-state actors perceive themselves under attack and, therefore, resort to offensive action. This is the case with Al Qaeda and affiliated organizations. Yet, these enemies face a strategic environment featuring nation states with an overwhelming dominance in conventional military forces. This includes but is not limited to the U.S. It's no surprise, then, that our actual and potential enemies have taken note of our conventional superiority and acted to dislocate it. State actors, such as North Korea and Iran, seek irregular means to engage their foes. Iran uses proxies such as Hizballah. Non-state actors like Al Qaeda have also developed asymmetric approaches that allow them to side-step conventional military power. They embrace terror as a tactic, but on such a level as to provide them strategic impact. Toward that end, they seek to acquire capabilities that can pose catastrophic threats, such as WMD, disruptive technologies, or a combination of these measures."

Henry Crumpton, Coordinator for Counterterrorism
U.S. Department of State, January 2006

---

[105] Henry Crumpton, "Remarks by Amb. Henry A. Crumpton, U.S. Coordinator for Counterterrorism at RUSI Conference on Transnational Terrorism," 16 January 2006; available from http://london.usembassy.gov/ukpapress17.html; Internet; accessed 12 August 2007.

This Page Intentionally Blank

3 | Terrorist Organizational Models

Chapter 3

Terrorist Organizational Models

Our [enemy] is proactive, innovative, well-networked, flexible, patient, young, technologically savvy, and learns and adapts continuously based upon both successful and failed operations around the globe.[106]

Honorable Lee Hamilton
Task Force Chairman for the Future of Terrorism Task Force 2007
Department of Homeland Security, Homeland Security Advisory Council

A terrorist organization's structure, membership, resources, and security determine its capabilities and reach. Knowledge of current and emergent models of terrorist organization improves an understanding and situational awareness of terrorism in a contemporary operational environment.

Popular images of a terrorist group operating in accordance with a specific political agenda and motivated by ideology or the desire for ethnic or national liberation dominated traditional appreciation of terrorism. While true of some terrorist organizations, this image is not universally valid. Terrorism threats range al-Qaida and affiliated cells with regional, international, or transnational reach to domestic hate groups and self-radicalized, unaffiliated terrorists with single issue agendas and finite capabilities.

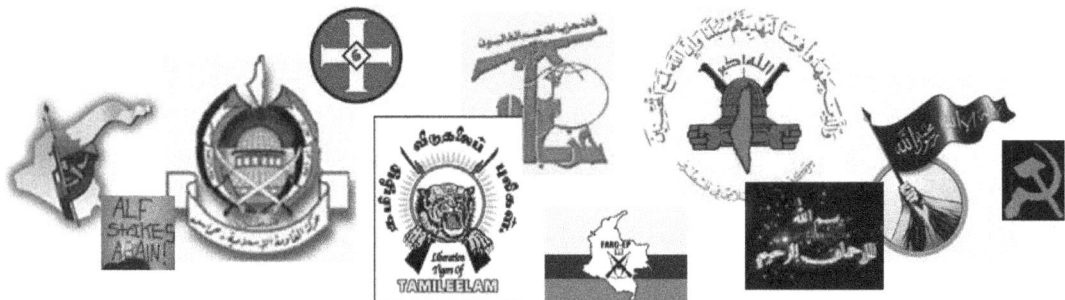

Figure 3-1. **Diverse Terrorism Intents and Capabilities in the COE**

---

[106] Don Philpott, "The Future of Terrorism Task force," *Homeland Defense Journal*, April 2007, 16-20.

What is one of the most significant adaptations in terrorist organization? "Perhaps the most fundamental shift rests in the enemy's downsizing. We will not see large al-Qaida armies. Rather, we will increasingly face enemy forces in small teams or even individuals. From an operational perspective, these are 'micro-targets with macro-impact' operating in the global exchange of people, data, and ideas. The enemy, their tradecraft, their tactics, their weapons, and their battlefield, our battlefield -- all evolve at the pace of globalization itself. We are facing the future of war today. The ongoing debate, sometimes disagreement, among allies reflects this new reality, this new way of war."[107]

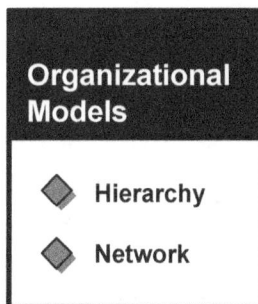

Organizational Models

◆ **Hierarchy**

◆ **Network**

In examining the structure of terrorist groups, this handbook presents two general categories of organization: network and hierarchy. A terrorist group may employ either type or a combination of the two models. The cell is the basic unit of organization in any of the models.

Contemporary groups tend to organize or adapt to opportunities available in the network model. Other variants professing an ideology can have more defined effects on internal organization. Leninist or Maoist groups can tend towards centralized control and hierarchical structure. Terrorist groups that are associated with a political activity or organization will often require a more hierarchical structure, in order to coordinate deliberate terrorist violence with political action. Examples include observing cease-fire agreements or avoiding particular targets in support of political objectives.

However, al-Qaida presents an example that has evolved from a hierarchical organization to a much more networked organization. Aspects of hierarchy still exist in senior leaders, cadre for functional coordination, and dedicated subgroups of terrorism. Current patterns display an increasing use of loosely affiliated networks that plan and act on generalized guidance on waging terror. Individuals with minimal or no direct connection to al-Qaida may take their inspiration for terrorism from ideological statements of senior al-Qaida leaders. Some individuals receive minimal training but act with no control by an organization such as al-Qaida. Richard Reid and his attempt to bomb an intercontinental flight in midair during December 2001 is an example of such a lone actor.

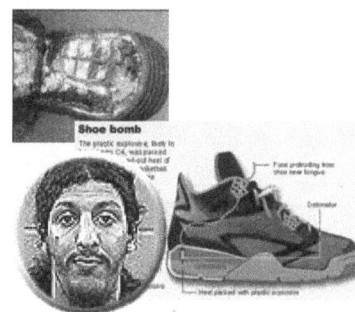

Fig. 3-1. **Reid and Shoe Bomb**

---

[107] Henry Crumpton, Coordinator for Counterterrorism, "Remarks at Transnational Terrorism Conference-12 January 2006," available from http://www.state.gov/s/ct/rls/rm/2006/59987.htm: Internet; accessed 12 May 2007.

Presenting any generalized organizational structure can be problematic. Terrorist groups can be at various stages of development in terms of capabilities and sophistication. Change in terrorist leadership, whether through generational transition or in response to enhanced security operations, may signal significant adjustments to organizational priorities and available means to conduct terrorism. Groups professing or associated with ethnic or nationalist agendas and limiting their operations to one country or a localized region tend to require fewer capabilities. Larger groups can merge from smaller organizations, or smaller groups can splinter off from larger organizations. Organizational method is situation dependent on specific circumstances of an operational environment during specified periods of time.

Section I: Organizational Commitment

Levels of Commitment

Typically, different levels of commitment exist within an organization. One way of display is four levels of commitment consisting of passive supporters, active supporters, cadre, and leaders. The pyramid diagram at Figure 3-2 is not intended as an organizational diagram, but indicates a relative number of people in each category. The general image of overall density holds true for networks as well as hierarchies. Passive supporters may intermingle with active supporters and be unaware of what their actual relationship is to the organization.

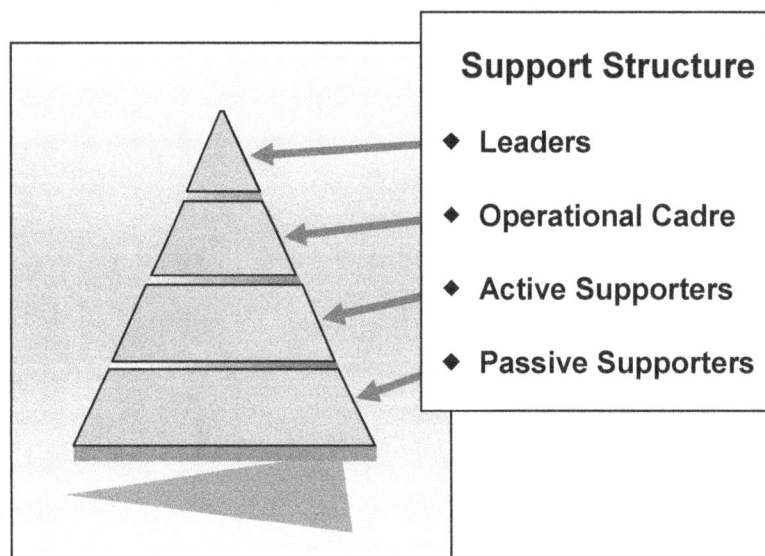

Support Structure

♦ **Leaders**

♦ **Operational Cadre**

♦ **Active Supporters**

♦ **Passive Supporters**

Figure 3-2. **Typical Levels of Organization**

- **Leaders** provide direction and policy; approve goals and objectives; and provide overarching guidance for operations. Usually leaders rise from within the ranks of an organization or create their own organization.

- **Cadres** are the active members of the terrorist organization. This echelon plans and conducts not only operations, but also manages areas of intelligence, finance, logistics, propaganda, and communications. Mid-level cadres tend to be trainers and technicians such as bomb makers, financiers, and surveillance experts. Low-level cadres are the bombers and similar direct action terrorists.

- **Active Supporters** are active in the political, fund-raising, and information activities of the group. Acting as a visible or tacit partner, they may also conduct intelligence and surveillance activities, and provide safehaven houses, financial contributions, medical assistance, and transit assistance for cadre members of the organization. Active supporters are fully aware of their relationship to the terrorist group but do not normally commit violent acts.

Figure 3-3. **HAMAS**

- **Passive Supporters** are typically individuals or groups that are sympathetic to the announced goals and intentions of an overarching agenda, but are not committed enough to take an active role in terrorism. They may not be aware of their precise relation to the terrorist group, and interface with a front that hides the overt connection to the terrorist group. Sometimes fear of reprisal from terrorists is a compelling factor in passive support. Sympathizers can be useful for political activities, fund raising, and unwitting or coerced assistance in intelligence gathering and other non-violent activities.

Terrorist groups will recruit from populations that are sympathetic to their goals. Legitimate organizations can serve as recruiting grounds for terrorists. Militant Islamic recruiting, for example, is often associated with the proliferation of fundamentalist religious sects. Some recruiting is conducted on a worldwide basis via schools financed from both governmental and non-governmental donations and grants. Recruiting may be conducted for particular skills and qualifications and not be focused on ideological commitment. Some terrorist organizations have sought current or former members of the U.S. armed forces as trained operatives and as agents within an organization.

Recruitment can gain operatives from many diverse social backgrounds. The approach to radical behavior or direct actions with terrorism can develop over the course of years or decades. One example is John Walker Lindh, the U.S. citizen captured in Afghanistan by U.S. military forces. His notoriety jumped into international attention, as did the situation of individuals from several counties that were apprehended in combat actions of Afghanistan. Lindh's change from an unassuming middle-class adolescent in the Western United States to a member of a paramilitary training camp in Pakistan and subsequent support for Taliban forces in Afghanistan spotlights that general profiling can be doubtful, and any assessment should be tempered with specific instances and a broad perspective. In the case of Jose Padilla, his simplistic and voluntary efforts to detonate a bomb in the U.S. may illustrate al-Qaida techniques to support, finance, and use less than sophisticated means to conduct terrorist acts.

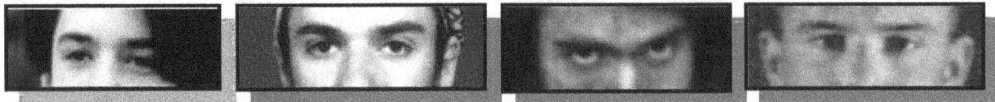

Figure 3-4. **Radicalization of U.S. Citizen**

Some groups will use coercion and leverage to gain limited or one-time cooperation from useful individuals. This cooperation can range from gaining information to conducting a suicide bombing operation.[108] Blackmail and intimidation are common forms of coercion. Threats to family or community members, as well as a targeted individual, may be employed.

Section II: Organizational Structure

Cellular Foundation

The cell is the smallest element at the tactical level of terrorist organization. Individuals, usually three to ten people, comprise a cell and act as the basic tactical component for a terrorist organization. One of the primary reasons for a cellular configuration is security. The compromise or loss of one cell should not compromise the identity, location, or actions of other cells. Compartmenting functions within organizational structure makes it difficult for an adversary to penetrate the entire organization. Personnel within one cell are often unaware of the existence of other cells and cannot provide sensitive information to infiltrators or captors.

Terrorists may organize cells based on family or employment relationships, on a geographic basis, or by specific functions such as direct action or intelligence. The terrorist group may also form multifunctional cells. Cell members remain in close contact with each other in order to provide emotional support and enhance security procedures. The cell leader is normally the only person who communicates and coordinates with higher levels and other cells. A terrorist group may form only one cell or may form several cells that operate in local or regional areas, across national borders, or among several countries in transnational operations.

A home page of the Earth Liberation Front (ELF) described its viewpoint of cellular organization. "Modeled after the Animal Liberation Front [ALF], the E.L.F. is structured in such a way as to maximize effectiveness. By operating in cells (small groups that consist of one to several people), the security of group members is maintained. Each cell is anonymous not only to the public but also to one another. This decentralized structure helps keep activists out of jail and free to continue conducting actions."

---

[108] Walter Reich, ed., *Origins of Terrorism: Psychologies, Ideologies, Theologies, States of Mind*, rev. ed. (Washington: Woodrow Wilson Center Press, 1998), 270-271.

Two basic methods define organizational structure of a terrorist group. These methods are hierarchical and networked models. A terrorist group may employ either type or a combination of the two models.

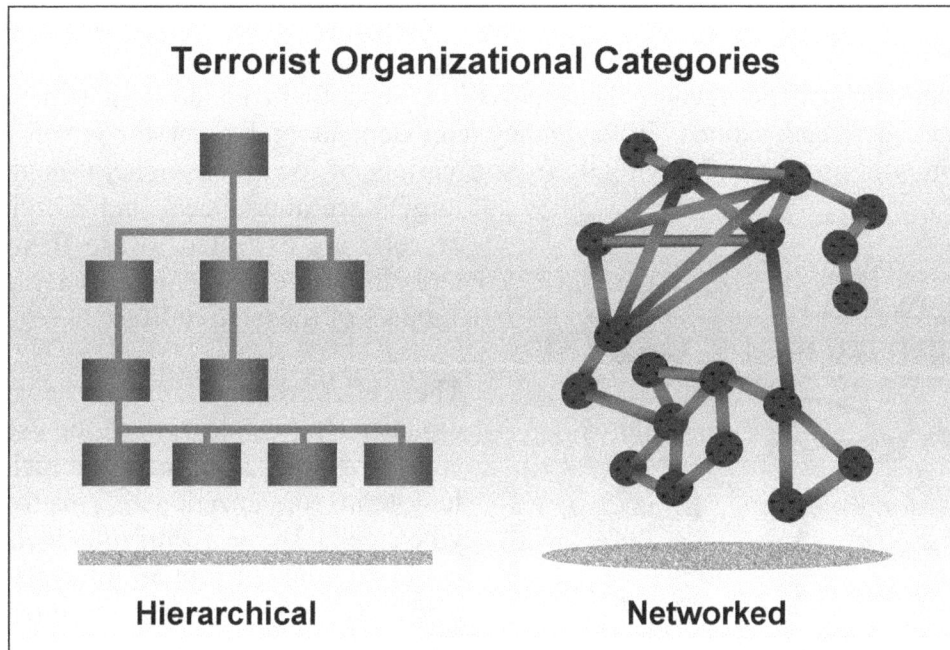

Figure 3-2. **Organizational Structure Categories**

Hierarchical Structure

Hierarchical structure organizations are those that have a well-defined vertical chain of command, control, and responsibility. Data and intelligence flows up and down organizational channels that correspond to these vertical chains, but may not necessarily move horizontally through the organization.

Hierarchical organizations feature greater specialization of functions in their subordinate cells such as support, operations, intelligence. Usually, only the cell leader has knowledge of other cells or contacts, and only senior leadership has visibility of the organization at large.

In the past, terrorism was practiced in this manner by identifiable organizations with a command and control structure influenced by revolutionary theory or ideology. Radical leftist organizations such as the Japanese Red Army, the Red Army Faction in Germany, the Red Brigades in Italy, as well as ethno-nationalist terrorist movements such as the Palestine Liberation Organization, the Irish Republican Army and the Basque separatist ETA group, conformed to this structure. These organizations had a clearly defined set of political, social or economic objectives, and tailored aspects of their organizations such as a political wing or social welfare group to facilitate their success. The necessity to coordinate actions between various subordinate cells such as political offices or non-violent support groups favored a strong and hierarchical authority structure.

Networked Structure

Terrorists are increasingly using a broader system of networks than previously experienced. Groups based on religious or single issue motives may lack a specific political or nationalistic agenda. They have less need for a hierarchical structure to coordinate plans and actions. Instead, they can depend and even thrive on loose affiliation with groups or individuals from a variety of locations. General goals and targets are announced, and individuals or cells are expected to use flexibility and initiative to conduct action in support of these guidelines.

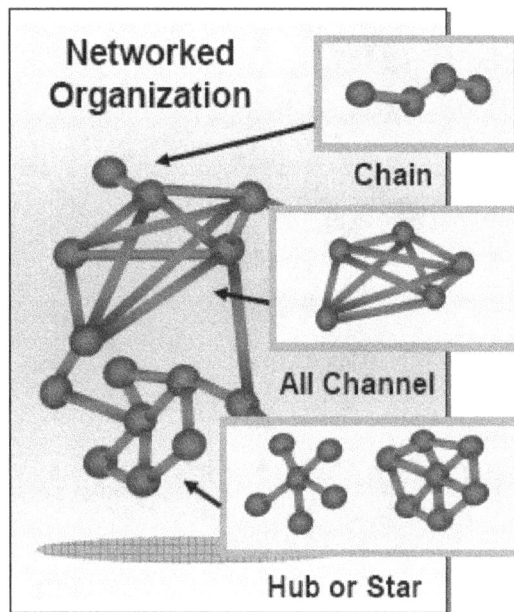

The effectiveness of a networked organization is dependent on several considerations. The network achieves long-term organizational effectiveness when cells share a unifying ideology, common goals or mutual interests.[109] A difficulty for network organizations not sharing a unifying ideology is cells can pursue objectives or take actions that do not meet the goals of the organization, or are counterproductive. In this instance, the independence of cells fails to develop synergy between their activities and limits their contribution to common objectives.

Figure 3-3. **Networked Organization**

Networks distribute the responsibility for operations and plan for redundancies of key functions. Cells do not contact or coordinate with other cells except for coordination essential to a particular operation or function. Avoiding unnecessary coordination or command approval for action provides ability for terrorist leaders to deny responsibility of specified acts of terror, as well as enhance operational security.

Networks are not necessarily dependent on modern information technology for effective command and control. The organizational structure and the flow of information and guidance inside the organization are defining aspects of networks. While information technology can make networks more effective, low technology means such as couriers, paper messages, and landline telephones can enable networks to avoid detection and operate effectively in certain circumstances.

---

[109] John Arquilla and David Ronfeldt, ed., *Networks and Netwars* (Santa Monica: RAND, 2001), 9.

Types of Structure.

There are various types of networked structure, depending on the ways elements are linked to other elements of the structure. There are three basic types: chain, hub, and all-channel. A terrorist group may also employ a hybrid structure that combines elements of more than one network type.

- **Chain Networks**

  Each cell links to the node next in sequence. Communication between the nodes is by passing information along the line. This organization is common among networks that smuggle goods and people or launder money.

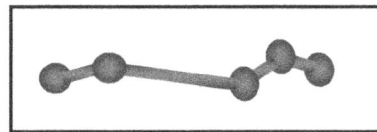

Fig. 3-4. **Chain Network**

- **Hub and Star**

  Cells communicate with one central element. The central cell need not be the leader or decision maker for the network. A variation of the hub is a wheel design where the outer nodes communicate with one or two other outer cells in addition to the hub. A wheel configuration is a common feature of a financial or economic network.

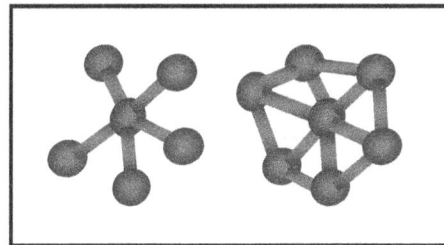

Fig. 3-5. **Hub and Star Network**

- **All-Channel**

  All nodes are connected to each other. The network is organizationally flat indicating there is no hierarchical command structure above it. Command and control is distributed within the network. This is communication intensive and can be a security problem if the linkages can be identified or tracked.

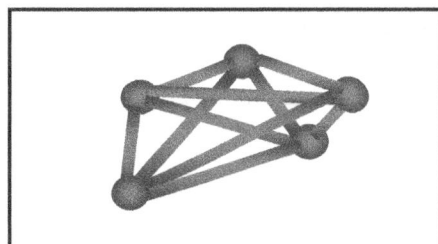

Figure 3-6. **All-Channel Network**

Despite their differences, the three basic types will be encountered together in hybrid organizations. A transnational terrorist organization might use chain networks for its money-laundering activities, tied to a wheel network handling financial matters, tied in turn to an all-channel leadership network to direct the use of the funds into the operational activities of a hub network conducting pre-targeting surveillance and reconnaissance.

Ideological Affiliation

A variation on network structure is a loosely affiliated method which depends more on an ideological intent, rather than any formalized command and control or support structure. These semi-independent or independent cells plan and act within their own means to promote a common ideological position with terrorist organizations that may have regional, international, or transnational reach.

Individuals may interpret a theology and acquire an extreme viewpoint of how to promote the ideology with personal action. Cells may form from a general inspiration of al-Qaida or similar ideological announcements.

Other independent actors may act as individuals or small terror cells to demonstrate a specific issue such as domestic terrorism in Environmental Liberation Front (ELF) or Animal Liberation Front (ALF) movements.

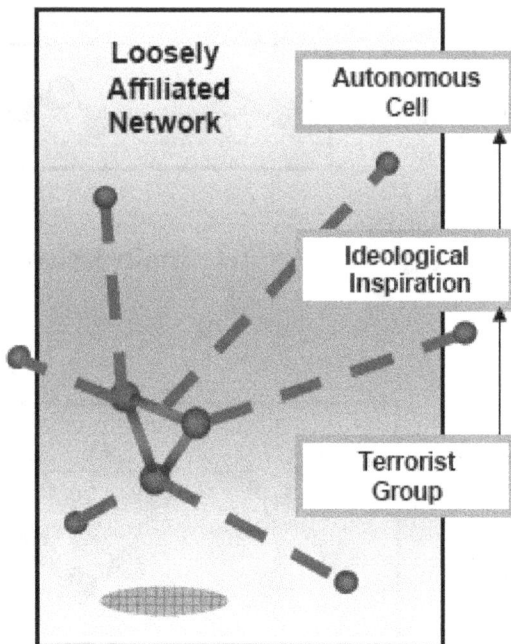

Figure 3-7. **Affiliated Network**

Section III: Organizational Categories

There are many different categories of terrorism and terrorist groups and their levels of capability. This section addresses several common classifications of support to terrorist organizations and provides explanation relationships.

Terrorist Affiliation

Categorizing terrorist groups by their affiliation with governments provides indications of their means for intelligence, operations, and access to types of weapons. U.S. joint doctrine identifies three affiliations: non-state supported, state-supported, and state-directed terrorist groups.[110]

---

[110] Joint Pub 3-07.2. *Antiterrorism*, 14 April 2006, II-4.

- **Non-state Supported.** These are terrorist groups that operate autonomously, receiving no significant support from any government.

- **State Supported.** These are groups that generally operate independently but receive support from one or more governments.

- **State Directed.** These groups operate as an agent of a government and receive substantial intelligence, logistic, and operational support from the sponsoring government.

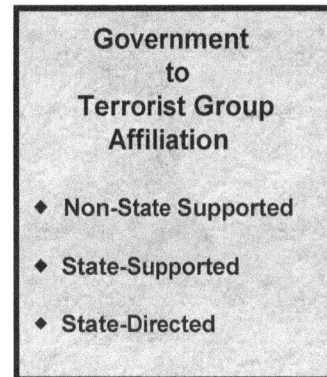

> **Government to Terrorist Group Affiliation**
>
> ◆ Non-State Supported
>
> ◆ State-Supported
>
> ◆ State-Directed

Association between or among terrorist groups increase their capabilities through the exchange of knowledge and other resources. Exchanges occur both directly and indirectly. Direct exchange occurs when one group provides the other with training or experienced personnel not readily available otherwise. An example of direct exchange is the provision of sophisticated bomb construction expertise by the IRA and ETA to less experienced groups. In 2001, three members associated with the IRA were arrested in Colombia. Traveling on false passports and with traces of explosives on their clothes and luggage,[111] the three individuals appeared to be an instance of inter-group terrorist support in use of explosives and other terrorist techniques. U.S. government reports state an IRA and FARC connection since at least 1998 with multiple visits of IRA operatives to Colombia. Terrorism techniques not previously observed as a norm in FARC operations, such as use of secondary explosive devices, indicate a transfer of IRA techniques.[112]

In order to disseminate knowledge, terrorist organizations often develop extensive training initiatives. By the 1990s, al-Qaida assembled thousands of pages of written training material, extensive libraries of training videos, and a global network of training camps.[113] This training material was distributed in both paper copy or via the Internet.

Indirect transfer of knowledge occurs when one group carries out a successful operation and is studied and emulated by others. The explosion of hijacking operations in the 1970s, and the similar proliferation of hostage taking in the 1980s were the result of terrorist groups observing and emulating successful attacks. However, this type of knowledge transfer is not restricted to just violent international terrorist groups. The same is true for many of the single issue groups located in the United States. The Stop

---

[111] Rachael Ehrenfeld, *IRA + PLO + Terror* [journal on-line] American Center for Democracy (ACD), 21 August 2002; available from http://public-integrity.org/publications21.htm; Internet; accessed 13 February 2004.

[112] Jan Schuurman, *Tourists or Terrorists?* [press review on-line] Radio Netherlands, 25 April 2002; available from http://www.rnw.nl/hotspots/html/irel020425.html; Internet; accessed 13 February 2004.

[113] Ben Venzke and Aimee Ibrahim, *The al-Qaeda Threat: An Analytical Guide to al-Qaeda's Tactics and Targets* (Alexandria: Tempest Publishing, LLC, 2003), 7.

Huntingdon Animal Cruelty (SHAC) group uses tactics initially used by British activists, which targets the homes of individuals that are related in some form to Huntingdon Life Sciences, an animal-testing lab. They use tactics just short of physical violence in terrorizing families and entire neighborhoods, such as showing up with sirens and bullhorns at 3 a.m., plastering the neighborhood with photographs of mutilated dogs, and posting home and work phone numbers on the Internet. An Oregon-based watchdog group, Stop Eco-Violence, stated that they are seeing a copycat effect within the eco-terror movement, with other groups now using similar tactics.[114]

These examples of knowledge exchange highlight the fact that assessments of terrorist threat capabilities cannot only be based upon proven operational abilities. Evaluating potential terrorist threats must consider what capabilities the specific terrorist cell may acquire through known or suspected associations with other groups.

Support

There are several types of support that provide information about a terrorist group's capabilities. These are measures of the strength of financial, political, and popular support for a group, as well as the number of personnel and sympathizers the group influences. These factors indicate an organization's abilities to conduct and sustain operations, gather intelligence, seek sanctuary and exploit the results of operations.

- **Financial.** Is the organization well funded? Money is a significant force multiplier of terrorist capabilities and involves the practical matters of income and expenditure. Many of the terror groups of significant durability such as the IRA, HAMAS, or Hizballah have large financial resources. Infrastructure costs consider the political and social support obligations that some groups promote to the population they exist within in order to gain active or passive support.

Fig. 3-8. **Money Laundering**

HAMAS is an example of a terrorist organization that has strong financial backing. Although the actual amount of money available to HAMAS is difficult to determine, estimates are that they receive several tens of millions of dollars per year. Sources for their funding include unofficial sources in Saudi Arabia and the Gulf States, including approximately several million dollars worth of support per year from Iran. They also receive funds that are siphoned from apparent charities or profitable economic projects.[115]

---

[114] Don Thompson, "British Ecoterror Tactics Spread to U.S. Activists," *The Mercury News*, 10 May 2003, 1-2; available from http://www.mercurynews.com/mld/mercurynews/news/local/5832723.htm?1c; Internet; accessed 21 April 2004.

[115] "Hamas," International Policy Institute for Counter-Terrorism, Profiles of International Terrorist Organizations, n.d., 5-6; available from http://www.ict.org.il/inter_ter/orgdet.cfm?orgid=13; Internet; accessed 26 April 2004.

Fig. 3-9. **HAMAS and Hizballah Politics**

- **Political.** Does the organization have political sponsors or representation, either within international, state, or sub-state political bodies? This measures the degree to which a group is state sponsored or supported, and considers whether the organization has its own political representatives or party that support its aims and methods. Political support can blur the distinction between terrorism and other forms of conflict and can generate sympathy and reduce negative consequences.

- **Popular.** What is the level of popular support or empathy? Passive or active support for the organization among populations it affects or operates within shapes the organizational tempo of activities. Support from a constituency increases the effectiveness of other types of support and increases the legitimacy and visibility of a group. Popular support from populations the terrorists operate within reduces the security risks and complicates the tasks of detection and defeat for the opposing security forces.

Fig. 3-10. **IRA Poster**

The size of a group in terms of the number of personnel is important but less so than other aspects of support. A small, well-funded, highly trained group may effectively attack targets, whereas a larger poorly funded and untrained group may be no direct threat to U.S. targets other than those in immediate proximity to its base area of operations. For instance, the Japanese Red Army (JRA) conducted numerous attacks around the world in the 1970s, including an attempted takeover of the U.S. Embassy in Kuala Lumpur. In 1988, the JRA was suspected of bombing a USO club in Naples, where 5 people were killed, including a U.S. servicewoman. Concurrent with this attack in Naples, a JRA operative was arrested with explosives on the New Jersey Turnpike, apparently planning an attack to coincide with the attack of the USO. Although the JRA conducted attacks around the world, the JRA only had six hard-core members, and at its peak, only had 30 to 40 members.[116]

Training

Training is the level of proficiency with tactics, techniques, technology and weapons useful to terrorist operations. Innovative application of tactics can render moderately harmless activities threatening. For example, the ability to stage a peaceful demonstration

---

[116] Department of State, Office of the Coordinator for Counterterrorism, *Patterns of Global Terrorism 2002* (Washington, D.C., April 2003), 137.

may be used to set the conditions for a riot that will provide cover for sniper assassinations of responding security forces.

 Training video tapes have shown al-Qaida operatives conducting live fire exercises for a number of scenarios. These scenarios include assassinations, kidnappings, bombings, and small unit raids on various types of targets. They often conduct detailed planning, diagramming, and walk-through rehearsals prior to the actual live-fire training exercise.

Fig. 3-11. **Training Video**

Proliferation of expertise and technology enables terrorist groups to obtain particular skills. In addition to the number of terrorists and terror groups that are willing and available to exchange training with one another, there are also experts in the technical, scientific, operational, and intelligence fields willing to provide training or augment operational capabilities on a contract basis.

The apocalyptic cult Aum Shinrikyo demonstrated its ability to produce weaponized chemicals and attempted to weaponize biological agents. It's most notable terrorist action was the release of sarin gas in five different subway trains in Tokyo in March 1995. However, the cult had released sarin previously in a Matsumoto residential area in June 1994. The cult had cultured and experimented with numerous biological agents, to include botulin toxin, anthrax, cholera, and Q fever. Fortunately these biological weapon efforts were unsuccessful.[117]

Weapons and Equipment

The weaponry and equipment available is an important part of any capabilities assessment of organizations that use violence. Terrorists use a broad range of weapons.

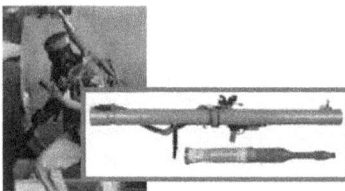 Virtually any type of firearm can be employed, as well as a wide variety of improvised explosive devices and conventional military munitions adapted for use in specific operational missions.

Fig. 3-12. **RPG-7 vs RPG-29**

See Appendix B, Firearms, and Appendix C, Conventional Arms and Munitions, of this Army TRADOC TRADOC G2 Handbook No. 1 for a sample of weapons data and illustrations used by terrorists.

---

[117] Kyle B. Olson, "Aum Shinrikyo: Once and Future Threat?" *Emerging Infectious Diseases*, 4 (July-August 1999): 513-514.

Terrorist intent to obtain and use weapons of mass destruction (WMD) or effect is one of the most serious contemporary threats to the United States. The means of attack can span from a highly sophisticated weapon system such as a nuclear bomb to a rudimentary improvised radiological device. The specter of chemical contamination or biological infection adds to the array of weapons. Although high explosives have not been traditionally recognized as a WMD, high yield explosives have caused significant devastating effects on people and places. See the 2007 version of Army TRADOC G2 Handbook No. 1.04, *Terrorism and WMD in the Contemporary Operational Environment*, for a primer on weapons of mass destruction and terrorism.

The threat of WMD terrorism to the U.S. is present across the entire spectrum of conflict. Potential exists for WMD terrorism with individual acts of wanton damage or destruction of property or person, to operations conducted by organized violent groups or rogue states with social, environmental, religious, economic, or political agendas. As the United States confronts terrorism, both foreign and domestic, the most significant U.S. concerns are terrorist organizations with demonstrated global reach capabilities and their intention to acquire and use weapons of mass destruction. Yet, recent events have demonstrated that devastating weapon effects can be caused by one or two people with the will and a way to terrorize.

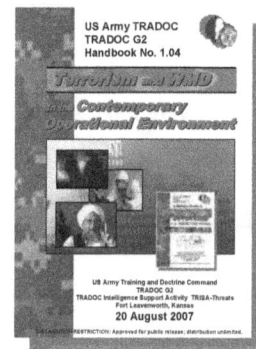

Figure 3-13. **WMD**

Conclusion

This chapter provided descriptions of the common organizational methods for terrorist groups. Discussion focused on hierarchical and networked structure. Levels of commitment exist within an organization and span senior leaders, active cadre, active supporters, and passive supporters. The cell is the foundation building block of either organization. Depending on how cells are linked to other elements, structure will display one of three basic configurations: chain, hub and star, or all-channel networks. Categorizing terrorist groups by their affiliation with governments can provide insight in terrorist intent and capability. Terrorist groups can align as state directed, state sponsored, or non-state supported organizations.

Know the Enemy. Principal themes in this knowing are: examine who will want to engage U.S. military forces with terrorism, (2) understand organizational models of significant terrorist groups, (3) determine probable capabilities of specific terrorist groups based on their affiliation with other terrorist groups or sovereign governments. Proactive knowledge and situational awareness of an operational environment enhances the ability for U.S. military forces to minimize the effects of terrorist activity in the conduct of unit missions.

4 Terrorist Targeting of U.S. Military Forces

Chapter 4

Terrorist Targeting of U.S. Military Forces

We are locked today in a war against a global extremist network that is fixed on defeating the United States and destroying our way of life...This foe will not go away, nor will he give up easily. And the next decade is likely to be one of persistent conflict. We are engaged in a long war.

General George Casey
U.S. Army Chief of Staff
April 2007

Terrorist targeting of U.S. military forces is a norm of the contemporary operational environment. This chapter examines terrorist targeting threats to U.S. military forces. The descriptions are neither a region specific product nor an exhaustive list of terrorist scenarios. Nonetheless, describing the targeting threat addresses three main components. Section I defines three operational areas of U.S. military forces: deployed, in-transit, and institutional.   Section II presents circumstances and influences on terrorist targeting of U.S. military forces. Section III provides an array of tactics and techniques that terrorists use to attack U.S. military forces.

Figure 4-1. **U.S. Armed Forces in a War on Terrorism**

Section I: Operational Environments and U.S. Military Forces

In many regions of the world, terrorism challenges political stability, economic progress, and democratic initiatives. To discuss the likelihood of particular terrorist threats to U.S. military forces, defining operational area and contemporary operational environment provides a setting of where and how particular threats may emerge. The operational environment (OE) is a composite of the conditions, circumstances, and influences that affect employment of capabilities and bear on the decisions of the commander. This environment includes physical areas and factors of land, air, maritime and space, as well as the cyber domain of information.[118]

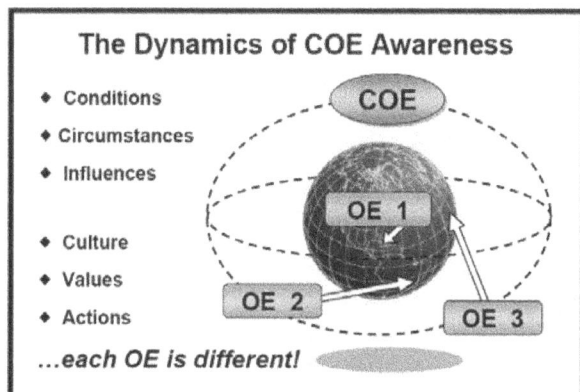

Figure 4-2. **Dynamics of COE Awareness**

The contemporary operational environment (COE) is a combination of all critical variables and actors that affect military operations today and in the near-term and mid-term.[119] US Army TRADOC appreciates this real-world context for analysis and situational awareness of the environment through use of critical variables. The US joint community use of a systems perspective on political, military, economic, social, information, and infrastructure (PMESII) components of several operational environments. Two additional domains complement this approach with an appreciation of varied physical environments such as geography-topography-hydrology and time (PMESII+PT).

The Contemporary Operational Environment (COE) is the overarching construct in which multiple operational environments exist. A model of PMESII+PT can be used to spotlight the complexity and uncertainty of the COE. Additional intangible yet significant issues for scrutiny include the culture, perceptions, beliefs, and values of all the actors in an OE. This complexity acknowledges a synergistic combination of all critical variables and actors that create the conditions, circumstances, and influences that can affect U.S. military operations.[120] Situational awareness is a holistic analysis of the OE rather than a discrete assessment of a specific issue or action.

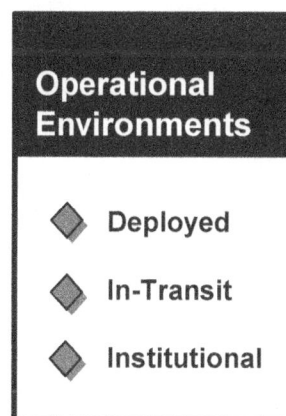

[118] Joint Publication 3-0. *Joint Operations*, U.S. Department of Defense; Washington, D.C., 17 September 2006, II-19 and II-20.
[119] U.S. Army Training and Doctrine Command, TRADOC G2, TRADOC Intelligence Support Activity (TRISA) White Paper, *The Contemporary Operational Environment*, July 2007.
[120] Ibid.

Deployed Forces

For this handbook, deployed forces are those U.S. military forces and individuals operating away from their permanent locations on either operational missions or training exercises. This category includes programmed unit rotations into stability operations or training assistance to foreign militaries, and can apply to all individual assignments in overseas locations such as military attachés or foreign study students. An example is an infantry battalion in Iraq.

In-Transit Forces

These U.S. military forces are either preparing for or in the process of deployment and redeployment phases of an operational mission. This includes active component units within the U.S. or positioned overseas, and reserve component units identified for operations, mobilization, or demobilization. Examples include an Army National Guard battalion returning from an operational mission in Iraq or an Army Reserve postal detachment deploying to Afghanistan.

Institutional Forces

These U.S. military forces are active and reserve component garrisons, training and logistic facilities, and other activities or installations that do not deploy to accomplish their organizational mission. Examples are an activity such as a provost marshal office assigned to an installation garrison or an institutional organization such as a military college located on an Army installation.

Section II: Circumstances and Influences

A principal consideration in terrorist targeting is the psychological impact of an attack on a selected audience. Attacking U.S. forces can provide a psychological impact that serves the goals of the terrorist. Assessing risk to potential targets will often focus less on specific military value, and consider the value to a terrorist intention to cause fear and anxiety.

During the post-colonial and nationalist insurgencies of the Cold War, terrorists might consider one civilian casualty more effective than several military casualties. With many insurgencies conducting simultaneous military and terror campaigns, military casualties usually caused less impact on the civilian population.[121] Terrorists also considered what soft targets could achieve the most significant attention while employing minimal risk to their own assets. A saying attributed to several terrorists is, "Why hunt wolves when

---

[121] Bruce Hoffman, *Inside Terrorism* (New York: Columbia University Press, 1998), 61.

there are so many sheep about?" However, recent operations by terrorists indicate that a recurring number of civilian deaths and mayhem can be an effective tool in a campaign of terror to break the resolve of a population and discourage a popularly elected representative government.

Reasons for Targeting

Why attack U.S. military forces? Large numbers of U.S. military forces located in varied areas of the world make military forces a lucrative target. Accessibility is one key factor. For example, during the 1970s to 1990s U.S. military installations and personnel were frequently targeted in by anti-NATO European terrorists and by state sponsored terrorists acting on behalf of a variety of regimes.[122] These attacks generally struck at military targets that were not engaged in hostilities but were accessible to terrorists of the geographic region. Today, the expansive presence of U.S. military forces is clearly evident in the Middle East and Persian Gulf region, and many other regions of the world due to political and economic factors as a global superpower.

Several terrorist rationales exist for targeting U.S. military forces. Whether terrorism comes from an individual with a single issue concern or a terrorist organization with global reach, many factors are considered in target selection, vulnerability analysis, and risk management before attacking a target. With the variety of terrorist motivations and goals, the reasons to target U.S. military forces or individuals are equally varied. The most common rationales are:

Identify Target Accessibility

Presence of military members, units, and activities in large numbers makes an inviting target. Presence of U.S. forces in some regions of the world may offend particular political or religious sensibilities and can be presented as a justification for terrorist attack.

Fig. 4-3. **USS** *Ashland*

Choose Symbolic Value

Commitment of military forces is a significant indicator of national interest and carries major political consequences. Targeting military forces can often achieve a greater notoriety for terrorists than targeting civilian targets such as diplomats, commercial businessmen, or government officials and facilities.

An example of successful terrorism is the Khobar Towers attack in Saudi Arabia. To Islamic fundamentalists, the presence of U.S. military forces in Saudi Arabia is considered particularly offensive due to the religious importance of the Saudi city of Mecca. In June of 1996, a housing facility for U.S. Air Force personnel near Dhahran, Saudi Arabia was attacked with a large truck bomb. [The acronym of VBIED for vehicle

---

[122] *International Encyclopedia of Terrorism*, 1997 ed., s.v. "Chronology of Terrorist Events."

borne improvised explosive device was not commonly used yet.] The Khobar Towers attack killed nineteen U.S. Air Force personnel and wounded about 400 other U.S. military members,[123] and demonstrated terrorist ability to back up terrorist threats with effective action. Members of Saudi Hizballah, a terrorist organization associated with Lebanese Hizballah, and an unnamed Iranian were indicted by the U.S. Department of Justice for this act of terrorism. Soon after this attack, terrorists declared war on American forces in the Persian Gulf region in August 1996, and announced that all U.S. forces must be withdrawn, or suffer further attacks. Terrorists could claim they caused U.S. military forces to relocate from this urban setting to remote locations in Saudi Arabia.

Man to Crater Proportion

Fig. 4-4. **Khobar Towers**

Demonstrate Organizational Capability

Terrorist action that demonstrates the capability to negate U.S. military operations security and force protection can promote individual terrorist or organizational terrorist agenda when they attack U.S. military forces.

Fig. 4-5. **General Haig**

Senior military officials are often a target. In the 1970s and 1980s, The Red Army Faction (RAF) conducted numerous terrorist activities against military presence in Germany and countries of the North Atlantic Treaty Organization (NATO). Shifting from original goals for a complete revolution of German society, the RAF concentrated much of their capabilities on a campaign to reduce NATO and U.S. military presence in Germany as a way to possibly build a more sympathetic understanding for societal change in Germany.[124] In 1979, the RAF attempted to assassinate General Alexander Haig, the Supreme Allied Commander in Europe and NATO. RAF surveillance confirmed that a road near Casteau, Belgium that was used frequently by General Haig. A remotely controlled bomb placed in a culvert of the road had a detonator of nine-volt batteries and a household switch with wire camouflaged by earth and grass. The blast lifted the general's car into the air and damaged the accompanying security

---

[123] Christopher C. Harmon, *Terrorism Today* (London: Frank Cass Publishers, 2000; reprint, Portland: Frank Cass Publishers, 2001), 71.

[124] Walter Reich, ed., *Origins of Terrorism: Psychologies, Ideologies, Theologies, States of Mind*, rev. ed. (Washington: Woodrow Wilson Center Press, 1998), 49-51.

vehicle; three guards in the security vehicle were lightly injured.[125] General Haig was physically unharmed.

Penetrating U.S. facilities and locations deemed secure can aim to cause a large number of casualties and increase the requirements for additional security forces and measures. An example is the individual terrorist suicide bombing of the military dining facility in Mosul, Iraq in 2004. A civilian was able to gain entry through security stations and detonated a suicide vest bomb in a group of U.S. military members and civilian workers eating in a large military tent. Fourteen U.S. soldiers were killed in the explosion. Four American civilian contractors and four Iraqi security soldiers were also reported killed in the blast.[126] Many more occupants were wounded by the explosion and ball bearings of the suicide vest bomb. Fortunately, rehearsed mass casualty medical plans and first aid medical response at the site quickly treated and stabilized casualties and prevented even more deaths from injuries.[127]

Fig. 4-6. **Mosul Dining Tent**

Delay or Prevent Movements

Fig. 4-7. **UK Child in Iraq 1990**

During Operation Desert Shield, Saddam Hussein called for terrorist activity to be directed against the countries of the coalition preparing to invade Iraq. Attacks conducted by indigenous terrorist groups Dev Sol and 17 November occurred against U.S. staging areas in Turkey and Greece. Iraq directly supported these overseas attacks with weapons components delivered via diplomatic pouch and other assistance.[128] Although Saddam Hussein did not have the influence to convince or compel a larger Middle East surge in terrorism, terrorist activities in general did increase during the period of the air campaign and subsequent invasion of Iraq, totaling 275 incidents.[129] Due to extensive counterterrorism efforts and international coordination, the overall effort to disrupt coalition deployments was ineffective. This period indicates a terrorist threat that deployed and deploying or redeploying units may encounter.

---

[125] John Vinocur, "Bomb Attempt on Gen. Haig's Life Not Tied to Major Terrorist Groups," *New York Times*, 27 June 1979, p. A13.

[126] Daisy Sindlelar, "Iraq: U.S. Military Investigating Deadly Mosul Blast,' available from http://www.rferl.org/featuresarticleprint/2004/12/17fac095-a36d-4a0e-abs9-635ee3e12ee3...; Internet; accessed 17 May2007.

[127] *Online NewsHour.pbs.org.*, "Deadly Day," available from http://www.pbs.org/newshour/bb/middle_east/july-dec04/mosul_12-22.html; Internet; accessed 17 May 2007.

[128] Christopher C. Harmon, *Terrorism Today* (London: Frank Cass Publishers, 2000; reprint, Portland: Frank Cass Publishers, 2001), 52.

[129] Ibid., 52.

During Operation Desert Shield and preparations for the liberation of Kuwait, Iraq conducted what amounted to the largest hostage taking crisis in modern time. They seized Kuwaiti citizens and hundreds of foreigners resident in Iraq and exploited them in the media as human shields. In one instance, about 350 passengers on a British Airways flight were held captive as the airplane attempted a refueling stop in Kuwait. Unfortunately, this event occurred on the first day if Iraq's invasion of Kuwait in 1990.[130] Most of the United Kingdom hostages and other UK citizens were released before the initiation of Operation Desert Storm.[131]

Disruption of transportation may take place by sabotage or direct attack upon the unit being transported and its mode of transportation. Methods of attack would be selected depending upon their effectiveness versus the mode of unit transport. Air, rail and sea are normal modes of transport for long voyages or distances, but may also be motor transportation means such as buses or organic unit vehicles to move to a destination. Weapons likely to be employed include bombs, antitank rockets, rocket propelled grenades, and small arms gunfire. In some cases, sophisticated shoulder fired missiles could be used. Sabotage may be designed to produce maximum casualties in the ensuing crash, derailment, or fire. In January 2003, intelligence sources detected the targeting of chartered aircraft participating in the build up of forces against Iraq.[132] In the past, U.S. domestic terrorists have derailed U.S. passenger and cargo trains.[133] Attacks on ships in port and at sea are within the capabilities of selected transnational and international terror groups.

Destroying facilities such as docks, airfields, refueling facilities, and cargo terminals at intermediate stops or at the final destination is another way for terrorists to prevent or delay deployment. Attacking critical private infrastructure through physical and cyber means could cause similar effects. Adding depth to a conflict does not necessarily require the projection of physical terrorist assets and weapons into more distant countries. If timed to coincide with the arrival or departure of military units, such destructive attacks could cause significant casualties. In 1975, the *Montoneras* terrorists of Argentina advanced from individual terrorist acts to paramilitary guerrilla operations and achieved significant physical and psychological effects to Argentine military forces. Placing explosives in an abandoned tunnel underneath an airfield runway, the bomb was detonated as a C-130 aircraft carrying an antiguerrilla unit was starting its departure. The C-130 was destroyed resulting in four killed and forty injured, as well as damaging the

---

[130] BBC NEWS, "UK hostages describe Kuwait ordeal," available from http://newsvote.bbc.co.uk/mpapps/pagetools/print/news.bbc.co.uk/2/hi/uk_news/politicsa/6...; Internet; accessed 16 May 2007.

[131] *International Encyclopedia of Terrorism*, 1997 ed., s.v. "Chronology of Terrorist Events."

[132] Thom Shanker, "Officials Reveal Threat to Troops Deploying to Gulf," *New York Times,* 13 January 2003; available from http://www.nytimes.com/2003/01/13/politics/13INTE.html; Internet; accessed 13 January 2003.

[133] Jim Hill, "Sabotage Suspected in 'Terrorist' Derailment," *CNN.com*, 10 October 1995; available from http://www.cnn.com/US/9510/amtrak/10-10/; Internet; accessed 15 January 2003.

runway. This was a psychological blow to the Army's image with its nation, and a publicized instance of a military force defeat.[134]

Reduce Operational Capability

Terrorists may target U.S. military forces to reduce or remove a specific capability or impair effectiveness. The intent would be to cause additional employment of military forces and further stress finite unit and soldier assets weaken morale. A likely method of attack would be a small to medium size improvised explosive device (IED) or an ambush conducted with light weapons (automatic weapons, grenades, and antitank rockets). Terrorists may seek to seize U.S. military members as prisoners and exploit them for media attention or a military reaction by U.S. forces. A May 2007 raid on a U.S. military observation post near Mahmoudiya, Iraq killed four U.S. soldiers and one Iraqi interpreter. Three missing U.S. soldiers were presumed to be captured. Reports stated about ten individuals attacked the two U.S. vehicles and their crews in limited visibility with small arms gunfire and grenades. Before departing the area, the terrorists belonging to an al-Qaida affiliated cell used IEDs to slow any U.S. response force into the attack site.[135] Subsequent search missions for the missing U.S. soldiers reduced available U.S. forces planned for other operations.

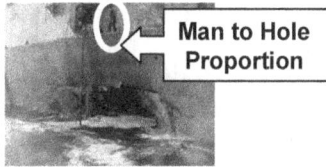

Fig. 4-8. **USS *Cole***

The suicide boat bombing of the USS *Cole* in 2000 occurred while the ship was moored at a refueling point in Aden, Yemen. Terrorists exploited access control measures and perimeter security vulnerabilities of waterside approaches to the naval ship while near the coastline. The result, besides the international media attention, killed 17 sailors killed and wounded 42 crewmembers.

The explosion caused extensive damage to the ship.[136] In more recent military operations, during the preparation for and conduct of Operation Iraqi Freedom, threat of terrorist attacks contributed to decisions by Turkey that significantly limited U.S. use of Turkish territory, facilities, and materiel.

A terrorist group with a rudimentary biological weapons capability could have the potential to infect enough of a unit with a debilitating or contagious disease. Quarantine

---

[134] Alan C. Lowe, "Todo o Nada: Montonerosa Versus the Army: Urban Terrorism in Argentina," ed. William G. Robertson and Lawrence A. Yates, in *Block by Block: The Challenges of Urban Operations* (Fort Leavenworth, KS: U.S. Army Command and General Staff College Press, 2003), 395.

[135] Robert Ried, "Search for missing soldiers intensifies," 15 May 2007, available from http://news.yahoo.com/s/ap/20070515/ap_on_re_mi_ea/iraq&printer=1;_ylt=AujoSQGJ62...; Internet; accessed 16 May 2007. See also, Kim Gamel, "Militants: stop hunt for U.S. soldiers," available from http://news.yahoo.com/s/ap/20070514/ap_on_re_mi_ea/iraq&printer=1;_ylt=ApG9rDwam...; Internet; accessed 16 May 2007.

[136] *Statement Before the 107th [U.S.] Congress, Chairman of the Joint Chiefs of Staff*, Senate Armed Services Committee May 3, 2001; [database on-line] available from http://www.dtic.mil/jcs/chairman/3MAY01_SASC_CJCS.htm; Internet; accessed 18 February 2004.

and other medical treatment would delay a planned deployment sequence. Additionally, terrorist capability and suspected or known intention to use biological weapons against U.S. military forces could cause extraordinary processes for vaccination of U.S. military forces. These additional preventive medicine and safety issues could complicate deployment timeframes for U.S. military forces.

Acquisition and use of chemical, biological, radiological, or nuclear material and weapons by terrorists is a significant concern. See Army TRADOC G2 Handbook No.1.04, *Terrorism and WMD in the Contemporary Operational Environment* published in 2007 for a discussion of this looming threat to U.S. military forces.

Degrade Social Environment

Terrorists prefer an environment that is chaotic. A fluid, poorly policed or uncontrolled situation often permits normally suspicious activities to go unnoticed. However, hostile environments put military forces on their guard, reduce the opportunities to get close to targets without being challenged or detained, and increase the difficulty of achieving any degree of operational surprise.

> The enemy today is not an empire, but a shadowy movement of terrorists cells; the threats today are not conventional, they're unconventional; and al-Qaida and other terrorists have...no hesitation to kill innocent men, women, and children.
>
> **Honorable Donald Rumsfeld**
> **U.S. Secretary of Defense**
> **March 2006**

Attacks on personnel at social gatherings can occur at clubs on military installations or during unit functions at private homes or commercial establishments off post. Traditional observances of organizational days, town hall meetings, and family support briefings are often publicized in advance and give attackers planning dates for possible gatherings in accessible locations. Attacks at commercial entertainment establishments such as bars, clubs and restaurants could be targeted because the density or presence of military personnel. The most likely attack method will be a small to large sized IED, although terrorists could employ improvised mortars or other weapons from a standoff distance.

In some cases urban terrain favors the terrorist in accomplishing these ends. Cities provide the terrorist with a population to conceal personnel, structures and facilities to hide and store equipment or weapons, and transportation nodes for movement. Terrorists may use the advantages of surprise and security by hiding within a population. Sometimes terrorists may forego specific terror activities and operate as guerillas in areas of active combat operations. They can also operate as part of an insurgency force in combat operations.

Disrupt Economic Environment

Other terrorist incidents indicate the potential for disrupting deployments or materiel in transit. The tensions of political, environmental, and economic impacts add to the specific damage or destruction of an incident. The terrorist suicide boat bombing in 2002 of the French tanker ship *Limburg* near Ash Shihr and east of Aden, Yemen spilled 90,000 barrels of oil into the ocean and contaminated 45 miles of coastline.[137] One immediate economic impact of this small boat attack on the *Limburg* was a maritime insurance increase in rates that tripled in the Yemeni area.[138]

Influence U.S. Policy

Terrorists can attack U.S. military forces with the intent to force a change in U.S. policy. Hizballah and Syrian sponsors were concerned that deployment of international peacekeeping forces into Lebanon in the spring of 1983 would reduce their freedom of action in the ongoing Lebanese Civil War. Suicide truck bomb attacks on the U.S. Marine Corps and French Army barracks in October of 1983 killed 241 U.S. Marines and 60 French soldiers. Combined with an earlier bombing campaign against the embassies of the U.S. and other countries, these attacks resulted in the withdrawal of the international military force.

Fig. 4-9. **USMC in Beirut 1983**

The desire to discredit U.S. Federal, state, and local governments can result in military members, units, or infrastructure being targeted by domestic terror groups. For example, during the Vietnam War anti-war extremist groups targeted Army cadet (ROTC) detachments, draft board offices, and university facilities involved in military research.[139] During the same period, the Weather Underground targeted recruiting offices in the late 1970's. In contemporary times, terrorists operating in foreign nations attempt similar influence with threats against U.S. military members or U.S. tourists in Germany. Several

---

[137] *"Evidence Points to Yemen Terror Attack," CBS News.com* [database on-line]; available from http://www.cbsnews.com/stories/2002/10/06/world/main524488.shtml; Internet; accessed 21 January 2004.

[138] *"The Terrorism Maritime Threat," United Press International* 2 December 2003 [Militarycom database on-line]; Internet; accessed 21 January 2004; and, *"French Tanker Explosion Confirmed as Terror Attack,"* [database on-line]; available from http://www.ict.org.il/spotlight/det.cfm?id=837; Internet; accessed 21 January 2004.

[139] *International Encyclopedia of Terrorism*, 1997 ed., s.v. "Student Terror: The Weathermen "

Islamic extremist organizations have threatened violence unless Germany withdraws its troops from the NATO force in Afghanistan.[140]

Table 4-1. Terrorist Targeting U.S. Military Forces		
Target Environment	Attack Means	Attack Rationale
Deployed Forces	◆ Threat-Hoax ◆ Arson ◆ Sabotage ◆ Kidnapping	**Select Accessible Target** within means of terrorist cell **Diminish Symbolic Prestige** of nation-coalition-alliance **Gain Notoriety** for terrorist cell or ideology
In-Transit Forces	◆ Hostage Taking ◆ Assassination ◆ Bombing ◆ Gunfire-RPG	**Delay-Prevent Movements** of US military forces **Reduce Operational Capability** of US military forces
Institutional Forces	◆ Raid-Ambush ◆ Seizure ◆ Aerial-MANPADS ◆ WMD	**Degrade Social Stability-Trust** of nation and region **Disrupt Economic Confidence** of nation-supporting nations **Influence Political Policy** of nation-supporting nations

In more recent decades, domestic antigovernment groups, some with bizarre conspiracy theories, targeted military bases or posts in the U.S. homeland believing them to be staging areas for United Nations directed foreign military forces. During the twenty year period from 1980 to 1999, thirteen specifically domestic military targets were attacked by terrorist activities. This does not count military facilities or personnel who were

---

[140] Brian Ross, Richard Esposito & Chris Isham, "U.S., Germans Fear Terror Attack," 11 May 2007, available from http://blogs.abcnews.com/theblotter/2007/05/us_germans_fear.html; Internet; accessed 17 May 2007.

collocated in the other 101 U.S. Government targets that were attacked.[141] A report by the FBI in 2004 stated that domestic terrorism cases nearly doubled in the previous five years from 3,500 in 1999 to more than 6,000 in 2004.[142] Based on new reporting procedures by the U.S. Federal Government after 2004, comparing current domestic terrorism statistics with pre-2004 data is not meaningful.

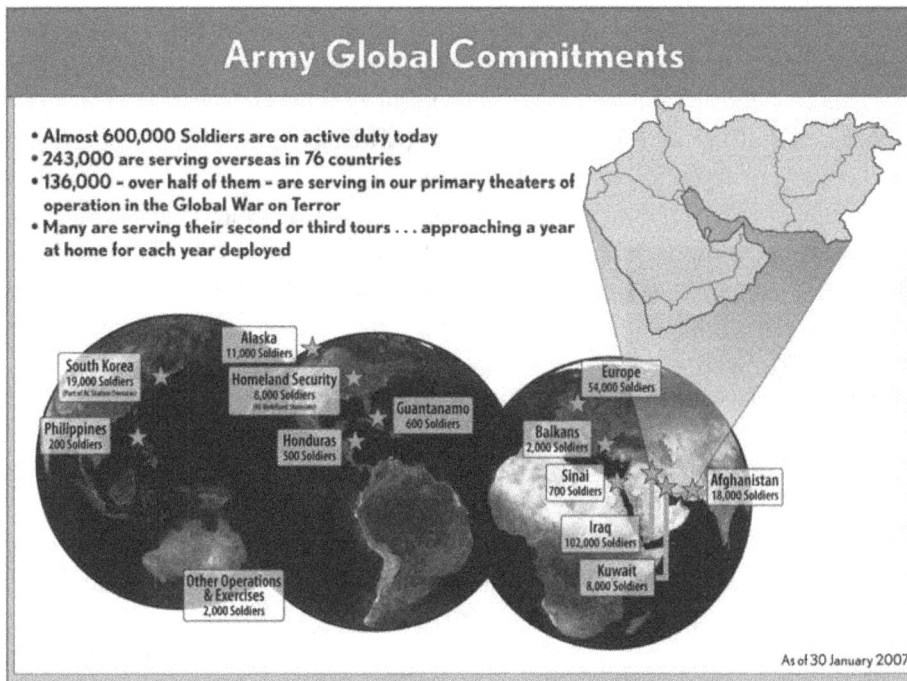

Army Global Commitments

- Almost 600,000 Soldiers are on active duty today
- 243,000 are serving overseas in 76 countries
- 136,000 - over half of them - are serving in our primary theaters of operation in the Global War on Terror
- Many are serving their second or third tours ... approaching a year at home for each year deployed

As of 30 January 2007

A January 2007 snapshot of global commitments of the U.S. Army highlights many areas of concentrated Army activity throughout the world. The illustration (above) from the U.S. Army's *2007 Posture Statement* displays almost 600,000 Soldiers on active duty. In early 2007 the Army was comprised of 507,000 active component, 46,000 Army National Guard and 28,000 Army Reserve. Over 40 percent (243,000) of them are deployed or forward stationed, serving in 76 countries worldwide. More than 4,600 Army Civilians are serving side-by-side with them in the field, performing a variety of missions vital to America's national defense.The other Services of the U.S. Armed Forces provide similar presence and mission conduct on a day to day basis on land in the continents of the world, in the maritime regions of the world, and in the air and space.

---

[141] Department of Justice, Federal Bureau of Investigation, Counterterrorism Threat Assessment and Warning Unit, Counterterrorism Division, *Terrorism in the United States 1999,* Report 0308, (Washington, D.C., n.d.), 53.
[142] "Preventing Terrorist Attacks on U.S. Soil," April 9, 2004, available from http://www.fbi.gov/page2/april04/040904krar.htm; internet; accessed 17 May 2007.

Section III: Terrorist Attack Threats to U.S. Forces

General

The terrorist uses a wide array of tactics and techniques in conducting terror. This section is not an exhaustive presentation of methods or approaches. One norm regarding terror operations is the use of surprise, secrecy, innovation, and indirect methods of attack. Tactics are as broad and diverse as the resources of the terrorist cell and the imagination of the group leader. Use of the Internet and training exchanges information among terrorists on tactics that yield success. Al-Qaida assembled written training material, training videos, and attempted to sustain training initiatives and encouragement even after much of its network of training camps were disrupted or destroyed.[143] Terrorists continue to improve techniques as field tests demonstrate degrees of effectiveness in real-world situations such as Chechnya, Kashmir, Afghanistan, the Balkans, and Iraq.

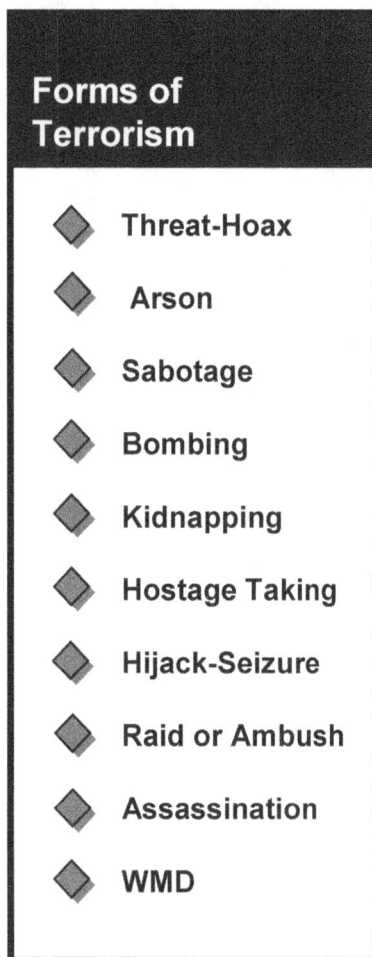

Forms of Terrorism

- ◆ Threat-Hoax
- ◆ Arson
- ◆ Sabotage
- ◆ Bombing
- ◆ Kidnapping
- ◆ Hostage Taking
- ◆ Hijack-Seizure
- ◆ Raid or Ambush
- ◆ Assassination
- ◆ WMD

Contemporary Setting

The terrorist will utilize tactics, forces, and weapons specifically tailored to a particular mission. Terrorist operations are individualistic in that each is planned for a specific target and effect. A terrorist relies upon prior planning and reconnaissance to counter and overmatch the target. If changes to the target or unexpected conditions render success unlikely, the terrorist may cancel the operation and return later or choose a different target and continue his planning and attack process.

Some groups will actually publish their targeting guidance. One example was noticed in March 2004. An al-Qaida affiliate published a nine page article in their training publication, "Camp al-Battar Magazine" that presented new targeting guidance to its members and other affiliated groups. This publication contained information on small arms skills, physical fitness, targeting, tactics, and secure communications. The new

---

[143] Ben Venzke and Aimee Ibrahim, *The al-Qaeda Threat, An Analytical Guide to al-Qaeda's Tactics & Targets* (Alexandria: Tempest Publishing, 2003), 7.

guidance specifically covered targets within cities addressing faith institution targets, economic targets, and human targets.[144]

Forms of Terrorism

Threat or Hoax

A terrorist cell can use threats to coerce or preclude actions by a targeted individual or population. Threats and hoaxes can dull the effectiveness of preventive or countermeasures when a targeted individual or population loses situational awareness of an actual terrorist target or disperses finite assets against many possible threats. At the less lethal end of the spectrum, hoaxes can simply be methods to annoy and wear down security forces and keep the population constantly agitated. Bomb threats, leaving suspicious items in public places, and ploys consume time and effort from other security operations and contribute to uncertainty and anxiety.

Fig. 4-10. **Ruse and Deception**

Such activities can be used to gain information about the target's response to a potential attack. Where the occupants go during the evacuation of a building, and how long it takes them to exit are useful elements of information in operational planning, and can be obtained through simply making an anonymous phone call or activating a fire alarm. Observation of regularly scheduled exercises or drills of emergency response procedures can provide similar information. This technique can also be combined with an actual attack to circumvent fixed security measures. For example, the occupants of a bomb-resistant building with controlled access and a guard force could be forced to evacuate by a plausible but false threat. Most security plans would respect the potential danger such a threat represented and evacuate the building. Unless assembly areas are properly secured, the evacuation could make the occupants more vulnerable to weapons such as a car bomb or other mass casualty technique placed near the exits or at designated assembly points.

Extortion is an example of a threat that obtains money, materiel, information, or support by force or intimidation. Extortion is often used during the formative period of a group or by groups that fail to develop more sophisticated financial resources. However, the opportunity to engage in more lucrative money making activities such as drug trafficking may eventually replace the need to extort by some groups. Depending on the structure of the terrorist organization, the cells may extort money from local businesses in exchange for protection. The Basque terrorists are an example of a group that uses extortion. They have extorted money for years from businesses to finance their battle for regional independence. When Spain converted from the peseta to the euro, ETA even sent letters to

---

[144] Ben N. Venzke, *al Qaeda Targeting Guidance* - Version 1.0 (Alexandria, VA: IntelCenter/Tempest Publishing, LLC, 2004), 3-5.

Basque businesses demanding payments ranging from 30,000 to 60,000 euros. Although many of the large companies in the Basque region refuse to pay ETA's revolutionary tax, ETA extorts money from smaller businesses that cannot afford to hire bodyguards.[145]

Intimidation is another form of extortion. Intelligence cells or a specialized team can intimidate people to obtain information on a target location or to provide resources. Death threats against an individual or his family may cause him to provide information or resources to a group with which he has no interest or allegiance. A terrorist cell can also intimidate people not to take an action. For example, enemy security personnel may not implement required security measures because of intimidation. The power of coercing individuals can be significant; several terrorist groups have successfully used these techniques to force individuals to carry out suicide bombing missions.

Arson

Arson uses fire to damage, sabotage, or destroy property. Effects can be accomplished with simple equipment and minimal training.[146] Since arson is primarily used against property, it is not normally planned as a casualty producer. However, arson can result in fatalities. Arson is most often used for symbolic attacks and economic effects. Single-issue groups, such as the Earth Liberation Front (ELF), particularly favor it for these purposes. Although ELF has claimed responsibility for dozens of arsons, probably the most costly arson committed by this group was in San Diego, California in August 2003. Claiming it was targeting rampant urban development, ELF started a fire that caused an estimated $50 million worth of damage in San Diego's fast-growing northern edge suburbs.[147]

Fig. 4-11. **Arson Terror**

Sabotage

Sabotage is the planned destruction of the enemy's equipment or infrastructure. The purpose of sabotage is to inflict both psychological and physical damage. This can result from an incident creating a large number of casualties or from a severe disruption of services for the population. Destroying or disrupting key services or facilities impresses the power of the saboteur on the public consciousness and either increases a target population frustration with the ineffectiveness of the government or may inspire others to resist.

---

[145] "Terrorists Demand Extortion Cash in Euros," *TCM Breaking News* (4 September 2001): 1; available from http://archives.tcm.ie/breakingnews/2001/09/04/story22584.asp; Internet; accessed 31 March 2004.

[146] Department of Justice, Federal Bureau of Investigation, Counterterrorism Threat Assessment and Warning Unit, Counterterrorism Division, *Terrorism in the United States 1999,* Report 0308, (Washington, D.C., n.d.), 41.

[147] Seth Hettena, "Earth Liberation Front Claims Responsibility for San Diego Arson," *The Mercury News*, 18 August 2003; available from http://www.mercurynews.com/mld/mercurynews/news/local/6562462.htm; Internet; accessed 17 March 2004.

A terrorist group normally aims its sabotage actions at elements of infrastructure, in order to reinforce the perception that nothing is safe. Oil pipelines, water purification plants, sewage treatment facilities, air traffic control hubs, and medical treatment or research facilities are several examples of potential targets. Terrorist groups use many techniques such as bombing, arson, cyber, or use of contaminates to conduct sabotage.

Examples of sabotage have been evident in Iraq since the end of major combat operations where attacks have been conducted against power generation facilities and water pipelines. Attacks on Iraq's oil pipeline were persistent in 2003 and estimates spotlighted that the country was losing $7 million daily because of damage to the pipeline that carried oil from the Kirkuk fields to a Mediterranean port in Turkey.[148]

Fig.4-12. **Sabotaged Oil Refinery**

Bombing

Bombs are a favored weapon for terrorists.[149] Bombs are highly destructive and can be easily tailored to the mission, do not require the operator to be present, and have a significant physical and psychological impact. To demonstrate their prominence in terrorist operations, 324 out of 482 total terrorist incidents or planned acts in the U.S. between 1980 and 2001 were bombings,[150] and 119 of 208 international terrorist incidents in 2003 were bombings.[151] In 2006, the U.S. National Counterterrorism Center (NCTC) reports that bombing incidents increased by 30 percent from those in 2005 and the death toll in these incidents during 2006 increased by 39 percent and injuries by 45 percent.[152] Given the NCTC parameters for measuring noncombatant terrorist incidents, over 6400 people were killed by terrorist bombs in 2006.[153]

Bombs have a significant historical record, and a particular place in early anarchist and revolutionary thought, where dynamite was viewed as the equalizing force between the state and the individual.[154] Interaction between Terrorist cells using the Internet and common training sites facilitate the proliferation of effective devices and tactics throughout the terrorist network. Bombings may be used as a technique to conduct other

---

[148] "Saboteurs Disable Critical Iraqi Oil Pipeline," *HoustonChronicle.com*, 8 September 2003; available from http://www.chron.com/cs/CDA/ssistory.mpl/special/iraq/2087438; Internet; accessed 16 January 2004.

[149] *Encyclopedia of World Terror*, 1997 ed., s.v. "Bombing."

[150] Department of Justice, Federal Bureau of Investigation, Counterterrorism Division, *Terrorism 2000/2001*, Report 0308, (Washington, D.C., 2004).

[151] Department of State, Office for Counterterrorism, *Patterns of Global Terrorism 2003* (Washington, D.C., April 2004, revised 22 June 2004), 5.

[152] National Counterterrorism Center (NCTC), *Reports on Terrorism Incidents - 2006*, 30 April 2007, 11; available from http://www.terrorisminfo.mipt.org/Patterns-of-global-terrorism.asp; Internet; accessed 2 May 2007.

[153] Ibid., 19.

[154] Walter Reich, ed., *Origins of Terrorism: Psychologies, Ideologies, Theologies, States of Mind*, rev. ed. (Washington: Woodrow Wilson Center Press, 1998), 264-265.

operations, such as sabotage or assassination, or can simply be a tactic to cause terror through the destruction and casualties produced by an explosion.

Numerous methods exist for emplacing and detonating bombs. For example, directional bombs have been disguised as bricks in roadside walls and radio command detonated in the Israeli-occupied territories. The Irish Republican Army (IRA) improved methods of remote detonation of a bomb using police laser speed detection devices. Detonation would occur from a particular laser pulse within line of sight.[155]

Car bombs, commonly referred to as vehicle borne improvised explosive devices (VBIED), are used regularly by terrorists. Besides the use of airplanes on September 11, 2001 to hit the World Trade Center and the Pentagon, probably the best-known U.S. domestic incident occurred on April 19, 1995, when a truck bomb exploded outside the Alfred P. Murrah building in Oklahoma City killing 168 people and injuring hundreds of other people. Timothy McVeigh was convicted and later executed for the bombing. Overseas, a suicide truck bombing of the U.S. Corps Marine Barracks in Beirut in October 1983 killing 241 Americans. A truck bomb that exploded near the Khobar Towers military complex in Dhahran, Saudi Arabia on June 25, 1996 killed 19 people and injured over 500 people.

The Department of Homeland Security distributed a warning reflecting new tactics being used by terrorists in this area based on the bombings in Riyadh, Saudi Arabia in May 2003. These included terrorists hitting multiple targets, conducting simultaneous attacks, using multiple vehicles per target, and using assault and breaching teams armed with small arms to accompany the VBIED to kill security personnel and gain access to the target area.[156] The NCTC report on terrorism incidents in 2006 notes that terrorists continue techniques of an initial bomb explosion followed by secondary bomb detonations as first responders or other people arrive at the attack site.[157]

Fig. 4-13. **Jeddah US Consulate**

In 2006, bombs and in particular improvised explosive devices (IEDs) increased in lethality and adaptation of techniques used by terrorists. Terrorists have mastered the employment of roadside explosives to attack both individuals and motorcades or convoys. Some IEDs are bulky devices often made from artillery shells and detonated with garage door openers or doorbells. However, terrorists are now producing smaller devices that can be planted quickly and can be detonated from longer distances.

---

[155]Bruce Hoffman, *Inside Terrorism* (New York: Columbia University Press, 1998), 181.

[156] National Security Institute, *Homeland Security Warns about Vehicle Bombs*, (Medway, MA, n.d.), 1-4; available from http://nsi.org/Library/Terrorism/Vehicle_Bombs.doc; Internet; accessed 14 January 2004.

[157] National Counterterrorism Center (NCTC), *Reports on Terrorism Incidents - 2006*, 30 April 2007, 11; available from http://www.terrorisminfo.mipt.org/Patterns-of-global-terrorism.asp; Internet; accessed 2 May 2007.

Another IED innovation is use a device called an explosively formed projectile (EFP). This penetrating principle is common to some types of munitions. The innovation in recent conflicts is its increasing use as an IED to outmatch armor protection. Although some technical skill and machining is required to obtain an optimum effect, a simple looking illustration of the EFP is a section of pipe filled with explosives and capped by a shaped copper disk. When the explosive detonates, the EFP liner is generally folded into its final shape, typically a rod, for maximum penetration of armor plating.

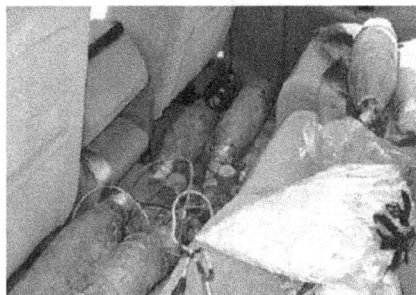

Fig. 4-14. **IED Artillery Shells**

Devices can be placed at a target site and remotely detonated. The terrorist bombing attack in Spain in March 2004 used ten backpack bombs with nails and screws packed around the explosives for shrapnel. Bombs were detonated on four trains almost simultaneously using cell phones as the initiation device.[158] The results were nearly 200 dead and over 1,800 injured people.

Kidnapping

Kidnapping is usually an action taken against a prominent individual for a specific reason. The most common reasons for kidnapping are ransom, release of a fellow terrorist, or the desire to publicize a demand or an issue. The terrorist cell conducts detailed planning, especially regarding movement of the kidnapped individual. The kidnapped victim is moved to a location controlled by the cell. The group makes demands and is often willing to hold a victim for a significant time.

Success of kidnapping relies on balancing the cost to the government represented by the threat of harm to the victim, with the costs of meeting the kidnappers' demands. Some kidnapping operations are actually assassinations with killing the victim as an intended outcome. The terrorists intended objective in this case being the intermediate concessions and publicity obtained during the negotiation process that they would not receive from a simple assassination.

Kidnapping can also be used as a means of financing the organization. Ransom from seized individuals or groups are a significant slice of income for groups in several regions of the world. Latin America has long been a victim of terrorist kidnapping, especially by the FARC and ELN in Colombia. The Abu Sayyaf Group in the Philippines uses this method to finance their operations. Ransoms vary but often demand significant payment. Ten employees of a Spanish energy consortium were kidnapped in Ecuador in October

---

[158] Lou Dolinar, "Cell Phones Jury-rigged to Detonate Bombs," *Newsday.com*, 15 March 2004; available from http://www.newsday.com/news/nationworld/ny-wocell153708827mar15,0,1644248.story?coll=ny-nationworld-headlines; Internet; accessed 15 March 2004.

2000 by kidnappers believed to be linked to the Popular Liberation Army of Colombia. The oil companies eventually paid $13 million in ransom for their release. Some regions experience kidnapping as a regular means of terror. In Nepal in 2006, Maoist rebels continued acts of kidnapping, extortion, and murder. Even with some accommodations and cease fire agreements that ended the insurgency between Nepal and the Communist Party of Nepal (CPN/M), a separatist terror group emerged from the Maoist rebels declaring their intent to secede a portion of the plains and countryside from Nepal.[159] In Nigeria in 2007, kidnapping of foreigners remains a regular danger as rebels struggle for control of oil and mineral wealth in the Niger Delta.[160]

Fig. 4-15. **Abu Sayyaf Kidnapping**

An example of kidnapping a U.S. military member is Lieutenant Colonel William Higgins, USMC. He disappeared on May 17, 1988, while serving as the Chief, Observer Group Lebanon and Senior Military Observer, United States Military Observer Group, United Nations Truce Supervision Organization. He was kidnapped and held by Iranian-backed Hizballah terrorists and later murdered. A picture of his body hanging from a noose was released to the news media in July 1989. His remains continued to be held until they were released in December 1991.

Another example was the kidnapping of Brigadier General James Dozier, senior American official at a NATO headquarters in Verona, Italy, by Red Brigade terrorists on

December 17, 1981. The targeting of General Dozier broke the pattern of previous terrorist activities in Italy since terrorist groups had previously concentrated their actions against key Italian personalities such as senior Italian politicians, industrialists, jurists, newspaper publishers and police officials. Following General Dozier's kidnapping, numerous additional threats were received which provided a clear indication that the terrorism situation had changed in Italy and other Americans and U.S. facilities were potential targets for terrorist actions.[161]

Fig. 4-16. **Dozier Kidnapping**

The terrorists conducted surveillance of General Dozier's residence for at least 30 days from positions in a park and at a bus stop across from the building. The techniques used were young people standing at the bus stop and young couples in the park area. Additionally, the terrorists had been in his apartment at least twice while posing as meter

---

[159] Department of State, *Country Reports on terrorism 2006*, April 2007, 120; available from http://www.terrorisminfo.mipt.org/Patterns-of-global-terrorism.asp; Internet; accessed 2 May 2007.
[160] "Nigeria Gunmen Seize Six Foreigners,' available from http://www.cnn.com/2007/WORLD/Africa/06/03/Nigeria.kidnap.reut/; Internet; accessed 5 June 2007.
[161] COL Thomas D. Phillips, "The Dozier Kidnapping: Confronting the Red Brigades," *Air and Space Power Chronicles* (February 2002): 1; available from http://www.airpower.maxwell.af.mil/airchronicles/cc/phillips.html; Internet; accessed 31 March 2004.

readers. Two men pretending to be plumbers conducted the actual kidnapping. They told General Dozier that there was a leak in the apartment below and wanted to determine if it was coming from Dozier's apartment. Since leaks were common in the building, he let them into the apartment, at which time the kidnapping was executed. After being held for 42 days, he was rescued by Italian police.[162]

Consider the amount of media attention given the abduction and eventual murder of reporter Daniel Pearl in 2002, and how the video of his murder was nearly presented on cable television networks. Subsequent murders since then have involved kidnapping and beheading. Nicholas Berg was kidnapped in Iraq and beheaded in May 2004. Another American, Paul Johnson who worked in Saudi Arabia as a contractor, was kidnapped and beheaded in June 2004. In both cases, the terrorists distributed videos or photographs to the media and posted similar exploitation means on websites.

A May 2007 attack on a U.S. two vehicle army observation post in Iraq resulted in several killed soldiers, an Iraqi soldier, and three missing U.S. soldiers. U.S. officials had credible evidence that the attack was conducted by al-Qaida or an al-Qaida affiliated cell with the intention to capture prisoners. Previous incidents of capturing U.S. soldiers had created immediate media attention. Website postings in May 2007 by terrorists mocked U.S. attempts to find the soldiers and gained significant international media attention of this small squad-size tactical raid.[163]

Hostage Taking

Hostage taking is typically an overt seizure of people to gain publicity for a cause, gain political concessions, political asylum, release of prisoners, or ransom. Many times the terrorists will take hostages with the intent to kill them after they believe they have fully exploited the media coverage from the situation.

Unlike kidnapping where a prominent individual is normally taken and moved to an unknown location, the hostages are usually not well known figures in the enemy's society. While dramatic, hostage situations are frequently risky for the terrorist group especially when conducted in enemy territory. They expose the terrorists to hostile military or police operations, and carry significant possibility of both mission failure and capture. Therefore, terrorists will usually attempt to hold hostages in a neutral or friendly area, rather than in enemy territory.

An example of a hostage crisis was the Moscow theater siege in October 2002. Thirty-four Chechen terrorists seized a movie theater, threatening to kill all of the hostages if the

---

[162] U.S. Marine Corps, Marine Corps University, Corporals Noncommissioned Officers Program, Force Protection, Course CPL 0302, (Quantico, VA, January 1999), 12-13; available from http://www.tecom.usmc.mil/utm/Force_Protection1_LP.PDF; Internet; accessed 31 March 2004.

[163] Kim Gamle, "Militants: stop hunt for U.S. soldiers," 14 May 2007, available from http://news.yahoo.com/s/ap/20070514/ap_on_re_mi_ea/iraq&printer=1;ylt=ApG9r; Internet; accessed 16 May 2007. See also, Robert H. Reid, "Search for missing soldiers intensifies,' 15 may 2007, available from http://news.yahoo.com/s/ap/20070515/ap_on_re_mi_ea/iraq&printer=1;_ylt+AujoSQGJ62...; Internet; accessed 16 may 2007.

Russians did not meet their demands. The rebels were demanding that Russian forces end the war in Chechnya. Following a long stalemate, Russian forces assaulted the theater. Over 60 hostages and over 30 terrorists died. However, 750 hostages were released. In another hostage crisis in 2004, an extremist regional group of over 30 men and at least two women seized a middle school and over 1000 people in Beslan, Russia. A three day crisis culminated in mayhem when an explosion erupted and caused an assault of the school facilities. Over 300 children, men, and women died in the assault.

Fig. 4-16. **Beslan Hostage Crisis**

See Chapter 6 of US Army TRADOC G2 Handbook No. 1.01, *Terror Operations: Case Studies in Terror*, for a case study of Beslan events and insights on domestic and foreign terrorism.

Similar issues could arise with captured U.S. soldiers. A case in point occurred during the air campaign against Serbia in the spring of 1999. Three U.S. Army soldiers patrolling the Yugoslav-Macedonian border became separated from a larger patrol and were captured by the Serbians. Serbian President Slobodan Milosevic orchestrated an international media campaign during their month long captivity. Maintaining an ambiguous stance on the status of the prisoners and their possible fate, Milosevic eventually released the three U.S. soldiers to an unofficial mission of prominent American political figures that resulted in even more media coverage. The political and psychological impact far outweighed any operational impact caused by the capture of three soldiers and one vehicle.

Fig. 4-17. **Milosevic and US Soldiers**

Hijack-Seizure

Hijacking involves the forceful commandeering of a conveyance. Although normally associated with planes, it can also include naval vessels or other craft. There are many purposes to hijacking, such as hostage taking activities, obtaining a means of escape, or as a means of suicide. While hijacking of aircraft for hostage taking has declined in frequency since the implementation of improved security measures, the use of hijacked aircraft for escape or as a weapon continues. The attacks on the World Trade Center and the Pentagon in September 2001 are vivid reminders of the hijacking abilities of terrorist groups and the destructive power of hijacked airliners.

Another example is the hijacking of TWA Flight 847 from Athens to Rome in 1985 by members of Hizballah. They held the plane and 153 hostages for 17 days demanding the release of Lebanese and Palestinian prisoners. The hostages from Flight 847 were released after Israel freed 435 prisoners. However, terrorists murdered a U.S. Navy diver, Robert Stethem, and dumped his body on the airport tarmac.

Fig. 4-18. **Hijackers TWA 847**

The use of hijacked vehicles for destructive devices is not restricted to aircraft. Trucks carrying cargoes of explosive or flammable materials have also been seized to use as delivery devices. The possibility of such a technique being used with a ship carrying oil, refined petroleum products, or liquefied natural gas (LNG) is of great concern. The results of several accidental explosions and fires from mishaps in handling such vessels in port show the catastrophic potential of this technique.[164] Although not related to terrorism, ships exploding in the harbors of Texas City, Texas in 1947 and Halifax, Nova Scotia in 1917 destroyed significant portions of these towns and caused a combined death toll of over 2500 people.

Seizure of a critical element of infrastructure, similar to hostage taking intentions, can be a physical site such as a facility of importance to a target population, or a cyber node that disrupts or precludes use of selected cyber functions.

Raid or Ambush

A terrorist raid is similar in concept to a conventional operation but is usually conducted with smaller forces against targets marked for destruction, hijacking, or hostage operations. A raid permits control of the target for the execution of some other action. The kidnapping or assassination of a target that has a security force can often require a raid to overcome the defenses. Successful conduct of these type attacks requires extensive preoperational surveillance and detailed planning.

Examples of this type tactic are the raids conducted by terrorists on three Riyadh western housing compounds in Saudi Arabia on 11 May 2003. Attackers penetrated each compound and then detonated vehicle borne IEDs. The attack at the al-Hamra compound demonstrates the tactics used in a raid such as this. A sedan pulled up to the gate, followed by another vehicle. A number of terrorists dismounted, shot the guard, and then forced their way into the compound. As both vehicles drove to the center of the compound, terrorists shot into buildings and at any moving targets. Once they reached

---

[164] Gerald Pawle, *Secret Weapons of World War II* (New York: Ballantine Books, 1967), 53-54.

the housing area, one of the suicide terrorists driving a vehicle detonated the explosive device as a VBIED.[165]

An ambush is a surprise attack characterized by violent execution and speed of action. The intended objective may be to cause mass casualties, assassinate an individual, or disrupt hostile security operations. Explosives, such as bombs and directional mines, are a common weapon used in terrorist ambushes. Other weapons frequently used are rocket launchers, automatic weapons, and other small arms.

An example of a compound attack was the bombing in Bali on 12 October 2002 attributed to Jemaah Islamiyah, an Islamic terrorist group linked to al-Qaida. Initially, an electronically triggered bomb was detonated in a bar that forced the patrons out into the street. A much more powerful car bomb was detonated in the street in front of another establishment. The sequential bombing caused casualties of 202 killed and 209 injured.[166]

Fig. 4-19. **Bali Sequential Bombings**

Terrorist ambushes are frequently conducted from a variety of mobile platforms. Cars, vans and motorcycles have been used to conceal the attackers, isolate or immobilize the target, and then allow the attackers to escape. Ambushes from mobile platforms can be conducted while moving, or can be designed to bring the target to a halt in order to allow the attack team to physically close with and attack a target. A more recent example is the March 2004 attack on five U.S. civilians working for a private volunteer organization (PVO) in Iraq. Four were killed and one was wounded in this mobile ambush in the city of Mosul.

Assassination

An assassination is a deliberate action to kill specific individuals, usually VIPs such as political leaders, notable citizens, collaborators, particularly effective officials. The terrorist group assassinates people it cannot intimidate, people who support their enemy, or people who have some symbolic significance for the enemy or world community. Terrorist groups often refer to these killings as punishment or justice as an attempt to legitimize their actions. In 1981, President Anwar Sadat of Egypt was assassinated by fundamentalist Islamics for his support of the peace process in the Middle East and his relationship with Western nations. In September 2001, Northern Alliance leader Ahmed Shah Massoud was assassinated in Afghanistan by two suicide bombers believed to be

---

[165] Department of State, U.S. Embassy, Jakarta, Indonesia, *Threats Involving Vehicle Borne Improvised Explosive Devices* (Jakarta, Indonesia, 2003), 2; available from http://www.usembassyjakarta.org/vbied_vehicles.html; Internet; accessed 14 January 2004.
[166] *Wikipedia*, 2004 ed., s.v. "2002 Bali Terrorist Bombing;" available from http://en.wikipedia.org/w/wiki.phtml?title=2002_Bali_terrorist_bombing&printable=yes; Internet; accessed 17 March 2004.

from al-Qaida. The assassination was due to Massoud's opposition of the Taliban regime and al-Qaida's presence in Afghanistan.

Many targets of assassination are symbolic and are intended to have great psychological impact on the enemy. For example, assassinating an enemy government official, a successful businessperson, or a prominent cleric can demonstrate the enemy's inability to protect its own people. Assassinating local representatives of social or civic order, such as teachers, contributes to disorder while demoralizing other members of the local government and discouraging cooperation with them. An example of this is the attempted assassination of Iraq's most prominent Shiite cleric, Grand Ayatollah Ali al-Sistani in February 2004. This incident was an attempt to create anger in the long oppressed Shiite community and increase the sectarian and ethnic violence in Iraq. Many assassinations have targeted Iraqis who have assumed leadership positions in support of a transition to a sovereign democratic government.

Fig. 4-20. **Intended Victim**

Extensive target surveillance and reconnaissance of engagement areas are required to select the optimum mode of attack. Although many factors play into the decision, the target's vulnerabilities determine the method of assassination. For example, a target driving to work along the same route each day may be vulnerable to an emplaced explosive device.[167]

A publicized assassination attempt during the 1981 Return of Forces to Germany (REFORGER) training exercise was directed against the U.S. military by the Red Army Faction. As the Commander in Chief of United States Army Europe (USAREUR) and Commander of NATO's Central Army Group (CENTAG), General Frederick Kroesen and his wife were attacked in their sedan as they drove near his headquarters in Heidelberg, Germany.

The assassination attempt used rocket propelled grenades and small arms gunfire when the sedan was at a halt for a city stoplight. After the attack, a site was discovered about 200 yards from the target point with an abandoned tent, radio transmitter, sleeping bag, and food.[168] The terrorists had conducted surveillance and developed detailed plans for the assassination attempt. Fortunately, sedan armor plating and bulletproof glass on his vehicle, combined with inaccurate rocket detonations, prevented any serious injuries.

Fig. 4-21. **General Kroesen**

---

[167] *Encyclopedia of World Terror*, 1997 ed., s.v. "Assassination."
[168] John Vinocur, "U.S. General Safe in Raid in Germany," *New York Times,* 16 September 1981, p. A1.

Unfortunately terrorists have been successful in some assassination attempts. In April 1989, Communist insurgents from the New People's Army in the Philippines assassinated an American military advisor, Col. James Rowe. He was killed in a moving ambush where small arms fire defeated the protection of his armored official vehicle. This terrorist group was attacking Americans they considered directly linked to the Philippine military campaign being conducted against their group.

Weapons of Mass Destruction (WMD)

Listing a category as weapons of mass destruction acknowledges a broad range of capabilities that specific terrorist groups would like to acquire. Once acquired, this capability would allow for catastrophic results through numerous delivery means. These type weapons include chemical, biological, radiological, nuclear, and high yield explosives.

See the 2007 version of US Army TRADOC G2 Handbook No. 1.04, *Terrorism and WMD in the Contemporary Operational Environment*, for a current guide on weapons of mass destruction and terrorism.

Aircraft Threats

A man portable air defense system (MANPADS) is a significant threat in the hands of terrorists. There are a number of surface-to-air weapons that terrorists can use to attack aircraft. Weapons can be as simple as a rocket propelled grenade (RPG) normally used in surface-to-surface combat or as sophisticated as a Stinger or similar Igla air defense missile.

One of the most notable incidents by terrorists-insurgents downing U.S. military aircraft was in Mogadishu, Somalia in 1993. The U.S. Army was conducting a raid to capture some of the close supporters of the leader of one of the rival Somali clans, Mohammed Farah Aideed. During this raid, two UH-60 Blackhawk helicopters were shot down using RPGs. The U.S. had underestimated the ability to shoot down its helicopters using this type system. Aideed had fundamentalist Islamic soldiers from Sudan who had experience shooting down Russian helicopters in Afghanistan. They trained his militia to use RPGs in an air defense role.[169]

Fig. 4-22. **MANPADS**

In a separate area of operations, U.S. military forces realized the threat posed by RPGs in an air defense mission in Afghanistan in 2002 when two MH-47 Chinook helicopters were shot down. Whether in Afghanistan or Iraq, attacks on U.S. military and civilian aircraft continue with various degrees of detail in the media on what type of weapon was used to hit or destroy targeted aircraft. Weapons descriptions in attacks during the last

---

[169] FM 3-06, *Urban Operations*, 1 June 2003.

several years include massed gunfire, RPGs, or air defense missiles.[170] Some missiles have infrared and ultraviolet detectors that assist in defeating flares.[171]

Shoulder-fired surface-to-air missiles offer a history of effective use in several regions of the world. These systems normally contain an infrared seeker with the speed of the missile providing little opportunity for warning or evasive maneuver by the aircraft. Afghan fighters demonstrated MANPADs lethality by probably destroying over 200 Soviet aircraft during the Soviet Union's war in Afghanistan.

Missiles are affordable to terrorist groups and they are available on the world weapons market. Unclassified estimates indicate several thousand shoulder-fired weapons are in terrorist control. Number estimates vary considerably. To demonstrate the number of systems in circulation, as of December 2002, coalition forces in Afghanistan had captured over 5,500 shoulder-fired systems from the Taliban and al Qaeda. Some of these weapons included U.S. Stinger and British Blowpipe missiles.[172] A consideration beyond numbers of missiles is the probable lack of maintenance and proper functioning of such missiles; the number of operational missiles could be quite limited.

Most experts consider aircraft departures and landings as the times when aircraft are most vulnerable to these weapons. A survey of 25 years of these incidents totaled 35 civilian aircraft have come under attack from these weapons. Results were 24 aircraft being shot down and causing more than 500 deaths. Of these encounters, five incidents involved large airliners.[173] Unclassified estimates reflect between 25 and 30 nonstate groups possess these MANPADS systems.

Fig, 4-23. **Missile Hit in Iraq**

In November 2004, a civilian cargo airplane was hit by a shoulder-fired missile while departing Baghdad International Airport in Iraq. The missile hit damaged the left wing of the plane. Fortunately, the crew was able to make an emergency landing with no loss of life. The airplane was declared a total loss.[174] The U.S. Department of State estimates that since the 1970s and up until 2003, 40 civilian aircraft have been hit by MANPADS and caused about 25 crashes with a cumulative death toll of over 600 people.[175]

---

[170] "Two soldiers die as another U.S. military helicopter goes down in Iraq," available from http://www.today.com/news/world/iraq/2007-202-02-sectarian-violence_x.htm; Internet; accessed 11 June 2007.
[171] "MANPADS Proliferation," available from http://www.fas.org/asmp/campaigns/MANPADS/MANPADS.html; Internet; accessed 11 June 2007.
[172] Christopher Bolkcom, et al, *Homeland Security: Protecting Airliners from Terrorist Missiles* (Washington, D.C.: Congressional Research Service Report for Congress, 3 November 2003), 4-7; available from http://www.fas.org/irp/crs/RL31741.pdf; Internet; accessed 1 April 2004.
[173] Ibid., 7-9.
[174] Christopher Bolkcom, Andrew Feickert, an Bartholomew Elias, Congressional Research Service, CRS Report for Congress, *Homeland Security: Protecting Airliners from Terrorist Missiles*, October 22, 2004., 11.
[175] Department of State, Bureau of Political-Military Affairs and Bureau of International Security and Nonproliferation, "The MANPADS Menace: Combating the Threat to Global Aviation from Man-Portable

Maritime Threats

Terrorist attacks against maritime targets are fairly rare and constitute only two percent of all international incidents over a 30 year period and entry into the twenty-first century.[176] There is a history of maritime terrorism and maritime authorities worldwide are increasingly anxious about terrorist attacks on both ports and ships. In fact, some intelligence analysts believe that because land-based targets are better protected, terrorists will turn to the maritime infrastructure because they see these as soft targets.[177]

Likely operations conducted by maritime terrorism include suicide attacks on commercial and military vessels, and hijacking for the following purposes: (1) carrying out a subsequent suicide attack on a ship or port (2) seeking ransom (3) smuggling weapons and explosives (4) simple piracy.[178] Although few terrorist groups have developed a maritime capability there have been some exceptions to include the Provisional Irish Republican Army, Abu Sayyaf Group based in the Philippines, various Palestinian groups, al-Qaida, and the Liberation Tigers of Tamil Eelam (LTTE) in Sri Lanka. The LTTE claims a large maritime capability of coastal and deepwater craft.[179] They reportedly have roughly 3000 trained personnel and between 100 to 200 surface and underwater vessels, including attack vessels, logistics vessels, fast personnel carriers, suicide craft, and multi-purpose craft. The Tamil Tigers have employed a range of technologies, including suicide stealth craft, mini submarines, and one-man suicide torpedoes.[180]

Information presented at the Terrorism in the Asia Pacific Conference in September 2002 reported that al-Qaida had obtained a variety of vessels and systems capable of carrying out attacks against ships and seaports. These included mini-subs, human torpedo systems, and divers trained in underwater demolitions. The larger vessels are commercial ships that are used to generate revenue for al-Qaida. However, there is concern that they could be filled with explosives and used as floating bombs to ram into other ships or port facilities.[181]

Fig. 4-24. **Targeting LNG**

The International Maritime Organization has warned that liquefied natural gas (LNG) carriers and other ships carrying volatile cargo could be hijacked and used as weapons of

Air Defense Systems," September 20, 2005, available from http://www.sate.gov/t/pm/rls/fs/53558.htm; Internet; accessed 11 June 2007.

[176] Peter Chalk, "Threats to the Maritime Environment: Piracy and Terrorism," (RAND Stakeholder Consultation, Ispra, Italy 28-30 October 2002): 9.

[177] Graham Gerard Ong, "Next Stop, Maritime Terrorism," *Viewpoints* (12 September 2003): 1; available from http://www.iseas.edu.sg/viewpoint/ggosep03.pdf; Internet; accessed 2 April 2004.

[178] Ibid., 2.

[179] Ibid., 1.

[180] Peter Chalk, "Threats to the Maritime Environment: Piracy and Terrorism," (RAND Stakeholder Consultation, Ispra, Italy 28-30 October 2002): 12.

[181] Bob Newman, "Terrorists Feared to Be Planning Sub-Surface Naval Attacks," *CNS News.com,* 3 December 2002; available from http://www.cnsnews.com/ForeignBureaus/archive/200212/FOR20021203a.html; Internet; accessed 19 March 2004.

mass destruction. A briefing at the Maritime Security Council's annual International Maritime Security Summit in October 2002 stated that a large ship loaded with LNG could result in an explosion equivalent to a .7-megaton nuclear detonation. For comparison, the bomb dropped on Hiroshima, Japan was 15-kilotons.[182]

A maritime terrorist attack against a U.S. military ship is the attack on the USS *Cole*. Two suicide bombers in a small boat loaded with explosives attacked the ship while it was refueling in Aden Harbor, Yemen. The blast blew a 40 foot by 60 foot hole in the side of the USS *Cole*, killed 17 sailors, and injured 39 crewmen. The al-Qaida member who is believed to have planned the attack on the USS *Cole*, Abdulrahim Mohammed Abda Al-Nasheri, was captured in 2002. He confessed also to planning attacks on shipping in the Strait of Gibraltar by using bomb-laden speedboat attacks against U.S. and British warships as they pass through the strait. Fortunately, Moroccan intelligence service thwarted the plot.[183]

Suicide Tactics

Suicide tactics are particular methods of delivering a bomb or conducting an assassination. The tactic can be defined as "An act of terror, employing an explosive or incendiary device that requires the death of the perpetrator for successful implementation."[184]

The prevalent suicide tactic in use today involves an individual wearing or carrying an explosive device to a target and then detonating the bomb, or driving an explosive laden vehicle to a target and then detonating the bomb. Suicide attacks differ in concept and execution from other high risk operations. In a high-risk mission, the likely outcome is the death of the terrorist, but mission success does not require that the participants die. The plan will allow for possible escape or survival of the participants. Some terrorist cells have used people who are unknowingly part of a suicide attack. An example is an individual associated with a terrorist cell who believes he is only a courier, but is transporting an improvised explosive device in a vehicle that is command detonated by an observer against a selected target.

Fig. 2-25. **Foreign or Domestic Terror**

---

[182] Ibid., 2.

[183] Michael Richardson, "A Time Bomb for Global Trade: Maritime-related Terrorism in an Age of Weapons of Mass Destruction," *Viewpoints* (25 February 2004): 8; available from http://www.iseas.edu.sg/viewpoint/mricsumfeb04.pdf; Internet; accessed 5 April 2004.

[184] Martha Crenshaw, "Suicide Terrorism in Comparative Perspective," in *Countering Suicide Terrorism* (Herzilya, Israel: The International Policy Institute for Counter Terrorism, The Interdisciplinary Center, 2002), 21.

Another way of describing a suicide bomber is a highly effective precision-guided munition. Psychological impact increases when confronted by a person who plans to intentionally commit suicide and kill other people as a tactic. Although a suicide bomber can be a lone terrorist working independently, the use of suicide terrorism as a tactic is normally the result of a conscious decision on the part of the leaders of terrorist organizations to engage this form of attack. It is frequently conducted as a campaign for a specific objective.[185] Notwithstanding, suicide bombing can be an indication that a terror organization has failed to meet its goals through less extreme measures.[186]

Religiously motivated extremist groups as well as secular issue groups have employed this tactic. In addition to the Middle East; suicide attacks have been conducted in India, Panama, Algeria, Pakistan, Argentina, Croatia, Turkey, Tanzania, and Kenya.[187] Other locations include Russia and the United States. The single most prolific suicidal terrorist group is the Tamil Tigers (LTTE) in Sri Lanka.[188] A lone woman belonging to the Tamil Tigers assassinated former Prime Minister Ravij Gandhi with a suicide vest-belt bomb. Tamil Tigers also killed a President of Sri Lanka with a suicide bomber.

Fig. 2-26. **Moments to Suicide**

As in any other terrorist operation, extensive pre-operational surveillance and reconnaissance, exhaustive planning, rehearsals, and sufficient resources will be devoted to an operation employing suicide as a tactic.[189] Although suicide bombers have been historically a male dominated tactic, women are becoming more involved in conducting these type operations. Women participated in 30 to 40 percent of the LTTE's nearly 200 suicide bombings in Sri Lanka.[190] Suicide attacks have also been conducted by Chechen and Palestinian women, as well as attacks conducted by women in Iraq, Turkey and

---

[185] Yoram Schweitzer, "Suicide Terrorism: Development and Main Characteristics," in *Countering Suicide Terrorism* (Herzilya, Israel: The International Policy Institute for Counter Terrorism, The Interdisciplinary Center, 2002), 85.

[186] Ehud Sprinzak, "Rational Fanatics," *Foreign Policy,* 120 (September/October 2000): 66-73.

[187] "Suicide Terrorism: a Global Threat," *Jane's Intelligence Review* (October 2000): 1; available from http://www.janes.com/security/international_security/news/usscole/jir001020_1_n.shtml; Internet; accessed 20 January 2004.

[188] "Suicide Terrorism," *The Economist* (January 2004): 3; available from http://quicksitebuilder.cnet.com/supfacts/id396.html; Internet; accessed 17 March 2004.

[189] Rohan Gunaratna, "Suicide Terrorism: a Global Threat," *Jane's Intelligence Review* (20 October 2000): 1-7; available from http://www.janes.com/security/international_security/news/usscole/jir001020_1_n.shtml; Internet; accessed 7 September 2002.

[190] Clara Beyler, "Messengers of Death – Female Suicide Bombers," *International Policy Institute for Counter-Terrorism* (February 2003): 3; available from http://www.ict.org.il/articles/articledet.cfm?articleid=470; Internet; accessed 18 March 2004.

Morocco. Additionally an FBI report has expressed concern over the forming of al-Qaida female units.[191]

Teenagers have been suicide bombers. Palestinian teenagers have been involved in attacks against Israel for several years. In February 2004, three boys, ages 13, 14, and 15 were arrested because they were planning to carry out an attack in the northern Israeli town of Afula. Use of children in suicide attacks became evident on March 16, 2004, when an 11-year-old boy was stopped at an Israeli checkpoint with a bomb in his bag. Although investigation doubted that this boy was aware of the bomb, later that month a 14-year-old was stopped at a checkpoint wearing a suicide explosive vest.[192]

The first major suicide bombing that struck at U.S. military forces was Hizballah's attack on the Marine barracks in Lebanon in October 1983 where 241 Americans were killed. Suicide attacks have also been used against coalition forces in Iraq during Operation Iraqi Freedom (OIF). In a one day example on 27 December 2003, 12 Iraqis and six coalition troops were killed, and 100 Iraqis and 26 coalition troops were wounded when four suicide bombers conducted coordinated attacks in the city of Kabala.[193] Unfortunately, these type of mass casualty producing attacks have continued in Iraq, with no sign of relief in the near future. Suicide is an increasing danger given the number of attempted or successful suicide attacks. Between March 2006 and February 2007 in Iraq, over 30 suicide vest bomb incidents were reported as well as over 275 vehicle borne improvised explosive devices.

Fig. 2-27. **VBIED at Check Point**

Conclusion

Whether U.S. military forces are deployed, in-transit, or located at institutional locations, U.S. military forces can be vulnerable to terrorist targeting activities. Deployed forces include unit rotations in combat operations, stability missions and training assistance to foreign militaries, and can apply to all individual assignments in overseas locations. In-transit units and members can include active and reserve component units and members. Institutional forces and locations include garrisons, training and logistic facilities, and other activities or installations that do not deploy to accomplish their organizational mission. The operational environment (OE) is a composite of the conditions, circumstances, and influences that affect employment of capabilities and bear on the decisions of the

---

[191] Clara Beyler, "Female Suicide Bombers – An Update," *International Policy Institute for Counter-Terrorism* (March 2004): 1; available from http://www.ict.org.il/articles/articledet.cfm?articleid=508; Internet; accessed 31 March 2004.

[192] Greg Myre, "Palestinian Bomber, 14, Thwarted before Attack," *International Herald Tribune* (March 2004): 1; available from http://www.iht.com/articles/511745.html; Internet; accessed 26 March 2004.

[193] Tom Lasseter, "Suicide Attackers Strike Karbala," *Knight Ridder,* 27 December 2003; available from http://www.realcities.com/mld/krwashington/news/special_packages/iraq/7581568.htm; Internet; accessed 20 January 2004.

commander. This includes active component units within the U.S. or positioned overseas, and reserve component units identified for operations, mobilization, or demobilization.

A terrorist may view value as a function of the overall psychological impact that destruction of a target will have on a population, as well as the cascading physical effects of damaging or destroying a critical piece or aspect of an organization or infrastructure.

Reasons for targeting of U.S. military forces include: target accessibility, symbolic value, demonstrate terrorist organizational capability, delay or prevent U.S. movements, reduce U.S. operational capability, delay or prevent U.S. movements, degrade social confidence in supported government, disrupt economic productivity, or influence U.S. policy.

This Page Intentionally Blank

5 | Terrorism of the Foreseeable Future

Chapter 5

Terrorism of the Foreseeable Future

Today's extreme Islamist groups such as al-Qaida do not merely seek political revolution in their own countries. They aspire to dominate all countries. Their goal is a totalitarian, theocratic empire to be achieved by waging perpetual war on soldiers and civilians alike.

**Honorable Michael Chertoff
U.S. Secretary of Homeland Security
April 2007**

The *Report of the Future of Terrorism Task Force*, published in January 2007, assesses future threats to the United States for the next five years. The lead finding of the report states, "There is every indication that the number and magnitude of attacks on the United States, its interest and its allies will likely increase." Predicting the nature, timing, or location of the next attack is beyond the scope of this report, however, the task force spotlights, "The most significant terrorist threat to the homeland today stems from a global movement, underpinned by a jihadist/Salafist ideology."[194]

Terrorism threats range al-Qaida affiliated cells with regional, international, or transnational reach to individual self-radicalized and unaffiliated terrorists with single issue agendas and finite capabilities. These types of terrorist threat exist as foreign and domestic threats of the United States in the U.S. Homeland and in United States presence throughout the world.

Figure 5-1. **Terrorism Trends and Future Trauma**

---

[194] Department of Homeland Security, Homeland Security Advisory Council, *Report of the Future of Terrorism Task Force*, January 2007, Washington, D.C.: Department of Homeland Security, 2-3.

Section I: Future Trends in Terrorism

To appreciate the future of terrorism, understanding current trends of terror must consider the nature of terrorists, and study the capabilities and limitations of specific cells or movements in an evolving contemporary operational environment. As the regions of the world advance in technological areas, expand the mobility opportunities of people, and exploit the Internet and other media, extremists fuel grievances and alienate segments of populations to foster support for their agendas.

Terrorism Trends

◆ *Intensified* **Ideological Extremism**

◆ *Enhanced* **Operational Capabilities**

◆ *Flexible* **Organizational Networks**

◆ *Expanded* **Transnational Associations**

◆ *Emergent* **Independent Actors**

◆ *Increased* **Weapon System Lethality**

◆ *Intended* **Mass Casualties – Mayhem**

◆ *Targeted* **Economic Disruption**

◆ *Exploited* **Mass Media Marketing**

As a means to an end, terrorism is becoming a more physically dangerous and more psychologically effective weapon. While a simple description of terrorism remains, "The calculated use of unlawful violence or threat of unlawful violence to inculcate fear…," terrorism is rising from a tactical novelty to become, in many instances, a significant operational and strategic tool.

Terrorism is becoming a more network based that encourages a loosely organized, self-financed organizational structure. The motivation of some terrorist groups appears to be based increasingly on theological extremes and ideological absolutes. The international or transnational cooperation among terrorist groups provides an improved ability to recruit members, develop fiscal support and resources, gain skills training, transfer of technology, and when desired, political advice.[195]

Terrorists are adapting constantly to optimize their knowledge, training, logistical support, and readiness to conduct terror.

This chapter examines several key themes of the probable future of terrorism in an era of increasing globalization.[196] Nine aspects frame the assessment of terrorism trends. These trends are: intensified ideological extremism, enhanced operational capabilities, flexible organizational networks, expended transnational associations, emergent independent actors, increased weapon system lethality, intended mass casualties and mayhem, targeted economic disruption, and exploited mass media marketing.

---

[195] Raphael Perl, *Terrorism and National Security: Issues and Trends* (Washington, D.C.: Congressional Research Service Issue Brief for Congress, 22 December 2003), 1.
[196] Ibid., 3.

Section II: Assessing the Trends

Intensified Ideological Extremism

A U.S. Defense Intelligence Agency (DIA) assessment of global terrorism states, "Al-Qaida's strategic objectives – reestablishing the Islamic caliphate, unified by a common ideology rooted in a violent rejection of apostasy and characterized by fervent opposition to Western influence in traditionally Islamic countries – compel al-Qaida's commitment..."[197] Senior leaders of al-Qaida have repeatedly stated an aim of establishing Islamic states that would include Afghanistan, an Islamic state in the Levant, Egypt, and neighboring states in the Arabian Peninsula and Iraq.

Other regions of the world have terrorist organizations with similar ideological aims such as the Armed Islamic Group (GIA) in Algeria. GIA poses to oust the Algerian regime and replace it with an Islamic state.[198] In September 2006, al-Zwahiri used a 9/11 anniversary videotape to announce that the Algerian Group for Salafist Preaching and Combat was formally aligning itself with al-Qaida.[199] The Jemaah Islamiya (JI) has the aim of establishing an Islamic caliphate that would span Indonesia, Malaysia, southern Thailand, Singapore, Brunei, and the Southern Philippines.[200]

Fig. 5-1. **Bali and Jemaah Islamiya**

Theology extremism underlies much of the contemporary Islamic struggle. The Wahhabi movement in Saudi Arabia is a very conservative ideology that is also very powerful due to its significant wealth from Saudi Arabian oil profits. By some estimates, the Wahhabi movement controls 70 to 90 percent of the Sunni Islamic institutions in the world. Much of the radical madrassas emerge from this institutional support and ferment extremism in their religious doctrine and conduct. According to a former Director of the Central Intelligence Agency, the "...Wahhabi ideology is essentially the same ideology as that of al-Qaida. It is genocidal with respect to Shiite Muslims, Jews, homosexuals, apostates, and is fanatically repressive, particularly of women, but also of virtually everyone else."

---

[197] Michael D. Maples, *Current and Projected National Security Threats to the United States*, Statement for the Record, Senate Select committee on Intelligence Committee, 11 January 2007; Washington, D.C. : Defense Intelligence Agency, 6.

[198] Department of State, *Country Reports on Terrorism 2006*, April 2007; 241, available from http://www.terrorisminfo.mipt.org/Patterns-of-global-terrorism.asp; Internet; accessed 2 May 2007

[199] Michael D. Maples, *Current and Projected National Security Threats to the United States*, Statement for the Record, Senate Select committee on Intelligence Committee, 11 January 2007; Washington, D.C. : Defense Intelligence Agency, 8.

[200] Ibid., 255.

The two ideologies have an ultimate aim of establishing a worldwide caliphate – a theocracy – that equates to a religious dictatorship.[201]

◆ Enhanced Operational Capabilities

Terrorists use new electronic and cyber technologies, and adapt existing ones to their uses. The debate over privacy of computer data was largely spurred by the specter of terrorists planning and communicating over cyberspace with encrypted data beyond law enforcement's ability to intercept or decode this data. To exchange information, terrorists have exploited disposable cellular phones, over the counter long-distance calling cards, Internet cafes, and other means of relative anonymous communications. Embedding information in digital pictures and graphics and sending them over the Internet is another innovation employed to enable the clandestine global communication that modern terrorists require.[202]

Terrorist groups and other illegal sub-state organizations are rapidly becoming indistinguishable from each other. The increasing role of criminal activity in financing terrorism, either in partnership or competition with traditional criminal activities, is making it very difficult, if not impossible, to clearly determine where one stops and the other begins. These enterprises include well-publicized activities such as drug trafficking and smuggling, which some terrorists, insurgencies, and even less reputable governments have been engaged in for decades. They also include newer, less well-known illegal activities such as welfare fraud, tax evasion and fraud, counterfeiting, and money laundering. Many of these activities are offshoots of terrorist groups' evolving capabilities of false documentation and concealment of money transactions for their operational purposes. These activities now generate a profit for additional funding.

Fig. 5-2. **Crime and Terror**

Terrorists and criminal organizations are becoming more closely related, as terrorists utilize criminal networks and methods to operate, and as criminals become more politicized.[203] As national governments fail, their ruling elites frequently criminalize the nation itself, lending their sovereignty to smuggling, money laundering, piracy, or other illicit activities. Their security forces may retreat into terrorism to hold onto what power or authority they can, and use terrorist groups to function in place of the official arms of

---

[201] R. James Woolsey, "Intelligence and the War on Terrorism," *The Guardian*, 9, April 2007, 21-30.

[202] Thomas Homer-Dixon, "The Rise of Complex Terrorism", *Foreign Policy Magazine* (15 January 2002): 2.

[203] "The New Threat of Organized Crime and Terrorism" *Jane's Terrorism & Security Monitor* (6 June 2000): 1-5; available from http://www.janes.com/security/international_security/news/jtsm/jtsm000619_1_n.shtml; Internet; accessed 27 June 2000.

the government. Successful coups often generate governments that immediately resort to terror to consolidate their position.[204]

This interpenetration of a criminal element into the government while government officials are seeping down to the terrorists' level is the result of governments feeling that legality in the international sense is a luxury they cannot afford and perhaps do not need. The better-funded sub-state organizations such as terrorist organizations or criminal syndicates infiltrate or supplant the government. Eventually, there is no distinction between the two as they effectively merge.

Emerging and non-state entities are not compelled to obey any established rules regarding the uses of force. Terrorism and the use of terror to oppress may be viewed as logical and effective methods to accomplish objectives. The development of rules of war and the framework of international laws that attempt to protect the civilian from military action are irrelevant to these combatants. Thus the expansion of where and to whom violence may be applied will accelerate. The treatment of prisoners will rely more on the provision for ransom or retribution for mistreatment than on the rulings of the international agreements such as Geneva Convention.[205]

Terrorist basing and operations in urban environments will increase. Terrorists have typically operated in urban environments, but the emergence of megalopolis cities in undeveloped or poorly developed countries, with poor services, weak governance, and rampant unemployment and dissatisfaction has created a near perfect recruiting ground-cum-operating environment for terrorists. Many of these cities have adequate international communication and transport capacities for the terrorists' purposes; yet have ineffective law enforcement and a potentially huge base of sympathizers and recruits. The inability of external counterterror and law enforcement organizations to effectively intervene where the local government is unable to assert authority is another advantage.[206]

Fig. 5-3. **Urban Terror**

A development related to this is the emergence of gray areas where no government exercises actual control. Control is imposed by sub-state actors that can span criminal organizations, militias, and terrorists. These groups may as coalitions or in various states of coexistence ranging from truce to open hostility. These areas may be located in urban centers or rural regions and a lack or absence of any effective government control.[207]

---

[204] Robert Kaplan, *The Coming Anarchy: Shattering the Dreams of the Post Cold War* (New York: Random House, 2000), 48.

[205] Martin L. Van Creveld, *The Transformation of War* (New York: The Free Press, 1991), 202.

[206] Xavier Raufer, "New World Disorder, New Terrorisms: New Threats for the Western World," in *The Future of Terrorism*, ed. Max Taylor and John Horgan (Portland: Frank Cass Publishers, 2000), 32.

[207] Ibid.

Terrorists have demonstrated significant resiliency after disruption by counterterrorist action. Some groups have redefined themselves after being defeated or being forced into dormancy. The Shining Path of Peru (*Sendero Luminosa*) lost its leadership cadre and founding leader to counter-terrorism efforts by the Peruvian government in 1993.[208] The immediate result was severe degradation in the operational capabilities of the group. However, the Shining Path has returned to rural operations and organization in order to reconstitute itself. Although not the threat that it was, the group remains in being, and could exploit further unrest or governmental weakness in Peru to continue its renewal.

There are potential cyber-terrorism impacts in relation to the U.S. military forces transformation. As the U.S. military increases its battlefield information capabilities, vulnerabilities peculiar to networks such as overload feedback between nodes and destruction of key concentration nodes become available for terrorists to exploit.[209] Simple deception techniques can exploit a reliance on sophisticated technology.[210] When Usama bin Laden thought American satellites were being used to locate him tracing his satellite phone, he had an aid depart from his location carrying the phone. Evidently the aid was captured with the phone, while bin Laden escaped.

Expanded Transnational Associations

Terrorist groups display significant progress in emerging from a subordinate role in nation-state conflicts to become prominent as international influences in their own right. They are becoming more integrated with other sub-state entities such as criminal organizations and legitimately chartered corporations, and are gradually assuming various levels of control and identity with national governments. For example, the FARC and ELN of Columbia use extortion, kidnapping, money laundering, and other economic strategies to finance their operations. Reports estimate that the FARC collects half a billion dollars per year from protecting the drug trade of the region.[211] Other examples include Hizballah and HAMAS members who establish front companies to cover an illegal market system, conduct money laundering, fraud, and tax evasion. United States investigations have directly linked Hizballah and HAMAS to illegal cigarette trafficking and funneling the illicit profits to their organizations that include material support to terrorism.[212]

---

[208] *International Encyclopedia of Terrorism*, 1997 ed., s.v. "Terrorism in Peru."

[209] Ibid., 3-4.

[210] "Osama's Satellite Phone Switcheroo," *CBS News.com,* 21 January 2003, 1; available from http://www.cbsnews.com/stories/2003/01/21/attack/main537258.shtml; Internet; accessed 10 February 2003.

[211] Christopher C. Harmon, *Terrorism Today* (London, Portland, OR: Frank Cass, 2000), 65 and 139.

[212] William Billingslea, "Illicit Cigarette Trafficking and the Funding of Terrorism," *The Police Chief,* February 2004, 49-54.

Between 1996 and 2000, a group of individuals affiliated with Hizballah used bulk cash to purchase about $8 million in cigarettes in North Carolina, where the cigarette tax is 5 cents per pack. They then traveled to sell the cigarettes in Michigan, where the cigarette tax is 75 cents per pack. Avoiding the tax to the State of Michigan, profits were an estimated $1.5 million. A portion of this illegal profit was delivered to Hizballah in Lebanon to finance their operations in the region.

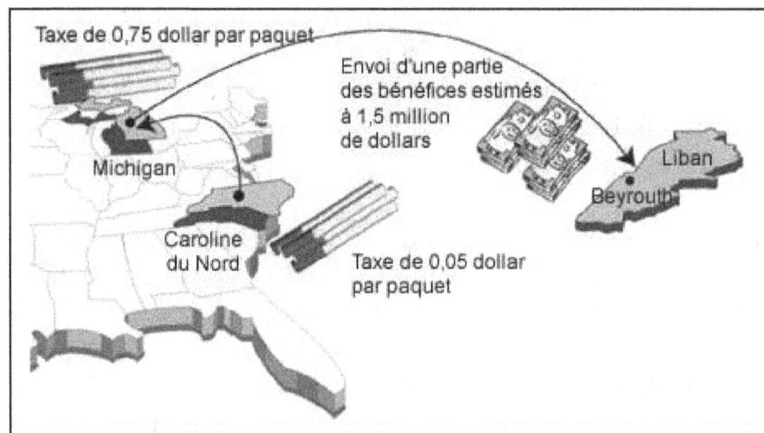

Fig. 5-4. **Criminal Activities in Support of Terrorism**

This evolutionary development has inverted the previous relationship between terrorists and governments.[213] In the earlier relationships, the nation-state sponsor had some measure of control. Due to the ability of terrorist groups to generate tremendous income from legitimate and illegal sources, it often becomes the terrorist organization that "sponsors" and props up its weaker partner, the national government. For example, during the period it was based in Afghanistan, al Qaeda was running an annual operating budget of approximately $200 million, while their hosts the Taliban had only $70 million annually.[214] In addition to financial supremacy, al Qaeda personnel also provided much of the technical expertise the Taliban lacked. The only asset the Taliban had to offer was sanctuary and the advantages their status as a recognized national government provided in some countries.

Although the increase in terrorist income has been tied to the increasing involvement of terrorists in international crime, simpler support by the more traditional means of donations, extortions, and extra-legal contributions can be leveraged into significant sums through investment. The PLO is an excellent example of financing through legitimate investments. The organization managed to acquire sufficient wealth by these means in the 1980s, receiving an estimated 80 percent plus of its annual operating budget of $600 million from investments.[215] This allowed the PLO progressively greater autonomy in dealing with other nations.

---

[213] Maurice R. Greenberg, Chair, William F. Wechsler and Lee S. Wolosky, Project Co-Directors, *Terrorist Financing: Report of an Independent Task Force Sponsored by the Council on Foreign Relations* (New York: Publication Office, Council on Foreign Relations, 25 November 2002), 5.
[214] David Albright, "Al Qaeda's Nuclear Program: Through the Window of Seized Documents," *Policy Forum Online* Special Forum 47 (6 November 2002): 8; available from http://www.nautilus.org/fora/Special-Policy-Forum/47_Albright.html; Internet; accessed 14 February 2003.
[215] Bruce Hoffman, *Inside Terrorism* (New York: Columbia University Press, 1998), 84.

◆ **Flexible Organizational Networks**

Terrorists have shown the ability to adapt to the techniques and methods of counterterror agencies and intelligence organizations over the long term. The decentralization of the network form of organization is an example. Adopted to reduce the disruption caused by the loss of key links in a chain of command, a network organization also complicates the tasks of security forces, and reduces predictability of operations.

Terrorists are improving their sophistication and abilities in virtually all aspects of their operations and support. The aggressive use of modern technology for information management, communication and intelligence has increased the efficiency of these activities. Cyber attack is a constantly expanding threat. Weapons technology has become more available, and the purchasing power of terrorist organizations is on the rise. The ready availability of both technology and trained personnel to operate it for any client with sufficient cash allows the well-funded terrorist to equal or exceed the sophistication of governmental counter-measures.[216]

Homegrown terrorists targeted key landmarks and security service locations in a plot that ended with a controlled delivery by police of three tons of material the terror suspects thought was ammonium nitrate. Internet chat rooms were used to develop the plot. An investigation grew to include Canadian, United States, and United Kingdom counterterrorism. By mid 2006, the investigation resulted in the arrest of 17 young men.[217]

Fig. 5-5. **Cyber Attack**

The advantage to terrorist organizations that use criminal activities to fund operations will continue to grow. Money is the great force multiplier for terrorists, and criminal activity produces more money than other strategies. The annual profit from criminal activity is estimated at 2 to 5 percent of the world Gross Domestic Product, or $600 billion to $1.5 trillion in profit.[218] Terrorists are emphasizing criminal activities for their

---

[216] Fred L. Fuller, "New Order Threat Analysis: A Literature Survey", *Marine Corps Gazette* 81 (April 1997): 46-48.
[217] Richard Esposito, "Terror Cell Targets," June 05, 2006, available from http://
http://images.google.com/imgres?imgurl...; Internet; accessed 11 June 2007.
C0GHpqY8HKM:&tbnh=89&tbnw=117&prev=/images%3Fq%3Dinternet%2Band%2Bterror%26start%3
D20%26gbv%3D2%26ndsp%3D20%26svnum%3D10%26hl%3Den%26sa%3DN
[218] Kimberly L. Thachuck, "Terrorism's Financial Lifeline: Can it Be Severed," *Strategic Forum,* 191 (May 2002): 2.

support funding because it allows them to compete more effectively with their adversaries, and conduct larger and more lethal operations.

Emergent Independent Actors

During the evolution of modern terrorism in the Cold War era, even nationalist insurgent groups sought and required a sponsor from one of the two competing ideological blocs. Sponsors could effectively influence the policy of their clients, and exercise a limited form of control over their actions. This gradually shifted to a less rigid control as more sponsors, such as Libya, entered the field. The collapse of the Soviet Union removed the motivations and capabilities of a large number of state sponsors. This loss of significant resources eliminated support for many terrorist groups, particularly those terrorist groups closely aligned with the communist bloc.[219]

Punitive actions against rogue states or states of concern have gradually reduced or denied some geographical sanctuaries and sources of support for terrorists. Although this can be temporarily disruptive, new support structures can replace previous systems. Groups based in Libya shifted to Iraq or Syria when support was restricted due to international sanctions and U.S. military action against Libya because of their sponsorship of terrorism. Similarly, al-Qaida shifted key functions from the Sudan to Afghanistan when U.S. action and diplomatic pressure were brought to bear in that geographical area.

In response, terrorists have adjusted their financial operations to become more self-sustaining in their activities, resulting in greater independence from any external control. Terrorist operations require extensive financial support. The facility with which groups can obtain and move funds, procure secure bases, and obtain and transport weaponry determines their operational abilities and the level of threat that they pose. The international nature of finance, the integration of global economies, and the presence of terrorists in the illegal economies of slaves, drugs, smuggling, counterfeiting, identity theft, and fraud have aided this new independence from traditional sources of sponsorship and support.[220]

Fig. 5-6. **Abu Mus'ab al-Suri**

---

[219] Christopher C. Harmon, *Terrorism Today* (London: Frank Cass Publishers, 2000; reprint, Portland: Frank Cass Publishers, 2001), 3.
[220] Kimberly L. Thachuck, "Terrorism's Financial Lifeline: Can it Be Severed," *Strategic Forum* no. 191 (May 2002): 2.

Terrorist Abu Mus'ab al-Suri published his vision for how to best carry on the jihad with the value of small semi-independent or independent cells in host countries. Minimal organizational structure or layering of supervision enhances security of individual terrorist operations, even though logistics and other support me be problematic. He writes, "The groups must move from the classical structure for an underground organization, which a hierarchical "pyramid" shaped chain of command, to a "secret gang-war [structure], which has different and numerous cells untied together [separate cells]." [221] Individuals plan their own missions and often will be responsible for their own financing.

Fig. 5-7. **Fort Dix Training**

Recent arrests of individuals planning to attack U.S. military members at Fort Dix, New Jersey illustrate this type of independent terrorist cell operation.

◆ **Increased Weapon System Lethality**

On a practical level, what changes to terrorist operations will concern U.S. forces? Terrorism will continue to increase in lethality. Who is the terrorist? Terrorism is merging and combining with various other state and sub-state actors, further blurring the difference between criminals, rogue governments, and terrorists. These are concerns regarding the impacts and interactions of mass media, technological advances, urbanization, and illegal fundraising with terrorism.

The Defense Intelligence Agency assess that non-state actors, specifically al-Qaida, continue to pursue weapons of mass destruction. In the areas of chemical, biological, radiological, and nuclear weapons, the DIA estimates that terrorists are interested in ricin, botulinum toxin, and anthrax. Chemical weapons might include cyanide or other industrial chemicals, mustard, and sarin. DIA estimates that "…al-Qaida and other terrorist groups the capability and intent to develop and employ a radiological dispersal device."[222]

---

[221] SITE Institute, "Abu Musab al-Suri Outlines Strategy for Attacks Against America, Britain, Russia, and NATO Countries," July , 13, 2005, available from http://siteinstitute.org/bin/articles.cgi?ID=publications67905&Category=publications&Subcategory=0; Internet; accessed 11 June 2007.

[222] Michael D. Maples, *Current and Projected National Security Threats to the United States*, Statement for the Record, Senate Select Committee on Intelligence Committee, 11 January 2007; Washington, D.C. : Defense Intelligence Agency, 9.

The ongoing conflict in Iraq displays that terrorist group attacks account for only a small fraction of insurgent violence but the high-profile nature of terrorist operations has a disproportionate impact.[223] Recent improvised explosive device (IED) attacks in Iraq combined with industrial chemicals have caused casualties but no where near the damage and destruction that would be caused by a weapon of mass destruction. Use of explosively formed projectiles (EFP) is a significant increase in weapon capability.

Of the technologies that are available to a well financed terrorist group or possibly individual actors, biological and nuclear threats may be the most significant near term WMD threats. The United Sates has already been attacked by anthrax with the crime still under investigation and no identified terrorist or terrorist group to hold accountable. In a government program to examine capabilities, a government sponsored group of experts produced a weaponized version of a harmless bacillus with properties similar to anthrax. The weaponization meant producing the extremely small size of particles required to infect a person via inhalation.[224]

Fig. 5-8. **Emplacing an EFP**

Intended Mass Casualties - Mayhem

Ongoing conditions in Iraq provide an example of changing dynamics in conflict with growing casualties and a perception by portions of the civilian population that "…unchecked violence is creating an atmosphere of fear, hardening sectarianism, empowering militias, and vigilante groups, hastening a middle-class exodus, and shaking confidence in government and security forces.[225] Terrorism plays a key role in much of this physical and psychological violence.

Fewer incidents with greater casualties appear to be the goal for many terrorist groups. This is not just a function of efficiency and developing skills, but a tendency by the increasing number of terrorists to view ever-larger casualty lists as a measure of their influence and power. The years from 1998 to 2001 show a large increase in the

---

[223] Ibid., 4.
[224] Randall J. Larsen, "Our Own Worst Enemy: Why Our Misguided Reactions to 9-11 Might Be America's Greatest Threat," *The Guardian*, 9. April 2007, 5-16.
[225] Michael D. Maples, *Current and Projected National Security Threats to the United States*, Statement for the Record, Senate Select Committee on Intelligence Committee, 11 January 2007; Washington, D.C. : Defense Intelligence Agency, 3.

number of casualties per incident due to catastrophic terrorism events: the embassy bombings in Kenya and Tanzania in 1998 and the 9/11 attacks in 2001. These three events caused for over 9000 casualties.

Conventional explosives have also been used by U.S. citizens in terrorist acts such as the 1995 bombings of the Murrah Federal Building in Oklahoma City, Oklahoma. That attack killed over 160 people and caused another 850 additional casualties. McVeigh was a U.S. citizen with personal beliefs that festered into a growing mistrust and eventual hatred of the U.S. government.[226] McVeigh selected the Murrah Building from a list of sites he developed as potential targets. He wanted his attack to target Federal law enforcement agencies and their employees. He recognized that many innocent people would be injured or killed. Awaiting execution, McVeigh remarked, "I like the phrase 'shot heard 'round the world,' and I don't think there's any doubt the Oklahoma blast was heard around the world."[227]

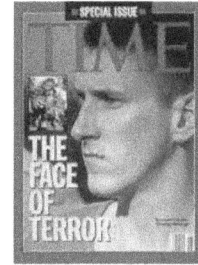

Fig. 5-9. **McVeigh**

Proliferation of weapons of mass destruction is a particularly alarming issue. The specter of their effects amplifies the dangers of a catastrophic terrorist act. Information is readily available on many aspects of chemical, biological, radiological, nuclear, and conventional high yield explosives. Materiel for attempting the construction of some forms of WMD is easily accessible in the public domain. The knowledge and technological means of specialists to produce WMD is a shadowy area of science, crime, and intrigue available to the terrorist.

In August 2006, an al-Qaida cell was disrupted that planned to bomb nearly a dozen airplanes while in flight enroute to the United States. In June 2006, Canadian authorities detained a group of individuals who were planning a series of attacks in Ontario, Canada that included bombings, seizing Canadian parlimentat4ry Buildings, and a broadcast center and hostages.[228]

Fig. 5-10. **Anthrax Letters**

The trend to exploit available technologies and the desire for more casualties will probably accelerate the eventual employment of Weapons of Mass Destruction (WMD) by terrorists. Documented uses of chemical (Tokyo 1995) and biological weapons (Oregon in 1984[229] and Florida and Washington D.C. in 2001) demonstrate the ability

---

[226] Lou Michel and Dan Herbeck, *American Terrorist: Timothy McVeigh and the Oklahoma City Bombing* (New York: Harper Collins Publishers Inc., 2001), 108.

[227] Ibid., 382.

[228] Michael D. Maples, *Current and Projected National Security Threats to the United States*, Statement for the Record, Senate Select committee on Intelligence Committee, 11 January 2007; Washington, D.C. : Defense Intelligence Agency, 7 and 8.

[229] Bruce Hoffman, *Inside Terrorism* (New York: Columbia University Press, 1998), 121.

to use WMD. Al-Qaida has stated an intention to acquire and attack the United States with WMD.

Targeted Economic Disruption

Modern, high-technology societies are susceptible to a concept of complex terrorism. Dependence on electronic networks, sometimes with minimal redundancy, and concentrating critical assets in small geographic locales can present lucrative targets for the terrorist. Ensuring redundant systems exist, dispersing critical assets physically, and creating buffers, firewalls, or other type safeguards can enhance defense and recovery from such complex terrorist attacks.[230]

The military will not be the only, or necessarily the primary target of new strategies useful against leading edge technologies and organizations. The dispersal of key civilian infrastructure nodes into locations remote from the urban complexes they serve increases their vulnerability and the reliance on computerized control systems to monitor and control these nodes increase their exposure to cyber-terrorism.

Many of the emerging entities that are rising to wield effective power in failing states are only concerned with the immediate tactical effects of their actions. They therefore look upon modern terrorism as an effective mode of conflict. They can point to the fact that al Qaeda invested only $500,000 in an attack that is estimated to eventually cost the U.S. Government $135 billion in damages and recovery costs.[231] Considering that these figures do not reflect the costs of military and law enforcement efforts to investigate and eliminate the organization responsible, the comparative return on the investment is even greater.[232] A terrorist attack on other critical infrastructure could be catastrophic too.

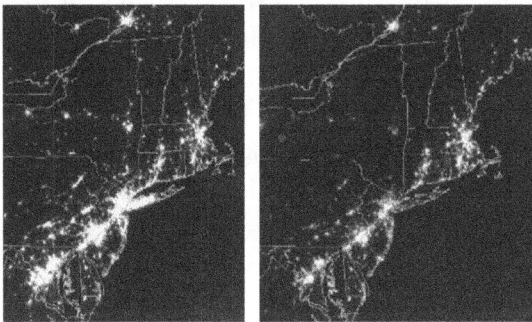

Fig. 5-11. **Electrical Grid Blackout 2003**

---

[230] Thomas Homer-Dixon, "The Rise of Complex Terrorism," *Foreign Policy Magazine* (January-February 2002): 1, 6, and 7; available from http://www.foreignpolicy.com/story/cms.php?story_id=170; Internet; accessed 26 August 2004.

[231] Kimberly L. Thachuck, "Terrorism's Financial Lifeline: Can it Be Severed," *Strategic Forum* no. 191 (May 2002): 4.

[232] Fred L. Fuller, "New Order Threat Analysis: A Literature Survey", *Marine Corps Gazette* 81 (April 1997): 46-48.

In the United States, the electric grid may be one of the prime terrorist targets. Several factors not linked to terrorism contributed the August 14, 2003 blackout that left 50 million people around the Great Lakes without power and cost the nation's economy an estimated $1 billion.[233] Although redundancies are built into the power systems, a simple natural event caused a power surge overload and shutdown of the electrical power grid servicing New York, New England, and eastern Canada.[234] Figure 5-11 illustrates the electrical power grid failure in August 2003. Two satellite images of the northeastern United States taken the day before the blackout condition and during the blackout on August 14, 2003 show the significant disruption and failure of electrical power.

Fig. 5-12. **Targeted for Terror - Abqaiq Oil Facility, Saudi Arabia**

Overseas, U.S. interests are different. Oil infrastructure gets more attention as a norm by many nations and vulnerability of critical aspects of the oil industry are at a primary source in the Middle East. Single points of failure in the infrastructure or denying critical services for a period of time might cripple many of the world's economies. On example is the Saudi oil production facility at Abqaiq; this facility handles about two-thirds of the Saudi crude oil daily output. The sulfur clearing towers of the facility are essential to processing the crude for shipment.[235]

---

[233] Evelyn Brown, "Creating stability in a world of unstable electricity distribution," Logos, 22, Spring 2004, available from http://www.anl.gov/Media_Center/logos22-1/electricity.htm; Internet; accessed 11 June 2007.

[234] R. James Woolsey, "Intelligence and the War on Terrorism," *The Guardian*, 9, April 2007, 26.

[235] Ibid., 26

In Nigeria, rebel factions, the government, and terrorists struggle over access and control of that nation's oil in the Niger Delta. Destruction of infrastructure, killings, and kidnapping have reduced oil production in the last year by 25 percent of its former output.[236]

Other critical infrastructure and support systems for the United States provide terrorists with a wide array of potential targets in land, maritime, cyber, and space environments.

Exploited Mass Media Marketing

Exploiting media coverage is as a norm for the terrorist. Effectiveness of information operations will be measured by ability to cause a dramatic impact of fear and uncertainty in a target population. Surprise and sustained violence will be normal against specified people representing elements of civil or military control and order, or common citizens as prey for terrorists in a culture of violence. Damage or destruction of community, regional, or national infrastructure and governance will be used to gain attention, provoke excessive reaction by host nation or coalition military forces, and attempt to alienate general population support of government policies and programs.

Fig. 5-13. **Interview**

Likewise, due to the increase in information outlets, and competition with increasing numbers of other messages, terrorism now requires a greatly increased amount of violence or novelty to attract the attention it requires. The tendency of major media to compete for ratings and the subsequent revenue realized from increases in their audience size and share produces pressures on terrorists to increase the impact and violence of their actions to take advantage of this sensationalism.[237]

There is an increasingly technological and informational nature to all conflict. Terrorism is no exception. Terrorists will continue to cultivate the ability to use new and innovative technologies, and methods of applying existing technologies to new uses. Terrorists will use sophisticated technology and will explore the improvement in capabilities that technology provides, especially the synergy between simple operations and selective technologies to ensure success.

A sinister yet simple aspect of media marketing is the indoctrination of children to hate and promote violence and terror in distorted views of the world they live in. For example,

---

[236] Michael D. Maples, *Current and Projected National Security Threats to the United States*, Statement for the Record, Senate Select committee on Intelligence Committee, 11 January 2007; Washington, D.C. : Defense Intelligence Agency, 24.

[237] *International Encyclopedia of Terrorism*, 1997 ed., s.v. "The Media and International Terrorism."

HAMAS al-Aqsa television broadcast a graduation ceremony of Kindergartens of the Islamic Association in Gaza. As adults guide the program and ask the children "What is your most lofty aspiration?" The children respond, "Death for the sake of Allah." The small boys dressed to resemble Palestinian militants march into view and drop to the floor to craw on their stomachs as if moving in a tactical manner. HAMAS conducts many charitable activities to assist Palestinians but concurrently promotes hate and terrorism.[238] In a similar adolescent example, Palestinian Authority schoolbooks reject Israel's right to exist, promote terror, and present maps that do not display Israel as a nation state and claiming this geography as Palestine.[239]

Terrorists will attempt to exploit US vulnerabilities to information dominance. Casualty avoidance and the media effect are interrelated perceptions held by many potential adversaries of the US social and political situation. Terrorists may believe the US. is extremely casualty averse and that images and news of casualties will be easy to deliver to the American public in their living rooms. While this effect may be overemphasized, promotion of goals, acts, and demands are significant part of terrorist operations.

Al-Qaida is steadily increasing its use of videotape releases. As of June 2007, al-Qaida has released 48 videos whereas 58 videos were released during the entire previous year of 2006. Techniques to reach a larger audience include broadcast anchors in periodic announcements, improved video engineering quality, and use of Arabic and English as subtitles in videos. Some speeches are issued in Arabic, English, French, and Urdu. The propaganda campaigns continue to recruit, and expose listeners to ideological rationale for terrorism.[240]

Wearing a white robe and a turban, Adam Yehiye Gadahn, who also goes by the name Azzam al-Amriki, spoke in English and the video carried Arabic subtitles. The video appeared on a Web site often used by Islamic militants and carried the logo of al-Qaida's media wing, as-Sahab. He warns, "Your failure to heed our demands ... means that you and your people will ... experience things which will make you forget all about the horrors of September 11th, Afghanistan and Iraq and Virginia Tech..." Gadahn has been charged in a U.S. treason indictment with aiding al-Qaida, and could face the death penalty if convicted.[241]

Fig.5-14. **al-Qaida Propaganda**

---

[238] Julie Stahl, "Palestinian Kindergarten Graduates Vow to Die for Allah," 1 June 2007, available from http://www.memritv.org/search.asp?ACT=S9&P1=1468; Internet; accessed 5 June 2007.

[239] "Palestinian Textbooks Incite hatred, US Funds Terror-Center Schools," 6 March 2007, available from http://www.justsixdays.co.uk/isblog/; Internet; accessed 12 March 2007.

[240] "Al-Qaida raises Tempo of Video Releases," available from http://www.iht.com/articles/ap/2007/06/01africa/ME-GEN- Al-Qaida-Video-Offensive.php; Internet; accessed 4 June 2007.

[241] Anna Johnson, "Al-Qaida video threatens attacks on U.S.," May 30, 2007, available from http://www.buffalonews.com/260/story/87272.html; Internet; accessed 11 June 2007.

In the techniques of media exploitation, terrorists were pioneers.[242] Since the terrorists prepare their operations around a desired media effect, they will be prepared and vocal or visual for reporting coverage. They can orchestrate supporting events and interviews to reinforce the desired message. Terrorists have well-established methods of presenting disinformation and false perspectives. Frequently, military reluctance to comment on ongoing operations in the media for operational security (OPSEC) reasons can assist the terrorist. If no balanced information comes from official sources in a timely manner, the media will use the information readily available from the terrorist as a primary source for reporting the story.

Terrorists will exploit the vulnerabilities of new technologies to attacks or disruption. Terrorists have a great deal of flexibility in their ability to acquire new technology. They also have the advantage of only needing to attack or neutralize specific systems or capabilities. Consequently, they can narrowly focus their expenditures on the limited countertechnology. They can neutralize some advanced systems or capabilities through the use of simple and unconventional techniques such as suicide bombers.

Fig. 5-15. **Encryption and Hacking**

Nonetheless, terrorism can have strategic impacts far beyond the physical damage of a terrorist attack. The terrorist bombings of commuter trains in Madrid just prior to a national election may indicate an alarming result on national resolve. A democratic election and political process appeared to react to these terrorist attacks, and caused a change in a sovereign government. National policies and coalition support to the War on Terrorism changed dramatically with this new government.

Section III: Enablers to Terror

Terrorism will be a condition in future conflicts. There are more unresolved international issues left over from the forty-plus years of the Cold War than from the conclusion of either of the two World Wars. However, now there is no balance of power or two-power system to regulate the conflicts that will arise from these issues.

The world order has changed significantly in recent decades. The number of new, sovereign nations that emerged from the end of the Cold War rivals the new nations created after the two World Wars and the retreat of the colonial empires in the 1950s and 1960s. However, not all of these nations are viable states and most of them do not have stable leadership other than that of local ethnic or tribal strongmen. Many have significant problems aside from poor leadership. The most significant of these problems include disease, resource depletion, factionalism, and incursions from neighboring states.

---

[242] Bruce Hoffman, *Inside Terrorism* (New York: Columbia University Press, 1998), 133-139.

The incidence of newer pandemics such as HIV/AIDS are just now beginning to equal the lethality of older scourges such as plague, malaria and other tropical fevers. The World Health Organization reports 1,000 to 3,000 cases of plague every year.[243] On the other hand, the 2004 United Nations report on AIDS reports almost five million new cases of HIV in 2003.[244]

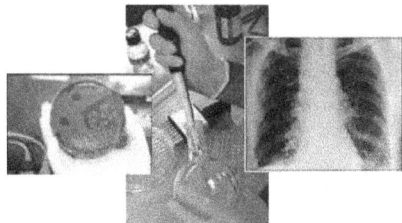 Gene research and the field of genomics may help combat new diseases, but offer the potential of a two-edged sword. Although it may provide advances in health care, it could also acquire a perverse tack toward biological warfare with very specific infections and target groups.[245]

Fig. 5-16. **Dual Bio-Technology**

State actors can destabilize regions with export of technologies and skills that promote the proliferation of weapons of mass destruction. Several state sponsors of terrorism as determined by the U.S. Department of State are Iran, North Korea, Syria, Sudan, and Cuba.[246] Iran appears determined to develop nuclear weapons, and is probably pursuing biological weaponry. North Korea continues to develop its WMD capability as evidenced by its first nuclear test in October 2006. North Korea could have already produced several nuclear weapons from plutonium, and has a biotechnology infrastructure capable of producing biological weapons. Large stockpiles of chemical weapons probably exist too.[247] Syria has a chemical warfare program capability and pursues similar biological weapon programs. Ballistic missiles and cruise missiles add a factor of concern related to sea and land attack.[248]

Countries may lack a base of sufficient industrial or technological production to sustain an economic system and attempt to rely on basic agriculture and resource extraction. Often, population pressure and lack of foresight encourage rapid depletion of finite resources. The establishment of a viable economic system to support a national government becomes impractical. Illegal activity may replace a gap in regular market development and create a setting prime for links to terror.

---

[243] "Plague," *CDC Plague Home Page;* available from http://www.cdc.gov/ncidod/dvbid/plague/index.htm; Internet; accessed 9 July 2004.

[244] *2004 Report on the Global AIDS Epidemic: Executive Summary* (Geneva: Joint United Nations Programme on HIV/AIDS, 2004), 5.

[245] "In My Humble Opinion: Genomics is the most important economic, political, and ethical issue facing mankind," *Fast Company*, November 1999; available from http://www.fastcompany.com/online/29/jellis.html; Internet; accessed 26 February 2004.

[246] Department of State, *Country Reports on Terrorism 2006*, April 2007; 145-149; available from http://www.terrorisminfo.mipt.org/Patterns-of-global-terrorism.asp; Internet; accessed 2 May 2007.

[247] Michael D. Maples, *Current and Projected National Security Threats to the United States*, Statement for the Record, Senate Select committee on Intelligence Committee, 11 January 2007; Washington, D.C. : Defense Intelligence Agency, 13.

[248] Ibid., 13-15.

Many nations are simply geographic fiction. They are results of an earlier international power strategy on a map and lack any sense of national or geographic identity. Tensions between tribal or ethnic factions, or a minority in one nation aligning with similar groups of a regional nation other than their own nation can be destabilizing. Non-state and sub-state organizations and power blocs are assuming military roles and utilizing organized forces in conflicts, and terror tactics in social or political conflicts. Major corporations, private security companies, and well-funded transnational terror groups have all played significant roles in failed or dysfunctional states

Two likely models in the nature of future conflicts emphasize struggle among cultures or a disintegration of a culture. The first model is strategic in nature, and reflects that past conflicts have moved from tribal to national to ideological struggles, culminating with World War II and the Cold War. This view predicts fighting along the parts of the world where cultures intersect, such as the Central Asian confluence of the Islamic and Eastern Orthodox cultures. The assumption is future conflicts will be between cultures, and wherever there is a line of engagement between two differing cultures, there will be conflict.[249]

A primary ideological conflict exists among Islamic extremists who seek domination of major areas of the world currently occupied by Muslims. Eventually, this theocratic radicalism seeks a secular expansion to other regions of the world.

Fig. 5-17. General Density Distribution of Sunni and Shia Muslims
Source: http://www.lib.utexas.edu/maps/world_maps/muslim_distribution.jpg

---

[249] Samuel Huntington, "The Clash of Civilizations," *Foreign Affairs* (Summer 1993): 2; available from http://www.lander.edu/atannenbaum/Tannenbaum%20courses%20folder/POLS%20103%20World%20Politics/103_huntington_clash_of_civilizations_full_text.htm#I.%20THE%20NEXT%20PATTERN%20OF%20CONFLICT; Internet; accessed 6 December 2002.

A transnational network like al-Qaida becomes more than a fundamentalist religious terror movement in such a setting. A goal of replacing the power structures in the historical Arab world with a new caliphate is impractical and unlikely, but when viewed at a clash of cultures, al-Qaida becomes a global transnational insurgency. The struggle fights against imposed Western political ideals and alien social order across multiple countries and regions simultaneously. Stateless for the moment, these cadres hope to organize the vanguard of an extremist religious revolution whose eventual success they consider inevitable.

The second model predicts the failure of numerous current nation-states in the developing regions of the world. Unable to exert authority, protect their citizens, or control their borders, they are disintegrating. Many of these countries are splintering into tribal and ethnic factions that might coalesce into a new, more stable form, or continue to devolve through violence into lawless zones of minor warlords and bandits.[250]

Regardless of which model more accurately describes the future, a most important occurrence common to both will be the merging of terrorists as they adapt and improvise flexible national, international, or transnational organizations.

Theories exist for using all of these levels of disorder, as well as economic warfare, information warfare, and conventional military force, in an orchestrated campaign against an adversary. This would be conducted as a long-term effort of undeclared conflict that might appear as amicable relations between the two adversaries, but with one pursuing the eventual defeat of the other through multiple, simultaneous methods.[251] Forms of terrorism easily fit into this construct of overt and covert conflict. The arena of cyber-war exemplifies the ability to impact on critical infrastructure, and its disruption and damage to national security, economic functions, and U.S. military response.[252]

The effectiveness of this approach is in the costs to the victim to defend against multiple threats with no clear foe. Operational control over the various tools employed by the aggressor is not required, as long as the tools perform their role of reducing the adversary of resources and resolve. Deniability is maintained and diplomacy pursued to keep the conflict from becoming focused before the aggressor is ready. Although all manner of unconventional threats may be employed, terrorism is a key component of this strategy.

The U.S. military unit leader, operator, and planner must be prepared to act in a chaotic and unstructured contemporary operational environment. Terrorism, unfortunately, will be a constant in the conditions of the future.

---

[250] Robert Kaplan, *The Coming Anarchy: Shattering the Dreams of the Post Cold War* (New York: Random House, 2000), 7-9.

[251] Qiao Liang and Wang Xiangsui, *Unrestricted Warfare,* trans. Department of State, American Embassy Beijing Staff Translators (Washington, D.C., 1999).

[252] President of the United States, *The National Strategy to Secure Cyberspace.* (Washington, D.C., February 2003), Preface; available from http://www.whitehouse.gov/pcipb/cyberspace_strategy.pdf; Internet; accessed 8 December 2003.

Conclusion

This chapter examined the future of terrorism with emphasis on concepts ideological extremism, world regional disorder, and morphing forms of terrorism. The evolution of some terrorist activity into non-state, politicized criminal action is an arena of growing concern. The merging of criminals, rogue political leaders, and terrorists into various groupings for their mutual benefit may be temporary as a collective identity, or may build some longevity as substantial bases of fiscal and materiel support and safehaven. International or transnational links and associations further complicate the issue.

Terrorism is foremost a political problem; yet, terrorism can have impact on other elements of power such as economic, social, and military. Common terms and definitions assist in focusing situational awareness of the Threat. Actions must consider aspects of terrorist activity that may include political demonstration, criminal conduct, and possible links to paramilitary operations or low intensity conflict.[253]

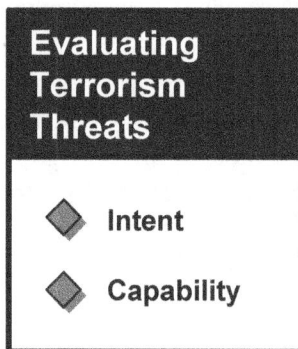

Evaluating Terrorism Threats
◆ **Intent**
◆ **Capability**

The psychological impact of terror on a target audience must be viewed as a means to an end. Threats cannot be assessed by knowing just functional capabilities. The sophistication of emergent tactics, techniques, and procedures will seek to attack vulnerabilities. Threats must be evaluated against two essential factors of terrorist intent and terrorist capability to act.

Participation in and use of terrorism will increase. Individuals and groups that are not currently employing terrorism will adopt it as a tactic, and those that are employing terror tactics at low levels of lethality will become more violent. This is a combination of existing terrorist groups trying to destabilize the existing order on an ever-widening basis, and the tendency of terrorist groups to increase the level of violence when not immediately successful.[254]

Accented by the U.S. Department of State, "a deeper trend is the shift in the nature of terrorism, from an international terrorism of the late twentieth century into a new form of non-state warfare that resembles a form of global insurgency. This represents a new era of warfare, and countering this threat demands the application of counterinsurgency techniques that focus on protecting, securing, and winning the support of at-risk populations, in addition to targeting violent extremist networks and individual terrorists." [255]

This handbook presented principal themes on the following aspects of terrorism: (1) explore who will want to engage U.S. military forces utilizing terrorism, (2) understand

---

[253] Long, *The Anatomy of Terrorism,* 11 and 13.

[254] Bruce Hoffman, *Inside Terrorism* (New York: Columbia University Press, 1998), 162-163.

[255] Department of State, *Country Reports on Terrorism 2006*, April 2007; 14, available from http://www.terrorisminfo.mipt.org/Patterns-of-global-terrorism.asp; Internet; accessed 2 May 2007.

why and how terrorist targeting is accomplished against U.S. military forces, and (3) describe what means are used and can will be used against U.S. military forces whether they are deployed on an operational mission, in-transit to or from an operational mission, or performing duties at an installation or institutional support location.

To Know the Enemy is an operational environment in itself.

Appendix A

Terrorist Planning Cycle

The main point is to select targets where success is 100% assured.

Dr. George Habash, Founder, PFLP
Popular Front for the Liberation of Palestine

Terrorist operations are typically prepared to minimize risk and achieve the highest probability of success. Terrorists avoid an adversary's strengths and concentrate on an adversary's weaknesses. Emphasis is on maximizing security and target effects. This normally means the minimum number of attackers to successfully conduct an operation with the most effective[256] weapons available. Detailed planning is a norm but can be deliberately shortened when an opportunity arises and a terrorist.

Collection against potential targets may continue for years before an operation is decided upon. While some targets may be "soft" enough for shorter periods of observation, the information gathering will still be intense. Operations planned or underway may be altered, delayed, or cancelled due to changes to the target or local conditions.

Tactical missions combine to complement operational objectives and strategic goals. The psychological impact on the target population is the overarching objective of any terrorist operation.

There is no universal model for terrorist planning but experience and success have demonstrated traditional principles for plans and operations. Terrorist organizations exchange personnel and training and study methods and operational successes of other groups. Innovation is a proven key component of operational success.

Terrorist operational planning can be analyzed according to requirements common to all operations. The planning and operation cycle in this appendix provides a baseline in assessing particular terrorist cells and organization. The differences among organizations center on factors of intent and capability.

Terrorist Planning Cycle

- ◆ Broad Target Selection
- ◆ Intelligence and Surveillance
- ◆ Specific Target Selection
- ◆ Pre-attack Surveillance and Planning
- ◆ Attack Rehearsal
- ◆ Actions on Objective
- ◆ Escape and Evasion

---

[256] Note: Effective in this case need not mean modern or destructive, but most suitable to cause the desired target effects. Knives, machetes, and other edged weapons have been used against terrorist victims in the modern era because of psychological impact on atarget populations is a key intention .

Current terrorist threats display the increasing desire and ability of a learning organization. Terrorist cells gather information and intelligence, analyze strengths and weaknesses, determine patterns, trends, and emerging actions, and identify vulnerabilities in an adversary's security to attack.

Phase I: Broad Target Selection

> **"Information gathering is a continuous operation..."**
>
> **Irish Republican Army's**
> *Handbook for Volunteers of Irish Republican Army,* **1956.**

This phase is the collection of information on a number of potential targets. Collection is gathered from diverse sources. Collectors may be core members of the terrorist cell, sympathizers, or people providing information without knowledge of the intended purpose. This phase also includes open source and general information collection. Some features of this type of collection are:

- Stories from newspapers and other media provide background information.

- Internet research provides data such as texts, pictures, blue prints, and video information.

- Potential targets are screened based on the intended objective and assesses areas such as symbolic value, critical infrastructure points of failure, expected number of mass casualties, and potential to generate high profile media attention.

The number of preliminary targets that can be screened is limited only by the capabilities of the group to collect information. Targets that are considered vulnerable and which would further terrorist goals are selected for the next phase of intelligence collection.

Phase II: Intelligence Gathering and Surveillance

Targets showing vulnerabilities may receive additional attention and priority of effort. This priority establishes the requirement to gather additional information on a target's patterns over time. This phase may be very short or can span years. Examples include the 2004 accounts of terrorist surveillance conducted for years on the International Monetary Fund, Prudential Building, New York Stock Exchange, as well as facilities in Las Vegas, Nevada. The type of surveillance employed depends on the target type. Elements of information typically gathered include:

- Practices/Procedures/Routines – For facilities this includes scheduled deliveries, work shift changes, identification procedures and other observable routines. For individuals, it can include regularly scheduled errands such as laundry pick up days or car parking locations.

- Residence and Workplace – This category applies primarily to the physical layout and individual activities at the two places the target typically spends the most time.

- Transportation/Routes of Travel – For individuals, this is the mode of transport and common routes to any regular destination such as house, work, gym, and school. For facilities, it addresses ingress and egress points, types of vehicles allowed on the grounds, or availability of transportation into the target site.

- Security Measures – This topic includes collection areas depending on the complexity of the security around the target: presence of a guard force; the reaction time of response units; any hardening of structures, barriers, or sensors; personnel, package, and vehicle screening procedures; and the type and frequency of emergency reaction drills are examples of key collection objectives. This is one of the most important areas of information for attack site selection, since an intent is to bypass and avoid security measures and be able to strike the target during any period.

Phase III: Specific Target Selection

Selection of a target for actual operational planning considers some of the following factors:

- Does success affect a larger audience than the immediate victim(s)?

- Will the target attract high profile media attention?

- Does success make the desired statement to the correct target audience(s)?

- Is the effect consistent with objectives of the group?

- Does the target provide an advantage to the group by demonstrating its capabilities?

- What are the costs versus benefits of conducting the operation?

A decision to proceed requires continued intelligence collection against the chosen target. Targets not receiving immediate consideration may still be collected against for future opportunities.

Phase IV: Pre-attack Surveillance and Planning

Members of the actual operational cells begin to appear during this phase. Trained intelligence and surveillance personnel or members supportive of the terrorist cell may be organized to conduct the operation conduct this phase. This phase gathers information on the target's current patterns, usually days to weeks. The attack team confirms information gathered from previous surveillance and reconnaissance activities. The areas of concern are essentially the same as in Phase II but with greater focus based on known or perceived vulnerabilities.

The type of surveillance employed depends on the target's activities. The information gained is then used to:

- Conduct security studies.

- Conduct detailed preparatory operations.

- Recruit specialized operatives (if needed).

- Procure a base of operations in the target area (safe houses, caches, etc.).

- Design and test escape routes.

- Decide on type of weapon or attack.

Phase V: Rehearsals

As with conventional military operations, rehearsals are conducted to improve the odds of success, confirm planning assumptions, and develop contingencies. Terrorists also rehearse to test security reactions to particular attack profiles. Terrorists use both their own operatives and unsuspecting people to test target reactions.

Typical rehearsals include:

- Equipment and weapons training and performance.

- Staging for final preparatory checks.

- Deployment into target area.

- Actions on the objective.

- Escape routes.

Tests in the target area will be conducted to confirm:

- Target information gathered to date.

- Target pattern of activities.

- Physical layout of target or operations area.

- Security force reactions such as state of alert, timing response, equipment and routes.

Phase VI: Actions on the Objective

Once terrorists reach this stage of their operation, the odds favor a successful attack against the target.

Terrorists conducting planned operations possess important tactical advantages. Since they are the attacker, they possess all the advantages of initiative and provide:

- Use of Surprise.

- Choice of time, place, and conditions of attack.

- Employment of diversions and secondary or follow-up attacks.

- Employment of security and support positions to neutralize target reaction forces and security measures.

Because of the extensive preparation through surveillance and reconnaissance, enemy security measures will be planned for and neutralized.

Phase VII: Escape and Exploitation

Escape plans are usually well rehearsed and executed. The exception is a suicide operation where the impact is enhanced by the willingness to die in achieving the attack. In suicide attacks, there are usually support personnel and handlers require escape or evasion from attack response forces.

Exploitation is the primary objective of the operation. The operation must be properly publicized to achieve an intended effect. Media control measures and prepared statements are examples of preparations to effectively exploit a successful operation. These will be timed to take advantage of media cycles for the selected target audiences.

Unsuccessful operations are disavowed when possible. The perception that a group has failed may severely damages the organization's prestige, indicate cell vulnerability, or ineffective conduct. In addition to the impact on the adversary, successful attacks bring favorable attention, notoriety and support such as funding and recruiting to the terrorist organization.

Appendix B

Firearms

General

Terrorists use a variety of firearms to include handguns, rifles, automatic rifles, submachine guns, as well as mortars and rocket launchers.[257] Access to sophisticated firearms is relatively easy for terrorist cells. Sources may include criminal links in the society, other terrorist cells, or indirect and direct sponsors of the terrorist activities.

This appendix presents a sample of firearms used by terrorists in five basic types: pistols, submachine guns, assault rifles, sniper rifles, and shotguns. Availability, simplicity, and efficiency are common requirements in acquiring firearms. Concealment of the weapon, especially in urban terrain, is often a key consideration too.[258] Terrorists standardize calibers of their weapon ammunition as much as possible to ease logistics of resupply and maintenance.[259]

Firearms Sample

- ◆ Pistol
- ◆ Submachine Gun
- ◆ Assault Rifle
- ◆ Sniper Rifle
- ◆ Shotgun

Pistols are standard weapons for terrorists. Although the revolver may be considered more reliable in field conditions, the semiautomatic handgun provides more ammunition per magazine than the cylinder capacity of a revolver. Submachine guns are basically short rifles that have a full automatic fire capability. They use pistol-caliber ammunition and typically have a large capacity magazine. Their range, accuracy and penetration are better than pistols due to the longer barrel and sighting performance.

Assault rifles are the primary offensive weapons of modern militaries and are used extensively by terrorist organizations. They normally have selective firing capability to allow single shot, 2 or 3 round bursts of fire, or full automatic fire. Their effective ranges often exceed 600 meters and have effective rates of fire up to 400 rounds per minute in the full automatic mode. Sniper rifles with telescopic sights and high performance ammunition provide a special capability. Ammunition caliber norms span 5.56 mm or 7.62 mm to the much larger caliber .50 chambered rifles. Shotguns are excellent weapons for close-range tactical tasks. Various types of ammunition provide wide area coverage, high impact hitting power, or special effects.

---

[257] Christopher C. Harmon, *Terrorism Today* (London: Frank Cass Publishers, 2000; reprint, Portland: Frank Cass Publishers, 2001), 111.

[258] Christopher Dobson and Ronald Payne, *The Terrorist: Their Weapons, Leaders, and Tactics* (New York: Facts on File, Inc, Revised Edition, 1982), 104.

[259] J. David Truby, *How Terrorists Kill: The Complete Terrorist Arsenal* (Boulder: Paladin Press, 1978), 7-8.

Handguns
CZ 75 (Czechoslovakia)

	Ammunition Types	Typical Combat Load
(*Source:* MCIA-1110-001-93, *Infantry Weapons Identification Guide,* September 1992, 94)	9mm Parabellum	Magazine Capacity: 16

SYSTEM	VARIANTS
A double-action semi-automatic pistol modeled after the Browning P-35. It can be carried cocked and locked and is considered a very accurate handgun. Its design has been copied frequently to produce such guns as the TZ75, EAA Witness, TA90, Springfield Armory P9, ITM AT84, ITM AT88, and Baby Eagle.	CZ 75B, 75BD, 75DAO, 75 Police: available in 9mm Luger, 9x21mm, .40 S&W CZ 75 Compact, 75D Compact, 75 Semi Compact: Available in 9mm Luger.
Weight (kg): 0.98 Length (mm): 203 Operation: Recoil operated double action. Fire Mode: Semi-automatic	AMMUNITION Name: 9mm Parabellum Caliber/length: 9 x 19 mm Effective Range (m): 50 Muzzle Velocity (m/s): 381
SIGHTS Iron sights.	

Glock 17 (Austria)

	Ammunition Types	Typical Combat Load
 (*Source*: Photograph Courtesy of GLOCK, Inc.)	9mm Parabellum	Magazine Capacity: 10, 17, 19, 31

SYSTEM

A semiautomatic handgun originally adopted by the Austrian Army and Police. It has a unique safe action striker-fired trigger mechanism that sets the striker in the half-cocked position after each round. When firing, the shooter pulls the trigger, which disengages the trigger safety, then cocks the striker to the full cock position prior to firing. The Glock has a polymer frame and steel slides.

Weight (kg): .905
Length (mm): 186
Operation: Recoil operated double action.
Fire Mode: Semiautomatic

SIGHTS

Iron sights. Adjustable on competition models.

VARIANTS

Glock 17L: Competition version
Glock 18: 3 round burst version
Glock 19: Compact version
Glock 34: Competition version
Numerous other models in a variety of calibers.

AMMUNITION

Name: 9 mm Parabellum
Caliber/length: 9 x 19mm
Effective Range (m): 50
Muzzle Velocity (m/s): 350

Makarov Pistol (USSR/Russia)

	Ammunition Types	Typical Combat Load
(Source: U.S. Army Special Forces Foreign Weapons Handbook, January 1967, I-13)	9mm Makarov	Magazine Capacity: 8

SYSTEM

A blowback operated, double action semiautomatic handgun that is extremely sturdy, simple to operate and maintain, and very reliable. It was designed for Soviet army officers and Soviet police. It is a Walther PP style weapon and provides good defense at short and medium distances. There are some disadvantages with this weapon, specifically the 9mm Makarov is considered to be underpowered. Additionally, the magazine capacity of 8 is low compared to other handguns available.

Weight (kg): .66
Length (mm): 160
Operation: Double action
Fire Mode: Semiautomatic

SIGHTS

Iron sites.

VARIANTS

PMM: 9x18mm
Izh 71: 9x17mm short/.380 ACP
Baikal IJ 70: 9mm Makarov/.380 ACP

AMMUNITION

Name: 9mm Makarov
Caliber/length: 9 x 18mm
Effective Range (m): 50
Muzzle Velocity (m/s): 315

Ruger GP100 (United States)

	Ammunition Types	Typical Combat Load
(UNCLASSIFIED) Figure 13. (U) Ruger GP100 .357 Magnum Revolver (*Source*: (S/NF/WN/NC) DST-2660H-481-89, *Terrorist Weapons Handbook – Worldwide* (U), 15 December 1989, 13. Unclassified Extract.)	.357 Magnum .38 Special	Cylinder Capacity: 6

SYSTEM	VARIANTS
The Ruger GP100 is a rugged double-action revolver, available in fixed and adjustable sight models. It was designed specifically for the law enforcement and security communities. It can be field stripped very quickly for easy maintenance. Although it is chambered for the .357 Magnum, it can also fire the .38 Special cartridge.	GP-141 KGP-141 GP-160 KGP-160 GP-161 KGP-161
Weight (kg): 1.28 Length (mm): 238 Operation: Double action Fire Mode: Single shot	AMMUNITION Name: .357 Magnum Caliber/length: .357 Cal/33 mm Effective Range (m): 60 Muzzle Velocity (m/s): 442
SIGHTS Adjustable iron sights.	

Submachine Guns

Heckler & Koch MP-5 (Germany)

	Ammunition Types	Typical Combat Load
 MP 5A3 Neg. 510058 (UNCLASSIFIED) Figure 21. (U) MP5A2 and MP5A3 9-mm Submachinegun (*Source*: (S/NF/WN/NC) DST-2660H-481-89, *Terrorist Weapons Handbook – Worldwide* (U), 15 December 1989, 19. Unclassified Extract.)	9 mm Parabellum	Magazine Capacity: 10, 15, 30

SYSTEM

A submachine gun with a recoil operated roller-locked bolt that fires from a closed position. Very accurate and reliable under adverse conditions with only a minimum requirement for maintenance. The smooth recoil characteristics provide optimum control when firing bursts or when firing full automatic. It is very conducive for concealed carrying or for use in confined areas.

Weight (kg): 3.07 loaded
Length (mm): 490/660
Cyclic Rate of fire (rd/min): 800
Operation: Blowback
Fire Mode: Semi-automatic, Full automatic

SIGHTS

Post front, select range peep rear.

Night sights, scopes, laser aiming devices available.

VARIANTS

MP5A1 – w/o stock
MP5A2 – fixed polymer stock
MP5A3 – telescopic metal stock
SD1 – SD3 – same as above with internal silencers
MP5N – US Navy model with 3 round burst capability

AMMUNITION

Name: 9 mm Parabellum
Caliber/length: 9 x 19 mm
Effective Range (m): 200
Muzzle Velocity (m/s): 400

PM 63 (Poland)

	Ammunition Types	Typical Combat Load
9 mm machine pistol M63	9 mm Makarov	Magazine Capacity: 15, 25

(Source: USAREUR Pam 30-60-1, Identification Guide, Part One: Weapons and Equipment, East European Communist Armies, Volume 1: General, Ammunition and Infantry Weapons, September 1972, 70)

SYSTEM

The PM 63 is a blowback operated SMG that fires from the open bolt position. Although it is capable of both semi-automatic and full automatic modes, there is no selector switch. The semi-automatic mode is achieved by a short pull of the trigger, whereas full automatic requires pulling the trigger completely. It was designed with Special Forces in mind and was one of the lightest SMGs when it was introduced. It has been used by Polish Special Forces, police and by military personnel requiring a compact weapon. Iranian terrorists used it during the siege of the Iranian embassy in London in 1980. It has been a very prolific weapon, with tens of thousands being produced.

Weight (kg): 2.0 Loaded
Length (mm): 333/583
Cyclic Rate of fire (rd/min): 650
Operation: Blowback, firing from open bolt position
Fire Mode: Semi-automatic, Full automatic

SIGHTS

Iron sights that can be set on 75 or 150 meters.

VARIANTS

9mm Parabellum developed in 1971.

Unlicensed copy by NORINCO of China.

AMMUNITION

Name: 9mm Makarov
Caliber/length: 9 x 18 mm
Effective Range (m): 75
Muzzle Velocity (m/s): 320

Uzi (Israel)

	Ammunition Types	Typical Combat Load
(*Source*: (S/NF/WN/NC) DST-2660H-481-89, *Terrorist Weapons Handbook – Worldwide* (U), 15 December 1989, 20. Unclassified Extract.)	9mm Parabellum	Magazine Capacity: 20, 25, 32

SYSTEM

The Uzi is a recoil operated, select fire submachine gun that fires from the open bolt position. It has a folding stock and can be equipped with silencers. The Uzi submachine gun is manufactured by IMI and has been adopted by more than 90 countries for their police and military. Special operations and security units to include the US Secret Service and the Israeli Sayeret (Special Forces) use the compact variants. It is considered one of the most popular SMGs in the world, with more than 10 million manufactured around the world.

Weight (kg): 4.0 loaded
Length (mm): 470/650
Cyclic Rate of fire (rd/min): 600
Operation: Blowback, firing from open bolt position
Fire Mode: Semi-automatic, Full automatic

SIGHTS

Front – Post; Rear – Aperture "L" Flip.
Tactical flashlights and laser aiming modules are available.

VARIANTS

Mini Uzi
Micro Uzi

AMMUNITION

Name: 9 mm Parabellum
Caliber/length: 9 x 19mm
Effective Range (m): 200
Muzzle Velocity (m/s): 400

Assault Rifles

AK 47 (Russia)

	Ammunition Types	Typical Combat Load
(*Source*: *OPFOR Worldwide Equipment Guide*, TRADOC ADCSINT-Threats, September 2001, 1-4.1)	7.62 x 39 mm	Magazine Capacity: 30

SYSTEM	VARIANTS
A gas operated, selective fire assault weapon adopted by the Soviet Army in 1949. It came with both a fixed wooden stock and a folding metal stock, the AKS, which was issued to paratroopers and armor units. All of the Kalashnikov assault rifles are very dependable and produce a high volume of fire. They are one of the most prevalent weapons used by terror groups today.	AKS: short stock AKM: updated version of the AK 47 Clones: Sako/Valmet: Finland Galil: Israel R-4/R-4C: South Africa
Weight (kg): 4.876 loaded Length (mm): 870 Cyclic Rate of fire (rd/min): 600 Operation: Gas operated Fire Mode: Semi-automatic, Full automatic	AMMUNITION Name: 7.62 Caliber/length: 7.62 x 39 mm Effective Range (m): 300 Muzzle Velocity (m/s): 710
SIGHTS Iron sites.	

AK 74 (Russia)

	Ammunition Types	Typical Combat Load
(Source: OPFOR Worldwide Equipment Guide, TRADOC ADCSINT-Threats, September 2001, 1-3)	5.45 mm	Magazine Capacity: 30

SYSTEM	VARIANTS
A gas operated assault weapon used by the Soviet Army. It is basically an AKM rechambered to fire a 5.45mm round. It has a higher muzzle velocity than the AK 47/AKM, which gives it a longer effective range. It does not have the accuracy of the M16, but reportedly has better reliability in a combat situation and less maintenance requirements than the M16.	AKS 74: Folding stock version

SYSTEM

A gas operated assault weapon used by the Soviet Army. It is basically an AKM rechambered to fire a 5.45mm round. It has a higher muzzle velocity than the AK 47/AKM, which gives it a longer effective range. It does not have the accuracy of the M16, but reportedly has better reliability in a combat situation and less maintenance requirements than the M16.

Weight (kg): 3.6 loaded
Length (mm): 933
Cyclic Rate of fire (rd/min): 600
Operation: Gas operated
Fire Mode: Semi-automatic, Full automatic

VARIANTS

AKS 74: Folding stock version

AMMUNITION

Name: 5.45mm
Caliber/length: 5.45 x 39 mm
Effective Range (m): 500
Muzzle Velocity (m/s): 900

SIGHTS

Front: Post, Rear: U-notch

Night sights are available.

Colt M16 (United States)

	Ammunition Types	Typical Combat Load
(*Source*: US Army File Photo)	5.56mm (.223 Rem)	Magazine Capacity: 20, 30

SYSTEM

A gas operated automatic assault rifle used by the US military as its primary weapon. Originally developed by Armalite as the AR 15, this was a scaled down version of the AR 10 redesigned to use the .223 Remington cartridge.

It has been modified numerous times and is used by nearly 30 different militaries and is very popular with law enforcement agencies.

Weight (kg): 2.89 empty
Length (mm): 986
Cyclic Rate of fire (rd/min): 800
Operation: Gas operated
Fire Mode: Semi-automatic, Full automatic

SIGHTS

Iron sites. Scope capable.

VARIANTS

M16A1, A2, A3: Various upgrades.

Civilian clones by Bushmaster, Armalite, Professional Ordnance, and many others.

AMMUNITION

Name: 5.56 NATO
Caliber/length: 5.56 x 45mm
Effective Range (m): 460
Muzzle Velocity (m/s): 991

Sniper Rifles

ArmaLite AR 50 (United States)

	Ammunition Types	Typical Combat Load
(*Source*: Photo courtesy of ArmaLite*)	.50BMG	Single Shot

SYSTEM	VARIANTS
A single shot bolt action rifle that uses the.50 Cal Browning Machine Gun ammunition. It has a unique octagonal receiver bedded into a sectional aluminum stock and has a modified M-16 type pistol grip. The butt stock is fully adjustable and is removable for transport.	
Weight (kg): 19.24 with scope Length (mm): 1499 Operation: Bolt Action Fire Mode: Single shot	AMMUNITION Name: .50BMG Caliber/length: 12.7x99mm Effective Range (m): 1200 Muzzle Velocity (m/s): 865-890
SIGHTS ArmaLite sells this with a Leupold Mk4 10-power scope.	
* ArmaLite is a registered trademark of ArmaLite.	

Remington Model 700 (United States)

(*Source*: US Army File Photo)	Ammunition Types .223 Rem .308 Win	Typical Combat Load Magazine. Capacity: 5

SYSTEM	VARIANTS
A bolt action, magazine fed rifle that is basically a re-stocked Remington Model 700 VS varmint rifle. This is one of the most widely used tactical rifles in the United States. The police, the US Army and the US Marine Corps, use it. Weight (kg): 4.08 empty without scope Length (mm): 1662 Operation: Bolt Action Fire Mode: Single Shot	M24 Sniper Weapon System (US Army) M40A1 Sniper Rifle (USMC) AMMUNITION Name: .223 Rem/.308 Win Caliber/length: 5.56x45mm / 7.62x51mm Effective Range (m): 800 Muzzle Velocity (m/s): 1005 / 780-840
SIGHTS Variable telescopic scopes. No iron sights.	

Steyr-Mannlicher SSG-69 (Austria)

	Ammunition Types	Typical Combat Load
(UNCLASSIFIED) Neg. 529276 (UNCLASSIFIED) Figure 44. (U) Steyr SSG-69 7.62-mm Sniper Rifle (*Source*: (S/NF/WN/NC) DST-2660H-481-89, *Terrorist Weapons Handbook – Worldwide* (U), 15 December 1989, 32-33. Unclassified Extract.)	7.62 x 51mm (.308 Win)	Magazine. Capacity: 5

SYSTEM	VARIANTS
A bolt action, magazine fed rifle, which has been used as a sniper rifle by the Austrian forces, as well as many police agencies. The rifle is extremely accurate and has been used to win a number of international competitions. Weight (kg): 4.6 with scope. Length (mm): 1130 Operation: Bolt Action Fire Mode: Single shot SIGHTS Scope	AMMUNITION Name: .308 Win Caliber/length: 7.62 x 51mm Effective Range (m): 800 Muzzle Velocity (m/s): 799 - 860

Shotguns

Franchi SPAS 12 (Italy)

	Ammunition Types	Typical Combat Load
(UNCLASSIFIED) Figure 46. (U) Franchi SPAS 12-Gauge Shotgun (UNCLASSIFIED) (*Source*: (S/NF/WN/NC) DST-2660H-481-89, *Terrorist Weapons Handbook – Worldwide* (U), 15 December 1989, 34. Unclassified Extract.)	12 Ga. Shot 12 Ga. Buckshot 12 Ga. Slug	Tubular Magazine capacity: 8

SYSTEM

This is a dual mode shotgun, which can be operated both as a pump-action style shotgun and as a semi-auto shotgun. It can rapidly fire full power loads such as buckshot set on semi-auto, and can be switched to pump to handle low power rounds -- or if auto functioning fails to function properly. It has a relatively short barrel, which makes it suitable for operation in tight quarters. Both military and the police use it.

Weight (kg): 4.0
Length (mm): 1070
Operation: Pump or gas operated
Fire Mode: Semi-automatic

SIGHTS

Iron Blade

VARIANTS

AMMUNITION

Name: 12 Gauge
Caliber/length: 12 Ga/ 2 ¾ inch
Effective Range (m): 60
Muzzle Velocity (m/s): 393 (00 Buckshot)

Mossberg Model 500 (United States)

	Ammunition Types	Typical Combat Load
(UNCLASSIFIED) Figure 47. (U) Mossberg Model 500 12-Gauge Shotgun (*Source*: (S/NF/WN/NC) DST-2660H-481-89, *Terrorist Weapons Handbook – Worldwide* (U), 15 December 1989, 34. Unclassified Extract.)	12 Ga. Shot 12 Ga. Buckshot 12 Ga. Slug	Tubular Magazine capacity: 6, 8, 9

SYSTEM	VARIANTS
This is a pump action shotgun that is common with the military and police departments, and is sold widely on the commercial market. It is available with both a traditional wood stock and with the pistol grip, as shown above.	Numerous variations of this model exist.
Weight (kg): 2.6 Length (mm): 711 Operation: Pump Action Fire Mode: Single shot	AMMUNITION Name: 12 Gauge Caliber/length: 12 Ga/ 2 ¾ inch and 3 inch Effective Range (m): 60 Muzzle Velocity (m/s): 393 (00 Buckshot)
SIGHTS Fixed iron sights	

Appendix C

Conventional Military Munitions

General

Although terrorists demonstrate innovation in fabricating improvised explosive devices, conventional weapons are often used in operations. These weapons range from highly sophisticated shoulder-fired air defense missiles to traditional grenades, rocket propelled grenades, and mines. This appendix a sampling of weapons U.S. military forces may encounter when dealing with terrorism.

Fragmentation Grenades

Grenades are a common weapon used by terrorists. In fact, in the annual report published by HAMAS on terrorist activities in 1998, they stated that a combination of time delayed bombs coupled with commando attacks using hand grenades were the major part of effective operations and caused the most casualties.[260] Although terrorists will use any grenade they can acquire, some of the common grenades available are listed below. These figures are courtesy of the Naval Explosive Ordnance Disposal Technology Division.[261]

- Figure E-1. U.S. Grenade, Fragmentation, M2A1, M2A2, U.S. Army

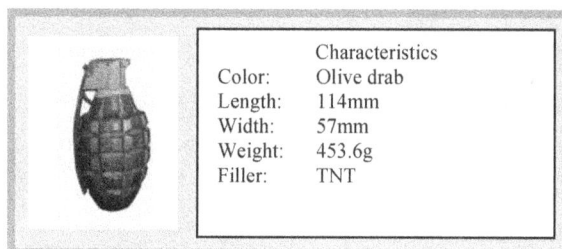

	Characteristics
Color:	Olive drab
Length:	114mm
Width:	57mm
Weight:	453.6g
Filler:	TNT

- Figure E-2. U.S. Grenade, Fragmentation, M26, M26A1, M61

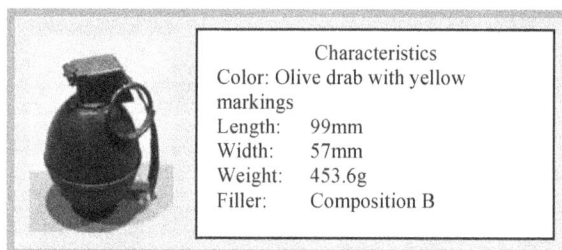

	Characteristics
Color:	Olive drab with yellow markings
Length:	99mm
Width:	57mm
Weight:	453.6g
Filler:	Composition B

---

[260] Reuven Paz, *Hamas Publishes Annual Report on Terrorist Activity for 1998* (Herzliya, Israel: International Policy Institute for Counterterrorism, May 3, 1999), 1; available from http://www.ict.org.il/spotlight/det.cfm?id=259; Internet; accessed 6 December 2002.

[261] Department of Defense, Naval Explosive Ordnance Disposal Technology Division, *ORDATA II - Enhanced Deminers' Guide to UXO Identification, Recovery, and Disposal,* Version 1.0, [CD-ROM], (Indian Head, MD: Naval Explosive Ordnance Disposal Technology Division, 1999).

- Figure E-3. French Grenade, Fragmentation, TN 733

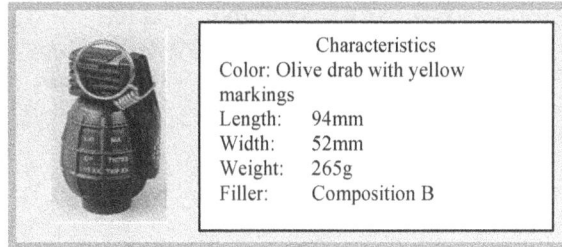

Characteristics
Color: Olive drab with yellow markings
Length: 94mm
Width: 52mm
Weight: 265g
Filler: Composition B

- Figure E-4. U.K. Grenade, Fragmentation, No. 36M MK1

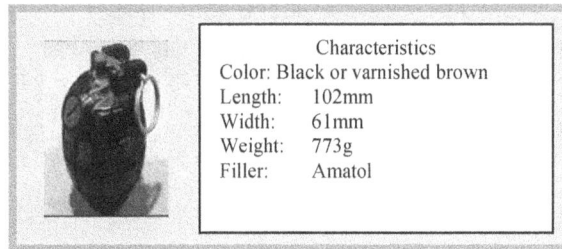

Characteristics
Color: Black or varnished brown
Length: 102mm
Width: 61mm
Weight: 773g
Filler: Amatol

- Figure E-5. Spanish Grenade, Fragmentation, POM 1

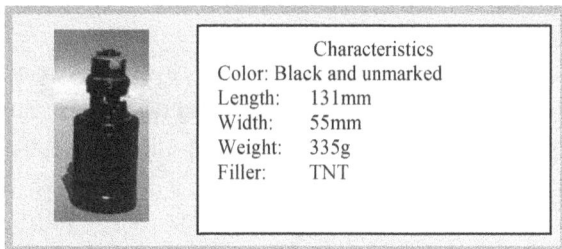

Characteristics
Color: Black and unmarked
Length: 131mm
Width: 55mm
Weight: 335g
Filler: TNT

- Figure E-6. U.S.S.R. Grenade, Hand, Defensive, RGD-5

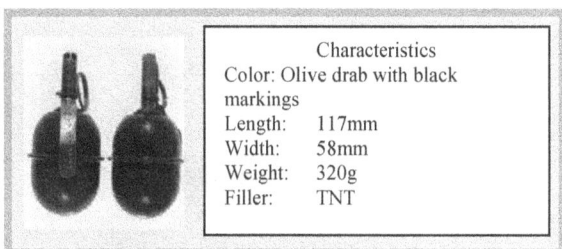

Characteristics
Color: Olive drab with black markings
Length: 117mm
Width: 58mm
Weight: 320g
Filler: TNT

- Figure E-7. U.S.S.R. Grenade, Hand, Defensive, F1

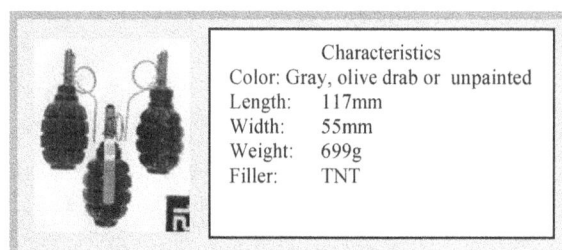

Characteristics
Color: Gray, olive drab or unpainted
Length: 117mm
Width: 55mm
Weight: 699g
Filler: TNT

- Figure E-8. North Korean Grenade, Fragmentation, Model Unknown

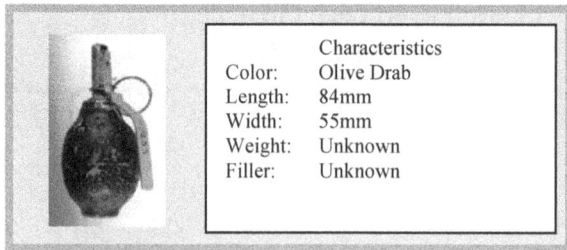

	Characteristics
Color:	Olive Drab
Length:	84mm
Width:	55mm
Weight:	Unknown
Filler:	Unknown

- Figure E-9. Chinese (P.R.) Grenade, Fragmentation, Type 86P

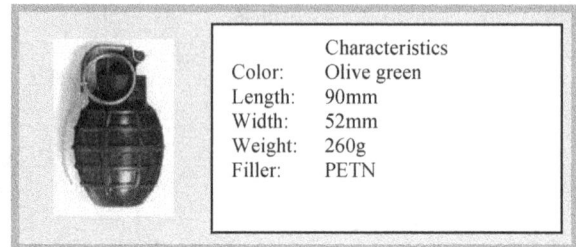

	Characteristics
Color:	Olive green
Length:	90mm
Width:	52mm
Weight:	260g
Filler:	PETN

Rocket Propelled Grenade

This weapon fires a motorized grenade from a tube-like launcher. Although it is an unguided weapon, a trained operator can negotiate targets at a long distance. Even though it was originally developed for an anti-tank weapon system, many terrorists use them as anti-aircraft weapons. RPGs were used to bring down two MH-47 Chinook helicopters in the Shah-e-Kot area of Afghanistan in 2002 and the same system was used in 1993 in Mogadishu, Somalia, when Somalis firing RPGs brought down a pair of UH-60 Black Hawk helicopters. Many armies use these systems and they are widely available on the weapons black market.

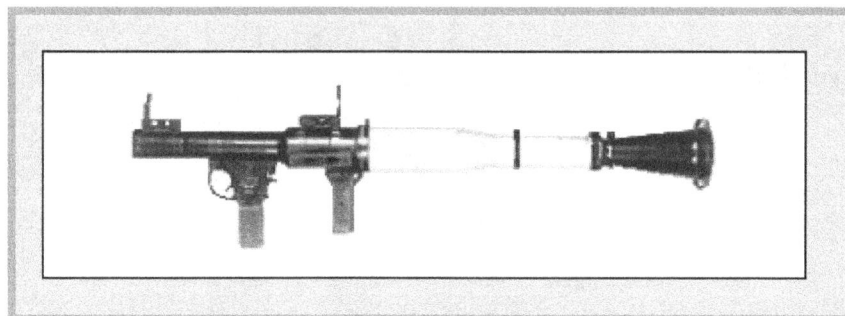

Figure E-10. RPG-7V Antitank Grenade Launcher (Source: WEG)

- Russian 40mm Anti-tank Grenade Launcher RPG-7V. The RPG-7V is abundant throughout the terrorist world and is being used extensively by terrorist organizations in the Middle East and Latin America and is thought to be in the inventory of many insurgent groups. The RPG-7V is a relatively simple and functional weapon, with an effective range of approximately 500 meters when used against a fixed target, and about 300 meters when fired at a moving target. [262] It can penetrate 330mm of armor. Photo is from the TRADOC *Worldwide Equipment Guide* (WEG).

- U.S. 66mm Light Anti-tank Weapon M72 LAW. Although the M72-series LAW was mainly used as an anti-armor weapon, it may be used with limited success against other targets such as buildings and light vehicles. It's effective range is not as good as the RPG-7V, since it's only effective to 200 meters for stationary targets, and 165 meters for moving targets. It can penetrate 350mm of armor.

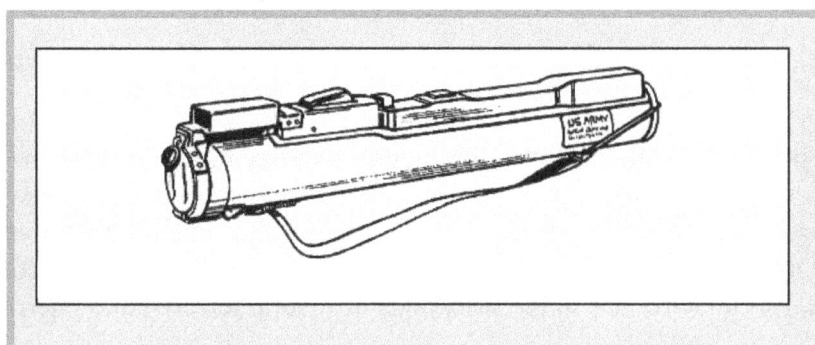

Figure E-11. M72 Series Light Antitank Weapon (*Source:* FM 23-25)

Air Defense Weapons

Although there are a myriad of air defense weapon systems, the man portable systems are the ones that will be covered in this section. As the name indicates, these systems are portable and can be employed by terrorists very quickly. Due to excellent performance and the large number of these air defense systems throughout the world, the two systems discussed below represent some of the most formidable threats to aircraft of all types. The fact that terrorists will use these weapons was demonstrated in November 2002 when two surface-to-air missiles were fired at a Tel Aviv bound Arkia airlines Boeing 757 as it departed Mombasa, Kenya. Fortunately the missiles missed their target, but it is an indication of possible employment of the systems in the future.

- U.S. FIM92A Stinger. The US-made Stinger is a man-portable infrared-guided shoulder-launched Surface-To-Air Missile (SAM). It proved to be highly effective in the hands of Afghan Mujahedeen guerrillas during their insurgency against the Soviets. Its maximum effective range is approximately 4,000+ meters. Its maximum effective altitude is approximately 3,500 meters. It has been used to target high-speed jets, helicopters, and commercial airliners.

---

[262] *Conventional Terrorist Weapons* (New York: United Nations Office for Drug Control and Crime Prevention, 2002), 3; available from http://www.undcp.org/odccp/terrorism_weapons_conventional.html; Internet; accessed 12 November 2002.

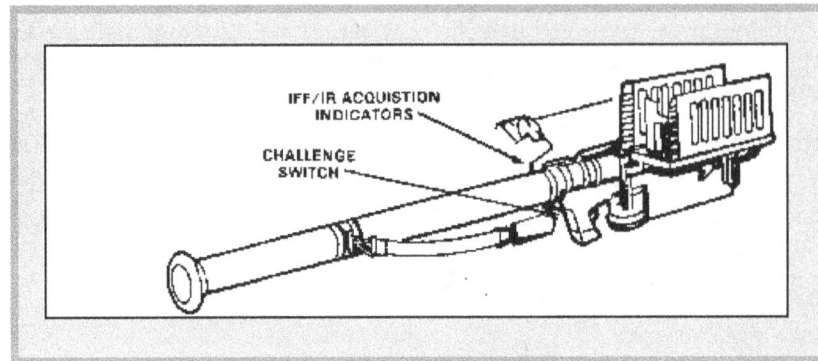

Figure E-12. U.S. FIM92A Stinger (*Source*: FM 44-18-1)

- Russian SA 7b/Grail. Sold by the thousands after the demise of the former Soviet Union, the SA-7 "Grail" uses an optical sight and tracking device with an infrared seeking mechanism to strike flying targets. Its maximum effective range is approximately 5,500 meters and maximum effective altitude is approximately 4,500 meters. It is known to be in the stockpiles of several terrorist and guerrilla groups.

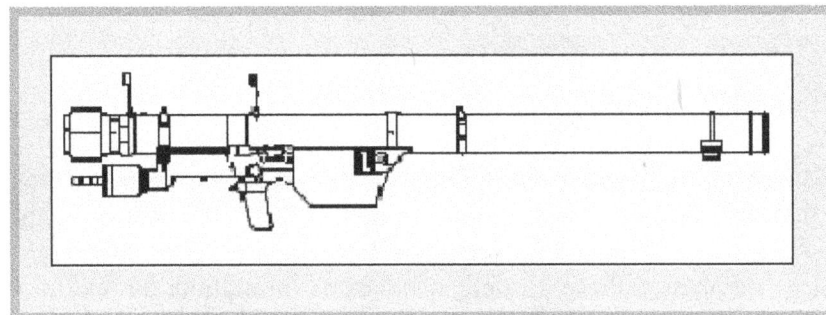

Figure E-13. Russian SA 7b/Grail (*Source:* WEG)

Bombs and Artillery

Although most bombs used by terrorists are fabricated devices, they do use some conventional munitions, especially as booby traps. They often use unexploded ordnance and modify it for their purposes. A 2001 report from the United Nations Mine Action Coordination Center on the former Yugoslav Republic of Macedonia indicates a plethora of unexploded munitions, to include 122 mm artillery rounds, 100 mm tank rounds, 82 mm and 120 mm mortar rounds, 20 mm and 30 mm cannon rounds, and 50 mm rocket rounds.[263] The following reflects some common munitions used by terrorist organizations. These figures are courtesy of the Naval Explosive Ordnance Disposal Technology Division.[264]

---

[263]C.J. Clark, *Mine/UXO Assessment: Former Yugoslav Republic of Macedonia* (New York: United Nations Mine Action Coordination Center, 8 October 2001), 2; available from

- Figure E-14. U.S. Artillery Projectile, 105mm, HE, M1

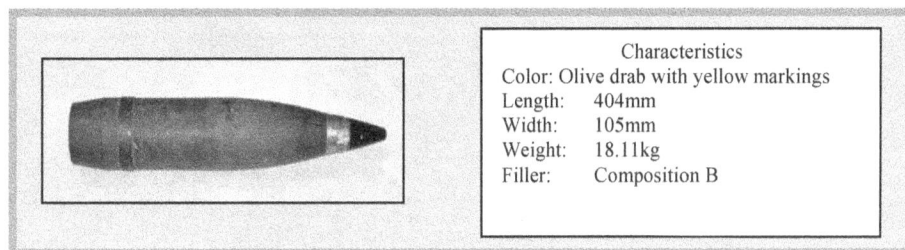

Characteristics
Color: Olive drab with yellow markings
Length: 404mm
Width: 105mm
Weight: 18.11kg
Filler: Composition B

- Figure E-15. U.S. Artillery Projectile, 155mm, HE, M107

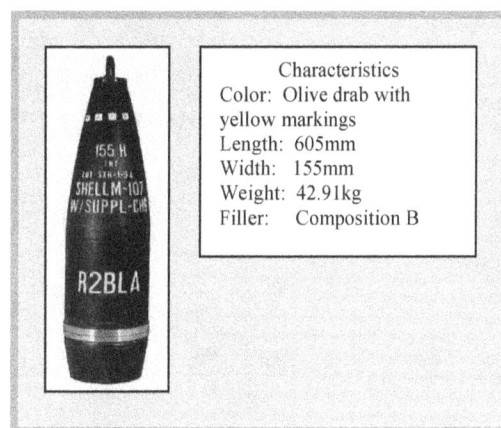

Characteristics
Color: Olive drab with yellow markings
Length: 605mm
Width: 155mm
Weight: 42.91kg
Filler: Composition B

- Figure E-16. U.S.S.R. Artillery Projectile, 122mm, HE, FRAG, Model OF-472

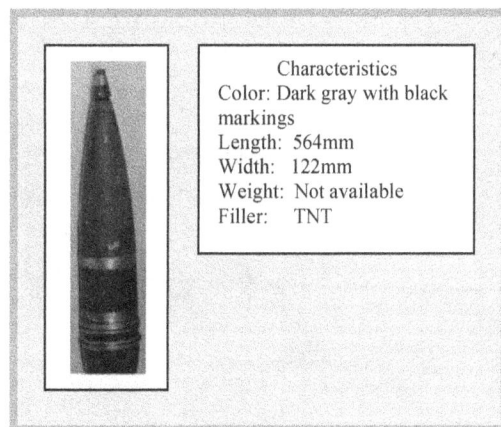

Characteristics
Color: Dark gray with black markings
Length: 564mm
Width: 122mm
Weight: Not available
Filler: TNT

---

http://www.mineaction.org/sp/mine_awareness/_refdocs.cfm?doc_ID=707; Internet; accessed 13 December 2002.
[264] Department of Defense, Naval Explosive Ordnance Disposal Technology Division, *ORDATA II - Enhanced Deminers' Guide to UXO Identification, Recovery, and Disposal,* Version 1.0, [CD-ROM], (Indian Head, MD: Naval Explosive Ordnance Disposal Technology Division, 1999).

- Figure E-17. U.S.S.R. Projectile, 100 mm, HEAT-FS, Model ZBK-5M

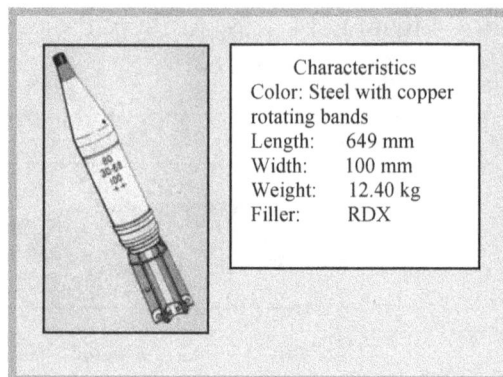

Characteristics	
Color: Steel with copper rotating bands	
Length:	649 mm
Width:	100 mm
Weight:	12.40 kg
Filler:	RDX

- Figure E-18. U.S.S.R. Projectile, 120 mm, Mortar, HE-FRAG, Model OF-843A

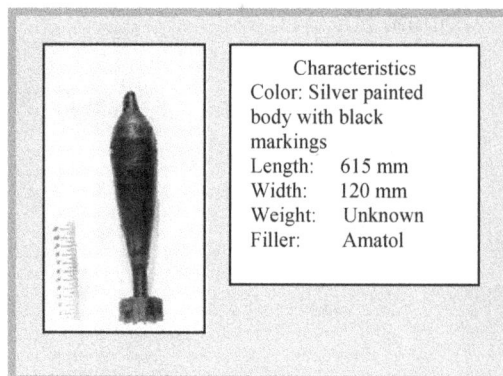

Characteristics	
Color: Silver painted body with black markings	
Length:	615 mm
Width:	120 mm
Weight:	Unknown
Filler:	Amatol

- Figure E-19. U.S. Bomb, 220 lb, Fragmentary, AN-M88

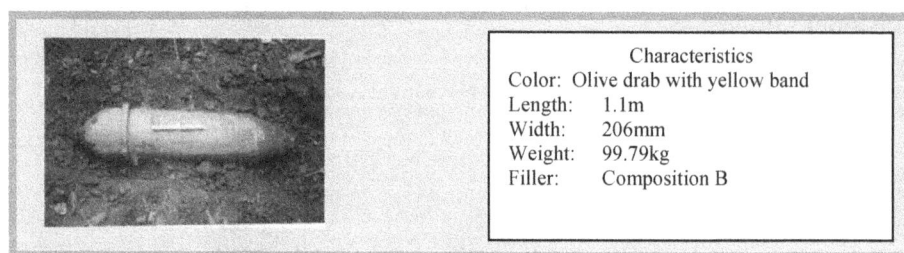

Characteristics	
Color: Olive drab with yellow band	
Length:	1.1m
Width:	206mm
Weight:	99.79kg
Filler:	Composition B

- Figure E-20. U.S. Bomb, 250 lb, GP, AN-M57 & AN-M57A1

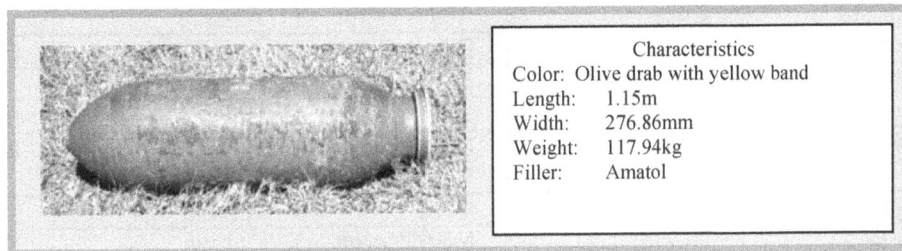

Characteristics
Color: Olive drab with yellow band
Length: 1.15m
Width: 276.86mm
Weight: 117.94kg
Filler: Amatol

- Figure E-21. U.S. Bomb, 500 lb, GP, MK3, MOD 1

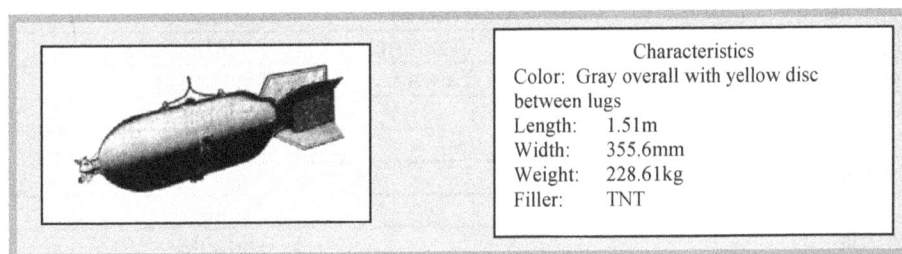

Characteristics
Color: Gray overall with yellow disc between lugs
Length: 1.51m
Width: 355.6mm
Weight: 228.61kg
Filler: TNT

Mines

Similar to the homemade bombs used by terrorists, mines are another means used to inflict damage by terrorist organizations. They use both anti-personnel and anti-tank mines. Unlike conventional military forces that use mines against an opposing military force, terrorists use mines to disrupt social, economic, and political operations. Consequently, mines are often placed around schools, on walking paths, or around wells, in order to gain terror effects.[265] When examining the proliferation of these type weapons throughout the world, it becomes readily apparent that it will be a true threat to U.S. forces. The information in Table E-1 is from the 2001 Landmine Monitor Report and shows the various countries of the world that are affected by landmines and unexploded ordnance. Many of these mines have been emplaced by terrorist organizations.

---

[265] Margaret Buse, "Non-State Actors and Their Significance," *Journal of Mine Action* (December 2002): 2; available from http://maic.jmu.edu/journal/5.3/features/maggie_buse_nsa/maggie_buse.htm; Internet; accessed 13 December 2002.

Africa	Americas	Asia-Pacific	Europe/ Central Asia	Middle East/ North Africa
Angola	Chile	Afghanistan	Albania	Algeria
Burundi	Colombia	Bangladesh	Armenia	Egypt
Chad	Costa Rica	Burma	Azerbaijan	Iran
Congo-Brazz.	Cuba	Cambodia	Belarus	Iraq
DR Congo	Ecuador	China	Bosnia & Herzegovina	Israel
Djibouti	El Salvador	India	Croatia	Jordan
Eritrea	Guatemala	North Korea	Cyprus	Kuwait
Ethiopia	Honduras	South Korea	Czech Republic	Lebanon
Guinea-Bissau	Nicaragua	Laos	Denmark	Libya
Kenya	Peru	Mongolia	Estonia	Morocco
Liberia	Falkland-Malvinas	Nepal	Georgia	Oman
Malawi		Pakistan	Greece	Syria
Mauritania		Philippines	Kyrgyzstan	Tunisia
Mozambique		Sri Lanka	Latvia	Yemen
Namibia		Thailand	Lithuania	Golan Heights
Niger		Vietnam	FYR Macedonia	Northern Iraq
Rwanda		Taiwan	Moldova	Palestine
Senegal			Poland	Western Sahara
Sierra Leone			Russia	
Somalia			Tajikistan	
Sudan			Turkey	
Swaziland			Ukraine	
Tanzania			Uzbekistan	
Uganda			Yugoslavia	
Zambia			Abkhazia	
Zimbabwe			Chechnya	
Somaliland			Kosovo	
			Nagorno-Karabakh	

Source: "Humanitarian Mine Action", *Landmine Monitor Report – 2001*; available from http://www.icbl.org/lm/2001/exec/hma.html#Heading514; Internet; accessed 13 December 2002.

Table E-1. **Landmine/UXO Problem in the World**

There are hundreds of different types of mines that can be employed against our troops. As Robert Williscroft stated in *Defense Watch*, "At least 800 different mine types populate the world's minefields. These range from homemade coffee can bombs to sophisticated 'smart' non-metallic devices that can distinguish between potential targets."[266] Manufactured mines used by terrorists originate from many of the former Warsaw Pact countries, the United States, China, Britain, and Iran, to name just a few

---

[266]Robert G. Williscroft, "The Economics of Demining Defines Success and Failure," *Defense Watch* (13 February 2002): 4; available from http://www.sftt.org/dw02132002.html; Internet; accessed 13 December 2002.

sources.[267] Some common mines are shown below. These can be detonated through the use of trip wires, pressure, or command detonation. These figures are courtesy of the Naval Explosive Ordnance Disposal Technology Division.[268]

- Figure E-22: Chinese (P.R.) Landmine, APERS, Type 59

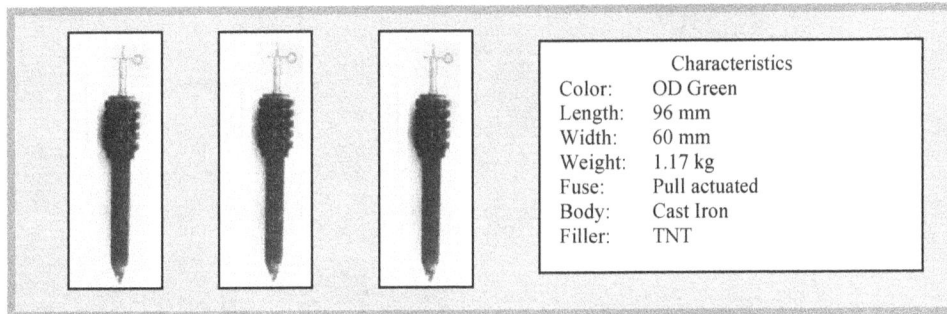

Characteristics	
Color:	OD Green
Length:	96 mm
Width:	60 mm
Weight:	1.17 kg
Fuse:	Pull actuated
Body:	Cast Iron
Filler:	TNT

- Figure E-23. Chinese (P.R.) Landmine, APERS, Type 66

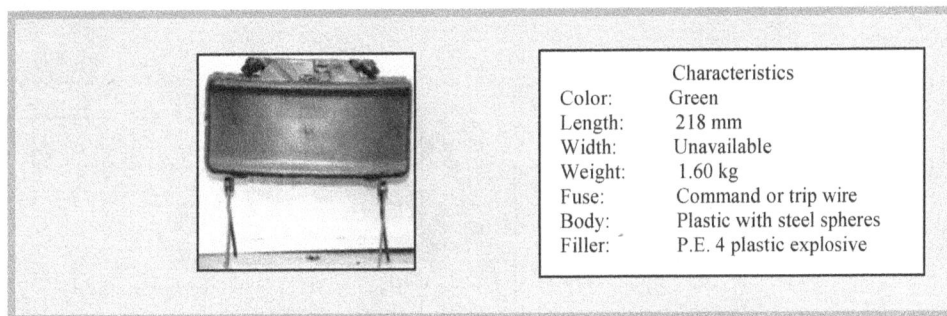

Characteristics	
Color:	Green
Length:	218 mm
Width:	Unavailable
Weight:	1.60 kg
Fuse:	Command or trip wire
Body:	Plastic with steel spheres
Filler:	P.E. 4 plastic explosive

- Figure E-24. Chinese (P.R.) Landmine, AT, Type 72

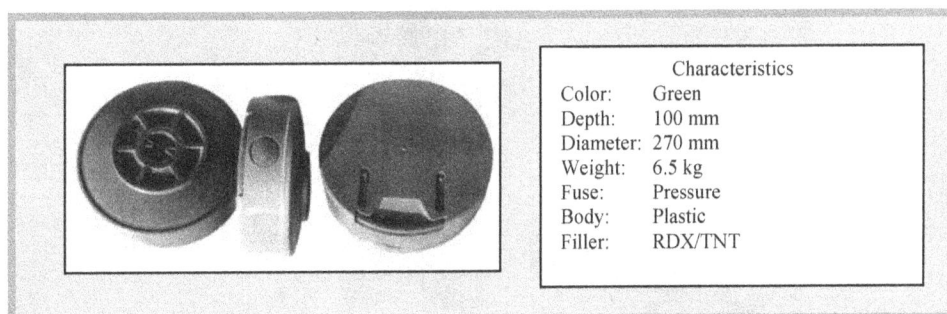

Characteristics	
Color:	Green
Depth:	100 mm
Diameter:	270 mm
Weight:	6.5 kg
Fuse:	Pressure
Body:	Plastic
Filler:	RDX/TNT

---

[267] C.J. Clark, *Mine/UXO Assessment: Former Yugoslav Republic of Macedonia* (New York: United Nations Mine Action Coordination Center, 8 October 2001), 2; available from http://www.mineaction.org/sp/mine_awareness/_refdocs.cfm?doc_ID=707; Internet; accessed 13 December 2002; and Jerry White, "Ridding the World of Land Mines," *Union-Tribune* (24 January 2002): 4; available from http://www.wand.org/9-11/discuss6.html; Internet; accessed 13 December 2002.
[268]Department of Defense, Naval Explosive Ordnance Disposal Technology Division, *ORDATA II - Enhanced Deminers' Guide to UXO Identification, Recovery, and Disposal,* Version 1.0, [CD-ROM], (Indian Head, MD: Naval Explosive Ordnance Disposal Technology Division, 1999).

- Figure E-25. U.S. Landmine, APERS, HE, M14

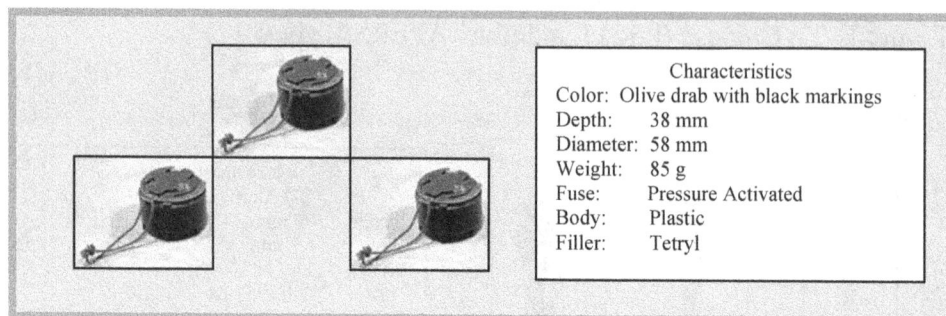

Characteristics
Color: Olive drab with black markings
Depth: 38 mm
Diameter: 58 mm
Weight: 85 g
Fuse: Pressure Activated
Body: Plastic
Filler: Tetryl

- Figure E-26. U.S. Landmine, APERS, HE, M18A1

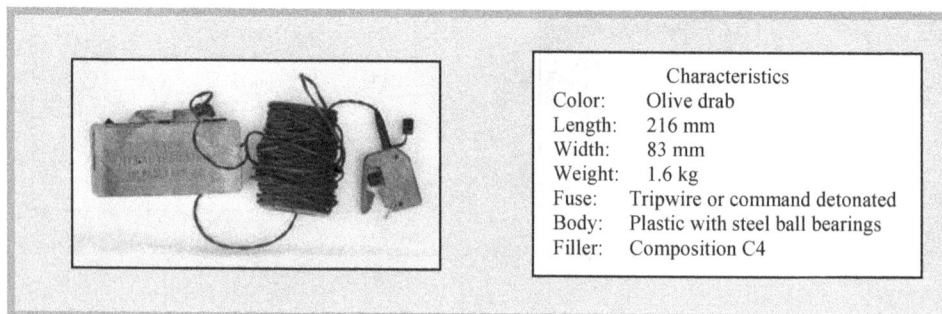

Characteristics
Color: Olive drab
Length: 216 mm
Width: 83 mm
Weight: 1.6 kg
Fuse: Tripwire or command detonated
Body: Plastic with steel ball bearings
Filler: Composition C4

- Figure E-27. U.S. Landmine, AT, HE, M21

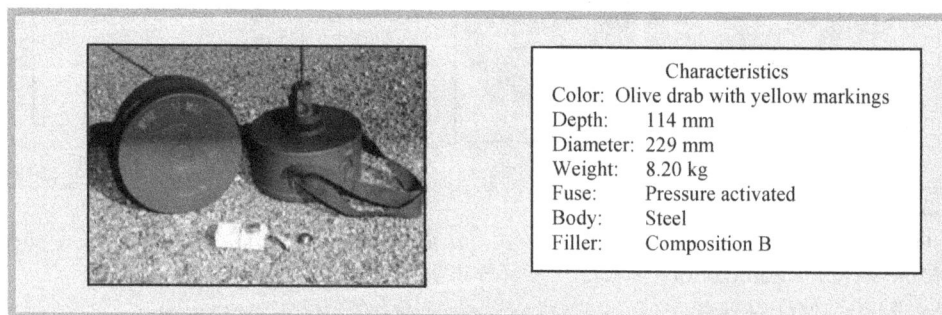

Characteristics
Color: Olive drab with yellow markings
Depth: 114 mm
Diameter: 229 mm
Weight: 8.20 kg
Fuse: Pressure activated
Body: Steel
Filler: Composition B

•   Figure E-28. U.S.S.R. Landmine, APERS, Directional, MON-50

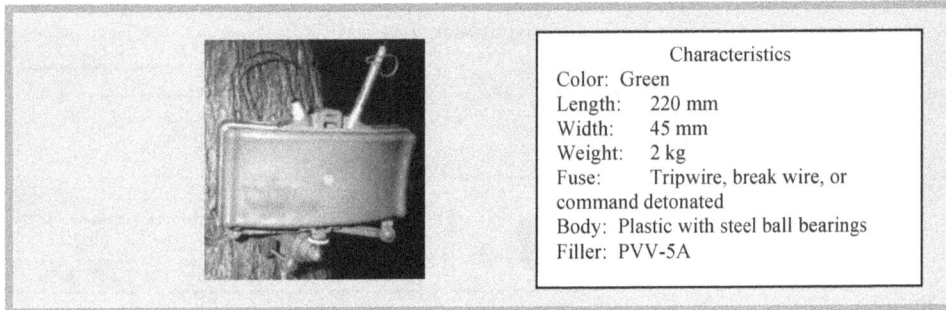

Characteristics
Color: Green
Length: 220 mm
Width: 45 mm
Weight: 2 kg
Fuse: Tripwire, break wire, or command detonated
Body: Plastic with steel ball bearings
Filler: PVV-5A

•   Figure E-29. U.S.S.R. Landmine, APERS, PMN-2

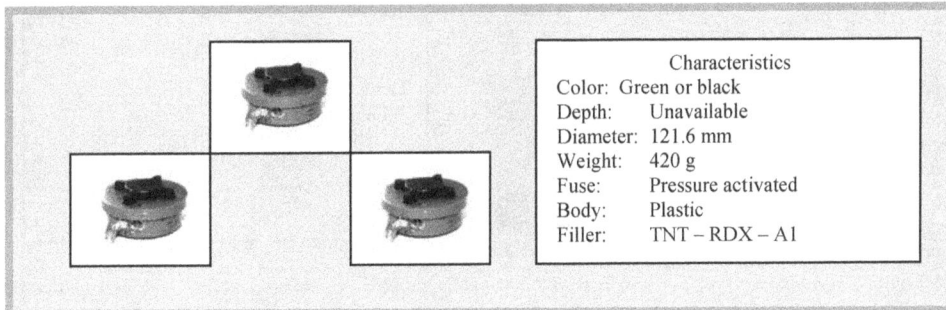

Characteristics
Color: Green or black
Depth: Unavailable
Diameter: 121.6 mm
Weight: 420 g
Fuse: Pressure activated
Body: Plastic
Filler: TNT – RDX – A1

•   Figure E-30. U.S.S.R. Landmine, AT, TM-62M

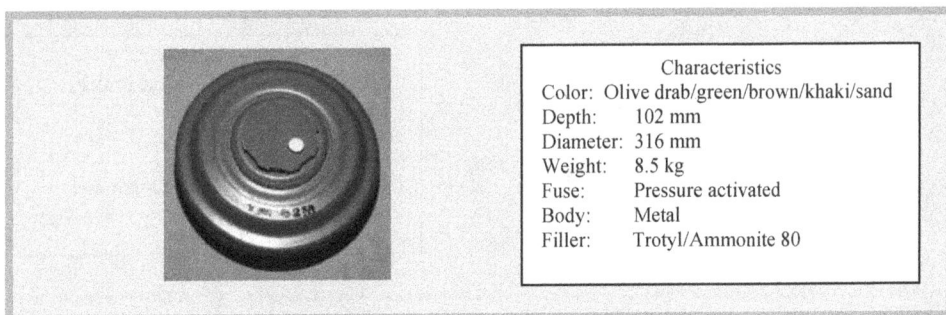

Characteristics
Color: Olive drab/green/brown/khaki/sand
Depth: 102 mm
Diameter: 316 mm
Weight: 8.5 kg
Fuse: Pressure activated
Body: Metal
Filler: Trotyl/Ammonite 80

- Figure E-31. Yugoslav Landmine, APERS, PMA-2

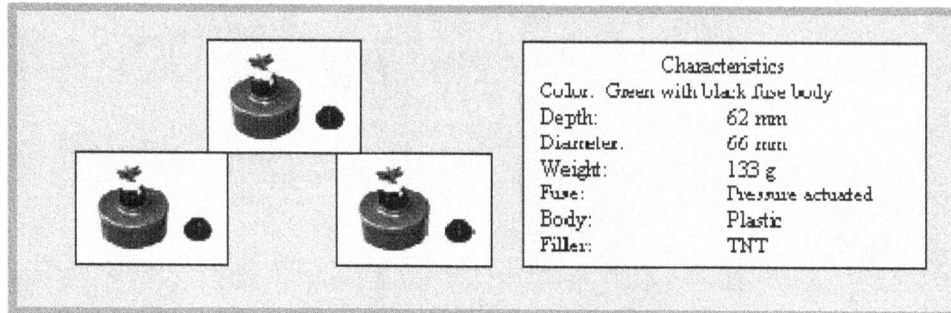

Characteristics	
Color:	Green with black fuse body
Depth:	62 mm
Diameter:	66 mm
Weight:	133 g
Fuse:	Pressure actuated
Body:	Plastic
Filler:	TNT

- Figure E-32. Yugoslav Landmine, APERS, PMR-2A

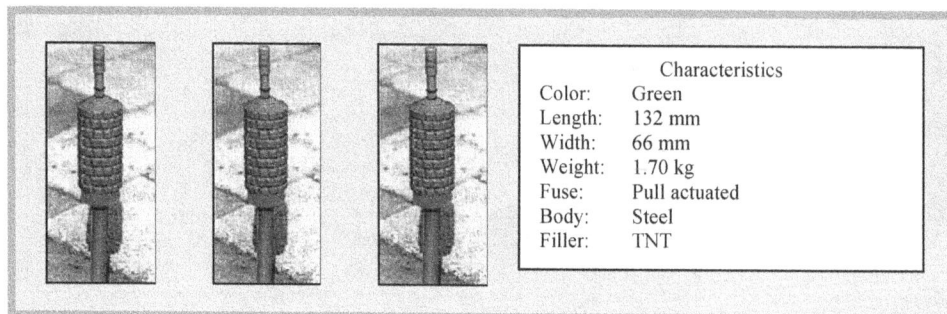

Characteristics	
Color:	Green
Length:	132 mm
Width:	66 mm
Weight:	1.70 kg
Fuse:	Pull actuated
Body:	Steel
Filler:	TNT

- Figure E-33. Yugoslav Landmine, AT, TMA-4

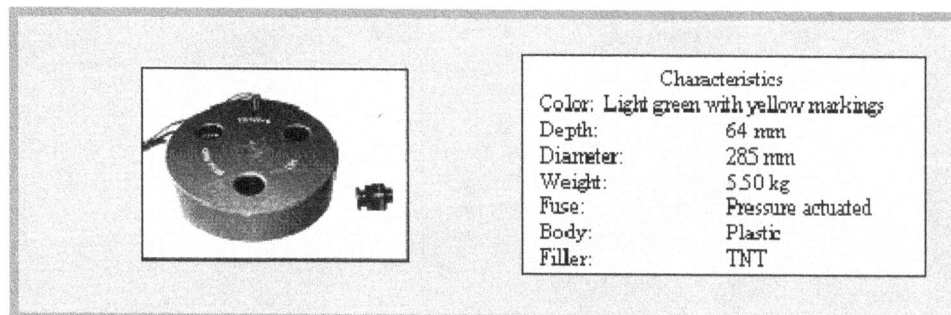

Characteristics	
Color:	Light green with yellow markings
Depth:	64 mm
Diameter:	285 mm
Weight:	5.50 kg
Fuse:	Pressure actuated
Body:	Plastic
Filler:	TNT

This Page Intentionally Blank

Glossary

17 November: Revolutionary Organization 17 November based in Greece

AAIA: Aden-Abyan Islamic Army, a.k.a. Islamic Army of Aden (IAA) based in Yemen

ABB: Alex Boncayao Brigade based in the Philippines

ADCON: Administrative control, that is, exercise of authority in administration and support. See Appendix H of terrorism handbook. (JP 1-02)

ADF: Allied Democratic Forces based in Uganda and the Congo

AI: Ansar al-Islam, a.k.a. Partisans of Islam, Helpers of Islam, Supporters of Islam, Jund al-Islam, and Jaish Ansar al-Sunna based in Iraq

AIAI: Al-Ittihad al-Islami, a.k.a. Islamic Union based in Somalia

AIIB: Anti-Imperialist International Brigade, a.k.a. Japanese Red Army (JRA) based in Lebanon and Japan

Al-Badhr: Al-Badhr Mujahidin based in Pakistan

ALF: Animal Liberation Front

ALIR: Army for the Liberation of Rwanda, a.k.a. Interahamwe, Former Armed Forces of Rwanda (ex-FAR)

anarchism: A political theory holding all forms of governmental authority to be unnecessary and undesirable and advocating a society based on voluntary cooperation and free association of individuals and groups. (Webster's)

ANO: Abu Nidal Organization, a.k.a. Fatah Revolutionary Council, Arab Revolutionary Brigades, Black September, and Revolutionary Organization of Socialist Muslims based in Iraq

anti-terrorism: (AT) (JP 1-02) — Defensive measures used to reduce the vulnerability of individuals and property to terrorist acts, to include limited response and containment by local military forces.

AOR: Area of responsibility.

ASG: Abu Sayyaf Group based in the Philippines

AUC: Autodefensas Unidas de Colombia, a.k.a. United Self-Defense Forces/Group of Colombia

AUM: Aum Supreme Truth, a.k.a. Aum Shinrikyo and Aleph based in Japan

backdoor: Used to describe a back way, hidden method, or other type of method of by passing normal computer security in order to obtain access to a secure area.

biological agent: (JP 1-02) A microorganism that causes disease in personnel, plants, or animals or causes the deterioration of materiel.

biological weapon: (JP 1-02) An item of materiel, which projects, disperses, or disseminates a biological agent including arthropod vectors.

blister agents: (JP 1-02) A chemical agent which injures the eyes and lungs, and burns and blisters the skin. Also called vesicant agent.

blood agents: (JP 1-02) A chemical compound, including the cyanide group, that affects bodily functions by preventing the normal utilization of oxygen by body tissues.

BR/PCC: New Red Brigades/Communist Combatant Party, a.k.a. Brigate Rosse/Partito Comunista Combattente based in Italy

CBRNE: Chemical, biological, radiological, nuclear, and high yield explosive categories normally associated with weapons of mass destruction.

CFF: Cambodian Freedom Fighters, a.k.a. Cholana Kangtoap Serei Cheat Kampouchea based in Cambodia

chemical weapon: (JP 1-02) — Together or separately, (a) a toxic chemical and its precursors, except when intended for a purpose not prohibited under the Chemical Weapons Convention; (b) a munition or device, specifically designed to cause death or other harm through toxic properties of those chemicals specified in (a), above, which would be released as a result of the employment of such munition or device; (c) any equipment specifically designed for use directly in connection with the employment of munitions or devices specified in (b) above.

chemical agent: (CBRN Handbook) A chemical substance that is intended for use in military operations to kill, seriously injure, or incapacitate people through its physiological effects. Excluded from consideration are riot control agents, and smoke and flame materials. The agent may appear as a vapor, aerosol, or liquid; it can be either a casualty/toxic agent or an incapacitating agent.

CIRA: Continuity Irish Republican Army based in Northern Ireland

conflict: (Army) — A political-military situation between peace and war, distinguished from peace by the introduction of organized political violence and from war by its reliance on political methods. It shares many of the goals and characteristics of war, including the destruction of governments and the control of territory. See FM 100-20.

COCOM: Combatant command, that is, command authority. (JP 1-02)

consequence management: Traditionally, consequence management has been predominantly an emergency management function and included measures to protect public health and safety, restore essential government services, and provide emergency relief to governments, businesses, and individuals affected by the consequences of terrorism. The requirements of consequence management and crisis management are combined in the NRP.

CONUS: Continental United States

counter-terrorism: (CT) (JP 1-02) — Offensive measures taken to prevent, deter, and respond to terrorism.

CPP/NPA: Communist Party of the Philippines/New People's Army based in the Philippines

crisis management: Traditionally, crisis management was predominantly a law enforcement function and included measures to identify, acquire, and plan the use of resources needed to anticipate, prevent, and/or resolve a threat or act of terrorism. The requirements of consequence management and crisis management are combined in the NRP.

cyber-terrorism: (FBI) — A criminal act perpetrated by the use of computers and telecommunications capabilities, resulting in violence, destruction and/or disruption of services to create fear by causing confusion and uncertainty within a given population, with the goal of influencing a government or population to conform to a particular political, social, or ideological agenda.

Defense Information System Network: (DISN) The global, end-to-end information transfer infrastructure of DOD. It provides long haul data, voice, video, and transport networks and services needed for national defense command, control, communication, and intelligence requirements, as well as corporate defense requirements.

DSWA: Defense Special Weapons Agency

Defense Support of Civil Authorities: DOD support provided by Federal military forces, DOD civilians, and contract personnel, and DOD agencies and components, in response to requests for assistance during domestic incidents to include terrorist threats or attacks, major disasters, and other emergencies. See National- Response plan (NRP).

denial of service attack: (DOS) An attack designed to disrupt network service, typically by overwhelming the system with millions of requests every second causing the network to slow down or crash.

Designated Foreign Terrorist Organization: (DFTO) A political designation determined by the U.S. Department of State. Listing as a DFTO imposes legal penalties for membership, prevents travel into the U.S., and proscribes assistance and funding activities within the U.S. or by U.S. citizens. From Patterns of Global Terrorism 2001, U.S. Department of State.

DIRLAUTH: Direct liaison authorized

DFLP: Democratic Front for the Liberation of Palestine based in the Occupied Territories

DHS: Department of Homeland Security

DHKP/C: Revolutionary People's Liberation Party/Front, a.k.a. Devrimci Sol, Revolutionary Left, or Dev Sol based in Turkey

distributed denial of service attack: (DDOS) Similar to a denial of service attack, but involves the use of numerous computers to simultaneously flood the target.

Domestic Emergency Support Team: (DEST) See NRP.

dysfunctional state: Used in this circular to mean a nation or state whose declared government cannot fulfill one or more of the core functions of governance, such as defense, internal security, revenue collection, resource allocation, etc.

ELA: Revolutionary People's Struggle based in Greece

ELF: Earth Liberation Front

ELN: National Liberation Army based in Colombia

e-mail spoofing: A method of sending e-mail to a user that appears to have originated from one source when it actually was sent from another source.

Emergency Response Team: (ERT) See NRP.

ETA: Basque Fatherland and Liberty based in Spain

ETIM: Eastern Turkistan Islamic Movement based in China

FACT: Federation of Associations of Canadian Tamils, a.k.a. World Tamil Movement (WTM), World Tamil Association (WTA), Liberation Tigers of Tamil Eelam (LTTE), Ellalan Force, and Sangilian Force based in Sri Lanka

failed state: For the purposes of this circular, a dysfunctional state which also has multiple competing political factions in conflict within its borders, or has no functioning governance above the local level. This does not imply that a central government facing an insurgency is automatically a failed state. If essential functions of government continue in areas controlled by the central authority, it has not "failed."

FALN: Fuerzas Armadas de Liberacion Nacional Puertorriquena, a.k.a. Armed Forces for Puerto Rican National Liberation

FARC: Revolutionary Armed Forces of Colombia

Federal Coordinating Officer: (FCO) A Federal representative who manages Federal resource support activities related to Stafford Act disasters and emergencies; supports and is subordinate to the Principle Federal Official (PFO) when one is designated by DHS.

FEMA: Federal Emergency Management Agency. See NRP.

force protection: Security program designed to protect Service members, civilian employees, family members, facilities, and equipment, in all locations and situations, accomplished through planned and integrated application of combating terrorism, physical security, operations security, personal protective services, and supported by intelligence, counterintelligence, and other security programs.

force protection condition (FPCON): There is a graduated series of Force Protection Conditions ranging from Force Protection Conditions Normal to Force Protection Conditions Delta. There is a process by which commanders at all levels can raise or lower the Force Protection Conditions based on local conditions, specific threat information and/or guidance from higher headquarters. The four Force Protection Conditions above normal are:

Force Protection Condition ALPHA--This condition applies when there is a general threat of possible terrorist activity against personnel and facilities, the nature and extent of which are unpredictable, and circumstances do not justify full implementation of Force Protection Conditions BRAVO measures. The measures in this Force Protection Conditions must be capable of being maintained indefinitely.

Force Protection Condition BRAVO--This condition applies when an increased and more predictable threat of terrorist activity exists. The measures in this Force Protection Conditions must be capable of being maintained for weeks without causing undue hardship, affecting operational capability, and aggravating relations with local authorities.

Force Protection Condition CHARLIE--This condition applies when an incident occurs or intelligence is received indicating some form of terrorist action against personnel and facilities is imminent. Implementation of measures in this Force Protection Conditions for more than a short period probably will create hardship and affect the peacetime activities of the unit and its personnel.

Force Protection Condition DELTA--This condition applies in the immediate area where a terrorist attack has occurred or when intelligence has been received that terrorist action against a specific location or person is likely. Normally, this Force Protection Conditions is declared as a localized condition.

FPM: Morzanist Patriotic Front based in Honduras

FPMR: Manuel Rodriquez Patriotic Front based in Chile

GIA: Armed Islamic Group based in Algeria

GICM: Moroccan Islamic Combatant Group based in Western Europe

Global Information Grid: (GIG) DOD's globally interconnected set of information capabilities, processes, and personnel for collecting, processing, storing, disseminating, and managing information on demand to warfighters, policymakers, and support personnel.

GRAPO: Grupo de Resistencia Anti-Fascista Premero de Octubre, a.k.a. First of October Antifascist Resistance Group based in Spain

GSPC: The Salafist Group for Call and Combat based in Algeria

guerrilla warfare: (JP 1-02, NATO) — Military and paramilitary operations conducted in enemy-held or hostile territory by irregular, predominantly indigenous forces. (See also unconventional warfare (UW).

WOT: War on terrorism

hacker: Advanced computer users who spend a lot of time on or with computers and work hard to find vulnerabilities in IT systems.

hactivist: These are combinations of hackers and activists. They usually have a political motive for their activities, and identify that motivation by their actions, such as defacing opponents' websites with counter-information or disinformation.

HIG: Hizb-I Islami Gulbuddin based in Afghanistan and Pakistan

Homeland Security Advisory System (HSAS): The advisory system provides measures to remain vigilant, prepared, and ready to deter terrorist attacks. The following Threat Conditions each represent an increasing risk of terrorist attacks. Beneath each Threat Condition are suggested protective measures, recognizing that the heads of Federal departments and agencies are responsible for developing and implementing appropriate agency-specific protective measures:

- **Low Condition (Green)**. This condition is declared when there is a low risk of terrorist attacks. Federal departments and agencies should consider the following general measures in addition to the agency-specific Protective Measures they develop and implement: refining and exercising as appropriate preplanned Protective Measures; ensuring personnel receive proper training on the Homeland Security Advisory System and specific preplanned department or agency Protective Measures; and institutionalizing a process to assure that all facilities and regulated sectors are regularly assessed for vulnerabilities to terrorist attacks, and all reasonable measures are taken to mitigate these vulnerabilities.

- **Guarded Condition (Blue)**. This condition is declared when there is a general risk of terrorist attacks. In addition to the Protective Measures taken in the previous Threat Condition, Federal departments and agencies should consider the following general measures in addition to the agency-specific Protective Measures that they will develop and implement: checking communications with designated emergency response or command locations; reviewing and updating emergency response procedures; and   providing the public with any information that would strengthen its ability to act appropriately.

- **Elevated Condition (Yellow)**. An Elevated Condition is declared when there is a significant risk of terrorist attacks. In addition to the Protective Measures taken in the previous Threat Conditions, Federal departments and agencies should consider the following general measures in addition to the Protective Measures that they will develop and implement: increasing surveillance of critical locations; coordinating emergency plans as appropriate with nearby jurisdictions; assessing whether the precise characteristics of the threat require the further   refinement of preplanned Protective Measures; and implementing, as appropriate, contingency and emergency response plans.

- **High Condition (Orange)**. A High Condition is declared when there is a high risk of terrorist attacks. In addition to the Protective Measures taken in the previous Threat Conditions, Federal departments and agencies should consider the following general measures in addition to the agency-specific Protective Measures that they will develop and implement: coordinating necessary security efforts with Federal, State, and local law enforcement agencies or any National Guard or other appropriate armed forces organizations; taking additional precautions at public events and possibly considering alternative venues or even cancellation; preparing to execute contingency procedures, such as moving to an alternate site or dispersing their workforce; and restricting threatened facility access to essential personnel only.

- **Severe Condition (Red)**. A Severe Condition reflects a severe risk of terrorist attacks. Under most circumstances, the Protective Measures for a Severe Condition are not intended to be sustained for substantial periods of time. In addition to the Protective Measures in the previous Threat Conditions, Federal departments and agencies also should consider the following general measures in addition to the agency-specific Protective Measures that they will develop and implement: increasing or redirecting personnel to address critical emergency needs; signing emergency response personnel and pre-positioning and mobilizing specially trained teams or resources; monitoring, redirecting, or constraining transportation systems; and closing public and government facilities.

HM: Hizb ul-Mujahidin based in Kashmir, India

HUA: Harakat ul-Ansar based in Pakistan

HUJI: Harakat ul-Jihad-I-Islami, a.k.a. Movement of Islamic Holy War based in Pakistan

HUJI-B: Harakat ul-Jihad-I-Islami/Bangladesh, a.k.a. Movement of Islamic Holy War based in Bangladesh

HUM: Harakat ul-Mujahidin, a.k.a. Movement of Holy Warriors, and Jamiat ul-Ansar (JUA) based in Pakistan

HUMINT: Human intelligence

IAA: Islamic Army of Aden, a.k.a. Aden-Abyan Islamic Army (AAIA) based in Yemen

IBDA-C: Great East Islamic Raiders – Front based in Turkey

IED: Improvised Explosive Device. Devices that have been fabricated in an improvised manner and that incorporate explosives or destructive, lethal, noxious, pyrotechnic, or incendiary chemicals in their design.

IG: Al-Gama'a al-Islamiyya, a.k.a. Islamic Group based in Egypt

IIPB: Islamic International Peacekeeping Brigade based in Chechnya

IMU: Islamic Movement of Uzbekistan based in Uzbekistan

incapacitating agent: (CBRN Handbook) Produce temporary physiological and/or mental effects via action on the central nervous system. Effects may persist for hours or days, but victims usually do not require medical treatment. However, such treatment speeds recovery.

Incident Command System (ICS): A standardized on-scene emergency management concept specifically designed to allow its user(s) to adopt an integrated organizational structure equal to the complexity and demands of single or multiple incidents without being hindered by jurisdictional boundaries. The national standard for ICS is provided by NIMS.

industrial agent: (CBRN Handbook) Chemicals developed or manufactured for use in industrial operations or research by industry, government, or academia. These chemicals are not primarily manufactured for the specific purpose of producing human casualties or rendering equipment, facilities, or areas dangerous for use by man. Hydrogen cyanide, cyanogen chloride, phosgene, chloropicrin and many herbicides and pesticides are industrial chemicals that also can be chemical agents.

INLA: Irish National Liberation Army based in Northern Ireland

insurgency: (JP 1-02, NATO) — An organized movement aimed at the overthrow of a constituted government through the use of subversion and armed conflict.

international: of, relating to, or affecting two or more nations (Webster's). For our purposes, affecting two or more nations.

IP address spoofing: A method that creates Transmission Control Protocol/Internet Protocol (TCP/IP) packets using somebody else's IP address

IRA: Irish Republican Army based in Northern Ireland

IMU: Islamic Movement of Uzbekistan

JEM: Jaish-e-Mohammed, a.k.a. Army of Mohammed based in Pakistan

JI: Jemaah Islamiya based in Malaysia and Singapore

Joint Field Office: (JFO) See National Response Plan.

JRA: Japanese Red Army, a.k.a. Anti-Imperialist International Brigade (AIIB) based in Lebanon and Japan

JUA: Jamiat ul-Ansar, a.k.a. Harakat ul-Mujahidin (HUM), and Movement of Holy Warriors

JUD: Jamaat ud-Dawa, a.k.a. Lashkar-e-Tayyiba, and Army of the Righteous (LT) based in Pakistan

JUM: Jamiat ul-Mujahidin based in Kashmir, India

KADEK: Kurdistan Freedom and Democracy Congress, a.k.a. Kongra-Gel (KGK), Kurdistan Workers' Party (PKK), and Freedom and Democracy Congress of Kurdistan based in Turkey

keylogger: A software program or hardware device that is used to monitor and log each of the keys a user types into a computer keyboard.

KGK: Kongra-Gel, a.k.a. Kurdistan Workers' Party (PKK), Kurdistan Freedom and Democracy Congress (KADEK), and Freedom and Democracy Congress of Kurdistan based in Turkey

KMM: Kumpulan Mujahidin Malaysia based in Malaysia

LFA: Lead Federal Agency. See NRP.

LJ: Lashkar I Jhangvi, a.k.a. Army of Jhangvi based in Pakistan

logic bomb: A program routine that destroys data by reformatting the hard disk or randomly inserting garbage into data files.

LRA: Lord's Resistance Army based in Uganda

LT: Lashkar-e-Tayyiba, a.k.a. Army of the Righteous and Jamaat ud-Dawa (JUD) based in Pakistan

LTTE: Liberation Tigers of Tamil Eelam, a.k.a. World Tamil Association (WTA), World Tamil Movement (WTM), Federation of Associations of Canadian Tamils (FACT), Ellalan Force, and Sangilian Force based in Sri Lanka

LVF: Loyalist Volunteer Force based in Northern Ireland

MAGO: Muslims Against Global Oppression, a.k.a. Qibla and People Against Gangsterism and Drugs (PAGAD), and Muslims Against Illegitimate Leaders (MAIL) based in South Africa

MAIL: Muslims Against Illegitimate Leaders, a.k.a. Muslims Against Global Oppression (MAGO), and Qibla and People Against Gangsterism and Drugs (PAGAD) based in South Africa

MCC: The Maoist Communist Center, a.k.a. Naxalites and Maoist Communist Center of India (MCCI) based in India

MCCI: Maoist Communist Center of India, a.k.a. The Maoist Communist Center (MCC) and Naxalites based in India

MEK: Mujahidin-e Khalq Organization, a.k.a. Holy Warriors of the People, National Liberation Army of Iran (NLA), People's Mujahidin of Iran (PMOI), National Council of Resistance (NCR), National Council of Resistance of Iran (NCRI), and Muslim Iranian Student's Society based in Iraq

> **millenarian**: Apocalyptic; forecasting the ultimate destiny of the world; foreboding imminent disaster or final doom; wildly unrestrained; ultimately decisive. (Merriam –Webster's)

MRTA: Tupac Amaru Revolutionary Movement based in Peru

narco-terrorism: (JP 3-07.4) Terrorism conducted to further the aims of drug traffickers. It may include assassinations, extortion, hijackings, bombings, and kidnappings directed against judges, prosecutors, elected officials, or law enforcement agents, and general disruption of a legitimate government to divert attention from drug operations.

nation: A community of people composed of one or more nationalities possessing a more or less defined territory and government or a territorial division containing a body of people of one or more nationalities usually characterized by relatively large size and independent status.

nation-state: A form of political organization under which a relatively homogeneous people inhabits a sovereign state; especially a state containing one as opposed to several nationalities.

NCR: National Council of Resistance, a.k.a. National Liberation Army of Iran (NLA), Mujahidin-e Khalq Organization (MEK), Holy Warriors of the People, People's Mujahidin of Iran (PMOI), National Council of Resistance of Iran (NCRI), and Muslim Iranian Student's Society based in Iraq

NCRI: National Council of Resistance of Iran, a.k.a. National Liberation Army of Iran (NLA), Mujahidin-e Khalq Organization (MEK), Holy Warriors of the People, People's Mujahidin of Iran (PMOI), National Council of Resistance (NCR), and Muslim Iranian Student's Society based in Iraq

nerve agents: (JP 1-02) A potentially lethal chemical agent which interferes with the transmission of nerve impulses.

National Incident Management System: (NIMS). See *National Incident Management System* published by the Department of Homeland Security, 1 March 2004. The NIMS represents a core set of doctrine, concepts, principles, technology and organizational processes to enable effective, efficient, and collaborative incident management. Nationwide context is an all-hazards, all jurisdictional levels, and multi-disciplines approach to incident management.

NIPR: Revolutionary Proletarian Initiative Nuclei based in Italy

NLA: National Liberation Army of Iran, a.k.a. Mujahidin-e Khalq Organization (MEK), Holy Warriors of the People, People's Mujahidin of Iran (PMOI), National Council of Resistance (NCR), National Council of Resistance of Iran (NCRI), and Muslim Iranian Student's Society based in Iraq

NPA: New People's Army based in the Philippines

National Response Plan (NRP): The *National Response Plan* is an all-discipline, all-hazards plan that establishes a single, comprehensive framework for the management of domestic incidents. It provides the structure and mechanisms for the coordination of Federal support to State, local, and tribal incident managers and for exercising direct Federal authorities ad responsibilities.

NTA: Anti-Imperialist Territorial Nuclei based in Italy

nuclear weapon: (JP 1-02) — A complete assembly (i.e., implosion type, gun type, or thermonuclear type), in its intended ultimate configuration which, upon completion of the prescribed arming, fusing, and firing sequence, is capable of producing the intended nuclear reaction and release of energy.

OPCON: Operational control, that is, transferable command authority. See Appendix H of terrorism handbook. (JP 1-02).

operations security: (OPSEC) A process of identifying critical information and subsequently analyzing friendly actions attendant to military operations and other activities to: a. Identify those actions that can be observed by adversary intelligence systems. b. Determine indicators hostile intelligence systems might obtain that could be interpreted or pieced together to derive critical information in time to be useful to adversaries. c. Select and execute measures that eliminate or reduce to an acceptable level the vulnerabilities of friendly actions to adversary exploitation. Also called OPSEC. (Joint Pub 1-02)

OV: Orange Volunteers based in Northern Ireland

PAGAD: Qibla and People Against Gangsterism and Drugs, a.k.a. Muslims Against Global Oppression (MAGO), and Muslims Against Illegitimate Leaders (MAIL) based in South Africa

Pathogen: (CBRN Handbook) Any organism (usually living) capable of producing serious disease or death, such as bacteria, fungi, and viruses

PFLP: The Popular Front for the Liberation of Palestine based in Syria

PFLP-GC: The Popular Front for the Liberation of Palestine – General Command based in Syria

physical security: That part of security concerned with physical measures designed to safeguard personnel; to prevent unauthorized access to equipment, installations, material and documents; and to safeguard them against espionage, sabotage, damage, and theft. (Joint Pub1-02)

PIJ: The Palestine Islamic Jihad based in Syria

PIRA: Provisional Irish Republican Army based in Northern Ireland

PKK: Kurdistan Workers' Party, a.k.a. Kongra-Gel (KGK), Kurdistan Freedom and Democracy Congress (KADEK), and Freedom and Democracy Congress of Kurdistan based in Turkey

PLF: Palestine Liberation Front based in Iraq

PMOI: People's Mujahidin of Iran, a.k.a. National Liberation Army of Iran (NLA), Mujahidin-e Khalq Organization (MEK), Holy Warriors of the People, National Council of Resistance (NCR), National Council of Resistance of Iran (NCRI), and Muslim Iranian Student's Society based in Iraq

Principle Federal Official: (PFO) Senior representative of Secretary of Homeland Security and lead Federal official on-scene to coordinate Federal domestic incidents management and resource allocation on-scene. See NRP.

PWG: Peoples War Group, a.k.a. Peoples War and Naxalites based in India

Radiological Dispersal Device: (RDD) (CBRN Handbook) A device (weapon or equipment), other than a nuclear explosive device, designed to disseminate radioactive material in order to cause destruction, damage, or injury by means of the radiation produced by the decay of such material.

Radiological Emitting Device: (RED) A device designed to disseminate radioactive material in order to cause destruction, damage, or injury by means of the radiation produced by the decay of such material. RED dissemination techniques can include intense, short duration exposure or progressive, long term exposure to radiation.

radiological operation: (JP 1-02) — The employment of radioactive materials or radiation producing devices to cause casualties or restrict the use of terrain. It includes the intentional employment of fallout from nuclear weapons.

RIRA: Real IRA, a.k.a. True IRA based in Northern Ireland

RHD: Red Hand Defenders based in Northern Ireland

RN: Revolutionary Nuclei based in Greece

RSRSBCM: Riyadus-Salikhin Reconnaissance and Sabotage Battalion of Chechen Martyrs based in Chechnya

RUF: Revolutionary United Front based in Sierra Leone

setback: Distance between outer perimeter and nearest point of buildings or structures within. Generally referred to in terms of explosive blast mitigation.

SL: Sendero Luminoso, a.k.a. Shining Path based in Peru

sniffer: A program and/or device that monitors data traveling over a network.

SPIR: Special Purpose Islamic Regiment based in Chechnya

SSP: Sipah-I-Sahaba/Pakistan based in Pakistan

state: A politically organized body of people usually occupying a definite territory; especially one that is sovereign.

steganography: The process of hiding information by embedding messages within other, seemingly harmless messages. The process works by replacing bits of useless or unused data in regular computer files (such as graphics, sound, text) with bits of different, invisible information. This hidden information can be plain text, cipher text, or images.

TACON: Tactical control, that is, command authority with detailed limitations and responsibilities inherent to operational control. See Appendix H of terrorism handbook. (JP 1-02).

TCG: The Tunisian Combatant Group, a.k.a. The Tunisian Islamic Fighting Group or Jama'a Combattante Tunisienne based in Tunisia

terror tactics: Given that the Army defines tactics as "the art and science of employing available means to win battles and engagements," then terror tactics should be considered "the art and science of employing violence, terror and intimidation to inculcate fear in the pursuit of political, religious, or ideological goals."

terrorism: (JP 1-02) — The calculated use of violence or threat of violence to inculcate fear; intended to coerce or to intimidate governments or societies in the pursuit of goals that are generally political, religious, or ideological.

terrorist: (JP 1-02) — An individual who uses violence, terror, and intimidation to achieve a result.

terrorist goals: The term *goals* will refer to the strategic end or end state that the terrorist objectives are intended to obtain. Terrorist organization goals equate to the strategic level of war as described in FM 101-5-1.

terrorist group: Any group practicing, or that has significant subgroups that practice, international terrorism (U.S. Dept of State)

terrorist objectives: The standard definition of *objective* is – "The clearly defined, decisive, and attainable aims which every military operation should be directed towards" (JP 1-02). For the purposes of this work, terrorist objectives will refer to the intended outcome or result of one or a series of terrorist operations or actions. It is analogous to the tactical or operational levels of war as described in FM 101-5-1.

toxin agent: (JP 1-02) — A poison formed as a specific secretion product in the metabolism of a vegetable or animal organism, as distinguished from inorganic poisons. Such poisons can also be manufactured by synthetic processes.

transnational: Extending or going beyond national boundaries (Webster's). In this context, not limited to or centered within a single nation.

trojan horse: A program or utility that falsely appears to be a useful program or utility such as a screen saver. However, once installed performs a function in the background such as allowing other users to have access to your computer or sending information from your computer to other computers.

virus: A software program, script, or macro that has been designed to infect, destroy, modify, or cause other problems with a computer or software program.

UDA/UFF: Ulster Defense Association/Ulster Freedom Fighters based in Northern Ireland

underground: A covert unconventional warfare organization established to operate in areas denied to the guerrilla forces or conduct operations not suitable for guerrilla forces.

unified command: As a term in the Federal application of the Incident Command System (ICS), defines agencies working together through their designated Incident Commanders at a single Incident Command Post (ICP) to establish a common set of objectives and strategies, and a single Incident Action Plan. This is NOT "unified command" as defined by the Department of Defense.

UVP: Ulster Defense Force based in Northern Ireland

UXO: Unexploded ordnance

VBIED: Vehicle borne improvised explosive device

WOT: War on terrorism

WTA: World Tamil Association, a.k.a. Liberation Tigers of Tamil Eelam (LTTE), World Tamil Movement (WTM), Federation of Associations of Canadian Tamils (FACT), Ellalan Force, and Sangilian Force based in Sri Lanka

WTM: World Tamil Movement, a.k.a. World Tamil Association (WTA), Liberation Tigers of Tamil Eelam (LTTE), Federation of Associations of Canadian Tamils (FACT), Ellalan Force, and Sangilian Force based in Sri Lanka

WCOTC: World Church of the Creator

WEG: Worldwide Equipment Guide. A document produced by the TRADOC G2 TRISA–Threats that provides the basic characteristics of selected equipment and weapons systems readily available for use by the OPFOR.

WMD: (JP 1-02) — Weapons of Mass Destruction. Weapons that are capable of a high order of destruction and/or of being used in such a manner as to destroy large numbers of people. Weapons of mass destruction can be high explosives or nuclear, biological, chemical, and radiological weapons, but exclude the means of transporting or propelling the weapon where such means is a separable and divisible part of the weapon.

WMD-CST: Weapons of Mass Destruction – Civil Support Team

WMD/E: Weapons of mass destruction or effect is an emergent term referenced in the 2004 U.S. National Military Strategy to address a broader range of adversary capabilities with potentially devastating results.

worm: A destructive software program containing code capable of gaining access to computers or networks and once within the computer or network causing that computer or network harm by deleting, modifying, distributing, or otherwise manipulating the data.

zombie: A computer or server that has been basically hijacked using some form of malicious software to help a hacker perform a Distributed Denial Of Service attack (DDOS).

Selected Bibliography

2004 Report on the Global AIDS Epidemic: Executive Summary. (Geneva: Joint United Nations Programme on HIV/AIDS, 2004), 5.

ABCNews.com, 18 October 2000. Available from http://www.abcnews.go.com/ sections/ world/DailyNews/cole001018b.html; Internet; Accessed 9 January 2003.

"Abu Nidal." *Encyclopedia of the Orient.* Available from http://i-cias.com/e.o/abu_nidal.htm; Internet; Accessed 24 February 2004.

"Abu Nidal Organization." *Terrorism Questions and Answers.* Available from http://cfrterrorism.org/groups/abunidal.html. Internet; Accessed 24 February 2004.

"Abu Nidal Organization (ANO)." *FAS Intelligence Resource Program.* Available from http://www.fas.org/irp/world/para/ano.htm; Internet; Accessed 24 February 2004.

"April 1983 US Embassy bombing." Available from http://encyclopedia.thefreedictionary.com/April%2011983%20US%20Embassy%20bombing; Internet; Accessed 1 July 2004

Albright, David. "Al Qaeda's Nuclear Program: Through the Window of Seized Documents." *Policy Forum Online* 47 (6 November 2002): 1-12. Available from http://www.nautilus.org/fora/Special-Policy-Forum/47_Albright.html; Internet; Accessed 13 February 2003.

Al-Qaeda in the Arabian Peninsula: Shooting, Hostage Taking, Kidnapping Wave – May/June 2004. (Alexandria: Tempest Publishing, LLC, 2004), 46-60.

"Al-Qaida raises Tempo of Video Releases." Available from http://www.iht.com/articles/ap/2007/06/01africa/ME-GEN- Al-Qaida-Video-Offensive.php; Internet; Accessed 4 June 2007.

Anderson, Sean K., and Stephen Sloan. *Historical Dictionary of Terrorism.* Lanham, MD: Scarecrow Press, Inc, 2002.

Arquilla, John and David Ronfeldt, ed. *Networks and Netwars.* Santa Monica: RAND, 2001.

BBC News, 21 December 1998. Available from http://news.bbc.co.uk/1/hi/special _report/1998/12/98/lockerbie/235632.stm; Internet; Accessed 12 December 2002.

BBC NEWS, "UK hostages describe Kuwait ordeal." Available from http://newsvote.bbc.co.uk/mpapps/pagetools/print/news.bbc.co.uk/2/hi/uk_news/politicsa/6...; Internet; Accessed 16 May 2007.

Beyler, Clara. "Messengers of Death – Female Suicide Bombers." *International Policy Institute for Counterterrorism* (12 February 2003): 3. Available from http://www.ict.org.il/articles/articledet.cfm?articleid=470; Internet; Accessed 18 March 2004.

Brook, Tom Vanden. "U.S. blames Iran for new bombs in iraq." 31 January 2007. Available from http://www.usatoday.com/news/world/iraq/2007-01-30-ied-iran_x.htm; Internet; Accessed 17 May 2007.

Billingslea, William. "Illicit Cigarette Trafficking and the Funding of Terrorism." *The Police Chief,* February 2004. 49-54.

Black, Andrew. "Al-Suri's Adaptation of fourth Generation Warfare Doctrine." *Global Terrorism Analysis,* The Jamestown Foundation, September 21, 2006. Available from http://www.jmaestown.org/terrorism/news/article.php?articleid=2370137; Internet; Accessed 1 November 2006.

Black, Cofer. "The International Terrorism Threat," Testimony before the House International Relations Committee, Subcommitteee on International Terrorism, Nonproliferation, and Human Rights. Washington, D.C., 26 March 2003; 6. Available from http://www.state.gov/s/ct/rls/rm/2003/19136.htm; Internet; Accessed 21 April 2005.

Bolkcom, Christopher, Bartholomew Elias, and Andrew Feickert. *Homeland Security: Protecting Airliners from Terrorist Missiles.* Washington, D.C.: Congressional Research Service Report for Congress, November 3, 2003. Available from http://www.fas.org/irp/crs/RL31741.pdf; Internet; Accessed 1 April 2004.

Bowman, Steve. *Weapons of Mass Destruction: The Terrorist Threat.* Washington, D.C.: Congressional Research Service Report for Congress, 7 March, 2002. Available from http://www.fas.org/irp/crs/RL31332.pdf; Internet; Accessed 23 December 2002.

Brown, Evelyn. "Creating stability in a world of unstable electricity distribution." Logos, 22, Spring 2004. Available from http://www.anl.gov/Media_Center/logos22-1/electricity.htm; Internet; Accessed 11 June 2007.

Buse, Margaret. "Non-State Actors and Their Significance." *Journal of Mine Action* (December 2002): 1-9. Available from http://maic.jmu.edu/journal/5.3/features/ maggie_buse_nsa/maggie_buse.htm; Internet; accessed 13 December 2002.

Carr, Caleb. *The Lessons of Terror: A History of Warfare Against Civilians: Why it has Always Failed and Why it will Fail Again.* New York: Random House, 2002.

Chalk, Peter. "Threats to the Maritime Environment: Piracy and Terrorism." RAND Stakeholder Consultation briefing presented at Ispra, Italy 28-30 October 2002. Available from http://www.rand.org/randeurope/news/seacurity/piracyterrorism.chalk.pdf; Internet; Accessed 4 April 2004.

Clark, C.J. *Mine/UXO Assessment: Former Yugoslav Republic of Macedonia.* New York: United Nations Mine Action Coordination Center, 8 October 2001. Available from http://www.mineaction.org/sp/mine_awareness/_refdocs.cfm?doc_ID=707; Internet; Accessed 13 December 2002.

CNN.com. "Official: Radicals wanted to create carnage at Fort Dix." Available from http://www.cnn.com/2007/US/05/08/fortdix.plot/index.html; Internet; Accessed 12 May 2007.

Conventional Terrorist Weapons. New York: United Nations Office for Drug Control and Crime Prevention, 2002. Available from http://www.undcp.org/odccp/terrorism _weapons_conventional.html; Internet; Accessed 12 November 2002.

Crenshaw, Martha. "The Logic of Terrorism: Terrorist Behavior as a Product of Strategic Choice." In *Origins of Terrorism: Psychologies, Ideologies, Theologies, States of Mind,* rev. ed., edited by Walter Reich. Washington: Woodrow Wilson Center Press, 1998.

Crumpton, Henry. "Remarks at Transnational Terrorism Conference." January 16, 2006. Available from http://www.state.gov/s/ct/rls/rm/2006/59987.htm; Internet; Accessed 12 August 2007.

Cyber-Terrorism. Statement by Major General James D. Bryan, U.S. Army Commander, Joint task Force-Computer Network Operations, U.S. Strategic Command and Vice Director, Defense Information Systems Agency. Washington, D.C., 24 July 2003, 5. Available from http://www.defenselink.mil/search97/s97is.vts?Action=FilterSearch&Filter=dl.hts&query=cyber-terrorism; Internet; Accessed 6 April 2004.

Dobson, Christopher, and Ronald Payne. *The Terrorist: Their Weapons, Leaders, and Tactics.* New York: Facts on File, Inc, Revised Edition, 1982.

Dolinar, Lou. "Cell Phones Jury-rigged to Detonate Bombs." *Newsday.com*, 15 March 2004. Available from http://www.newsday.com/news/nationworld/ny-wocell153708827mar15,0,1644248.story?coll=ny-nationworld-headlines; Internet; Accessed 15 March 2004.

Ehrenfeld, Rachael. *IRA + PLO + Terror.* Journal on-line. American Center for Democracy (ACD), 21 August 2002. Available from http://public-integrity.org/publications21.htm; Internet; Accessed 13 February 2004.

Esposito,Richard. "Terror Cell Targets," June 05, 2006. Available from http://images.google.com/imgres?imgurl...; Internet; Accessed 11 June 2007.

"Evidence Points to Yemen Terror Attack." CBS News.com [database on-line]. Available from http://www.cbsnews.com/stories/2002/10/06/world/main524488.shtml; Internet; Accessed 21 January 2004.

"Fact Sheet on the Accident at the Chernobyl Nuclear Power Plant." U.S. Nuclear Regulatory Commission, 1. Available at http://www.nrc.gov/reading-rm/doc-collections/fact-sheets/fschernobyl.html; Internet; Accessed 1 July 2004.

"Fatah Tricks 12-year-old Boy into becoming a Suicide Terrroist." 15 March 2004. Available from http://www.mfa.gov.il/MFA/Terrorism-+Obstacle+to+Peace/Terrorism+and+Islamic+Fund...; Internet; Accessed 8 June 2007.

"FBI Warns of growing Terrorist Threat from American-Based Islamic Extremists." Available from http://news.rgp.com/apps/pbcs.dll/article?AID=/20070513/NEWS18/705130372; Internet; Accessed 18 May 2007.

Fishman, Brian. *Zarqawi's Jihad.* Combating Terrorism Center at West Point, U.S. Military Academy. 26 April, 2006, 20.

Ford, Franklin L. *Political Murder: From Tyrannicide to Terrorism.* Cambridge: Harvard University Press, 1985.

Frances, Sabil. "Uniqueness of LTTE's Suicide Bombers." *Institute of Peace and Conflict Studies*, Article no. 321 (4 February 2000): 1. Available from http://www.ipcs.org; Internet; Accessed 7 September 2002.

Fuller, Fred L. "New Order Threat Analysis: A Literature Survey." *Marine Corps Gazette*, 81 (April 1997): 46-48.

Gamle, Kim. "Militants: stop hunt for U.S. soldiers." 14 May 2007. Available from http://news.yahoo.com/s/ap/20070514/ap_on_re_mi_ea/iraq&printer=1;ylt=ApG9r; Internet; Accessed 16 May 2007.

Greenberg, Maurice R., Chair; William F. Wechsler, and Lee S. Wolosky, Project Co-Directors. *Terrorist Financing: Report of an Independent Task Force Sponsored by the Council on Foreign Relations.* New York: Publication Office, Council on Foreign Relations, 25 November 2002.

"Group Profile, First Mechanical Kansas Militia." Available from http://www.tkb.org/Group.jsp?groupID=3418; Internet; Accessed 12 May 2007.

Gunaratna, Rohan. "Suicide Terrorism: A Global Threat." *Jane's Intelligence Review* (20 October 2000): 1-7. Available from http://www.janes.com/security/international _security/news/usscole/jir001020_1_n.shtml; Internet; Accessed 7 September 2002.

"Hamas." International Policy Institute for Counter-Terrorism, Profiles of International Terrorist Organizations, n.d., 5-6. Available from http://www.ict.org.il/inter_ter/orgdet.cfm?orgid=13; Internet; Accessed 26 April 2004.

Harmon, Christopher C. *Terrorism Today.* London: Frank Cass Publishers, 2000;Reprint, Portland: Frank Cass Publishers, 2001.

Hettena, Seth. "Earth Liberation Front Claims Responsibility for San Diego Arson." *The Mercury News*, 18 August 2003. Available from http://www.mercurynews.com/mld/mercurynews/news/local/6562462.htm; Internet; Accessed 17 March 2004.

Hill, Jim. "Sabotage Suspected in 'Terrorist' Derailment." *CNN.com.* 10 October 1995. Available from http://www.cnn.com/US/9510/amtrak/10-10/; Internet; Accessed 15 January 2003.

"History of Radiological Terrorism." *Introduction to Radiological Terrorism, 1 to 3*. Available from http://www.nti.org/h_learnmore/radtutorial/chapter03_01.html; Internet; Accessed 19 May 2004.

Hoffman, Bruce. *Inside Terrorism*. New York: Columbia University Press, 1998.

_____. *Insurgency and Counterinsurgency in Iraq*. Arlington: RAND Corporation, 2004.

Homer-Dixon, Thomas. "The Rise of Complex Terrorism." *Foreign Policy Magazine* 1, 6, and 7, January-Febraury 2002. Available from http:// www.foreighnpolicy.com/story/cms.php?story_id=170; Internet; Accessed 26 August 2004.

Huntington, Samuel."The Clash of Civilizations." *Foreign Affairs* (Summer 1993): 1-29. Available from http://www.lander.edu/atannenbaum/Tannenbaum%20courses%20folder/POLS%20103%20World%20Politics/103_huntington_clash_of_civilizations_full_text.htm#I.%20THE%20NEXT%20PATTERN%20OF%20CONFLICT; Internet; Accessed 6 December 2002.

"In My Humble Opinion: Genomics is the most important economic, political, and ethical issue facing mankind." *Fast Compan.*, November 1999. Available from http://www.fastcompany.com/online/29/jellis.html; Internet; Accessed 26 February 2004.

International Encyclopedia of Terrorism, 1997 ed., s.v. "The Media and International Terrorism."

_____. "Theories of Insurgency and Terrorism: Introduction."

Johnson, Anna. *"Al-Qaida video threatens attacks on U.S."* May 30, 2007. Available from http://www.buffalonews.com/260/story/87272.html; Internet; Accessed 11 June 2007.

Joint Chiefs of Staff. *National Military Strategy of the United States of America*. 1 May 2004.

Joint Chiefs of Staff, J5 War on Terrorism, Strategic Planning Division. Briefing (U) *The National Military Strategic Plan for the War on Terrorism (NMSP-WOT)*, Version 18 April 2005.

Joint Pub 1-02. *Department of Defense Dictionary of Military and Associated Terms*. 12 April 2001, as amended through 22 March 2007.

Joint Publication 3-0. *Joint Operations*. 17 September 2006.

Joint Pub 3-07.2. *Joint Tactics, Techniques, and Procedures for Antiterrroism*. 17 March 1998.

Juergensmeywer, Mark. *Terror in the Mind of God*. Berkeley and Los Angeles: University of California Press, 2000.

Kaplan, Robert. *The Coming Anarchy: Shattering the Dreams of the Post Cold War*. New York: Random House, 2000.

"Kashmir's Army Chief Fears Increased Suicide Attacks by Rebels." South Asia Monitor, 6 August 2003, 2. Available from http://www.southasiamonitor.org/focus/2003/july/24rebels.html; Internet; Accessed 20 April 2004.

Kepel, Gilles. *Jihad: The Trail of Political Islam*. Cambridge: The Belknap Press of Harvard University Press, 2002.

Krane, Jim. "U.S. Faces Complex Insurgency in Iraq." *Duluth News Tribune.com*. 4 October 2004. Available from http://www.duluthsuperior.com/mld/duluthsuperior/news/world/9833731.htm; Internet; Accessed 16 November 2004.

Larsen, Randall J. "Our Own Worst Enemy: Why Our Misguided Reactions to 9-11 Might Be America's Greatest Threat." *The Guardian*. April 2007.

Lasseter, Tom. "Suicide Attackers Strike Karbala," *Knight Ridder,* 27 December 2003. Available from http://www.realcities.com/mld/krwashington/news/special_packages/iraq/7581568.htm; Internet; Accessed 20 January 2004.

Liang, Qiao and Wang Xiangsui. *Unrestricted Warfare.* Translated by Department of State, American Embassy Beijing Staff Translators. Washington, D.C., 1999.

Long, David E. *The Anatomy of Terrorism.* New York: THE FREE PRESS, A Division of Macmillan, Inc., 1990.

Lowe, Alan C. "Todo o Nada: Montonerosa Versus the Army: Urban Terrorism in Argentina." In *Block by Block: The Challenges of Urban Operations,* ed. William G. Robertson and Lawrence A. Yates. Fort Leavenworth, KS: U.S. Army Command and General Staff College Press, 2003.

Manchester, William. *The Arms of Krupp.* Boston: Little, Brown, 1968.

"MANPADS Proliferation." Available from http://www.fas.org/asmp/campaigns/MANPADS/MANPADS.html; Internet; Accessed 11 June 2007.

Maples, Michael D. *Current and Projected National Security Threats to the United States.* Statement for the Record, Senate Select committee on Intelligence Committee, 11 January 2007. Washington, D.C.: Defense Intelligence Agency.

McGuire, Frank G., ed. *Security Intelligence Sourcebook, Including Who's Who in Terrorism.* Silver Spring, MD. : Interests, Ltd., 1990.

Merari, Ariel. "Terrorism as a Strategy of Insurgency." *Terrorism and Political Violence.* Vol 5, No. 4 Winter 1993.

Michel, Lou and Dan Herbeck. *American Terrorist: Timothy McVeigh and the Oklahoma City Bombing.* New York: Harper Collins Publishers Inc., 2001.

Moilanen, Jon H. "Engagement and Disarmament: A U.S. National Security Strategy for Biological Weapons of Mass Destruction." *Essays on Strategy XIII.* Washington, D.C.; National Defense University, 1996, 141-182.

Molnar, Andrew R. *See* DA Pamphlet 550-104.

Mueller, Robert. Statement Before the Senate Select Committee on Intelligence." January 11, 2007. Available from http://www.fbi.gov/congress/congress07/mueller011107.htm; Internet; Accessed 14 March 2007.

Murphy, Shelley. "White Supremacist Accused of Targeting D.C. Museum." *Globe,* 20 September 2001. Available from http://www.rickross.com/reference/supremacists/supremacists57.html; Internet; Accessed 16 February 2004.

"Murrah Federal Building Bombing." US Army TRADOC DCSINT Handbook No. 1, *Terror Operations: Case Studies in Terror.* Fort Leavenworth, KS: TRADOC Intelligence Support Activity-Threats, 10 August 2006.

Myre, Greg. "Palestinian Bomber, 14, Thwarted before Attack." *International Herald Tribune* March 2004: 1. Available from http://www.iht.com/articles/511745.html; Internet; Accessed 26 March 2004.

National Commission on Terrorist Attacks Upon the United States. Statement of Brian Jenkins to the Commission, March 31, 2003. Available from http://www.9-11commission.gov/hearings/hearing1/witness_jenkins.htm; Internet; Accessed 23 September 2004.

National Counterterrorism Center (NCTC). *Reports on Terrorism Incidents – 2006.* 30 April 2007. Available from http://www.terrorisminfo.mipt.org/Patterns-of-global-terrorism.asp; Internet; Accessed 2 May 2007.

National Security Institute. *Homeland Security Warns about Vehicle Bombs.* (Medway, MA, n.d.), 1-4. Available from http://nsi.org/Library/Terrorism/Vehicle_Bombs.doc; Internet; Accessed 14 January 2004.

"NCTC Revises, Raises Terror Incident List From 2004." 6 July 2005. Available from http://www,foxnews,com/printer_friendly_story/0,3566,161645,00.html; Internet; Accessed 6 July 2005.

Newman, Bob. "Terrorists Feared to Be Planning Sub-Surface Naval Attacks." *CNS News.com,* 3 December 2002. Available from http://www.cnsnews.com/ForeignBureaus/archive/200212/FOR20021203a.html; Internet; Accessed 19 March 2004.

"Nigeria Gunmen Seize Six Foreigners." Available from http://www.cnn.com/2007/WORLD/Africa/06/03/Nigeria.kidnap.reut/; Internet; Accessed 5 June 2007.

Olson, Kyle B. "Aum Shinrikyo: Once and Future Threat?" *Emerging Infectious Diseases.* 4, July-August 1999.

Ong, Graham Gerard. "Next Stop, Maritime Terrorism." *Viewpoints* (12 September 2003): 1-2. Available from http://www.iseas.edu.sg/viewpoint/ggosep03.pdf; Internet; Accessed 2 April 2004.

Online NewsHour.pbs.org., "Deadly Day." Available from http://www.pbs.org/newshour/bb/middle_east/july-dec04/mosul_12-22.html; Internet; Accessed 17 May 2007.

"Osama's Satellite Phone Switcheroo." *CBS News.com.* 21 January 2003, 1. Available from http://www.cbsnews.com/stories/2003/01/21/attack/main537258.shtml; Internet; accessed 10 February 2003.

"Palestinain Textbooks Incite hatred, US Funds Terror-Center Schools." 6 March 2007. Available from http://www.justsixdays.co.uk/isblog/; Internet; Accessed 12 March 2007.

Pawle, Gerald. *Secret Weapons of World War II.* New York: Ballantine Books, 1967.

Perl, Raphael. *Terrorism and National Security: Issues and Trend.* Washington, D.C.: Congressional Research Service Issue Brief for Congress, 22 December 2003.

Phillips, Thomas D. "The Dozier Kidnapping: Confronting the Red Brigades." *Air & Space Power Chronicles* (February 2002): 1. Available from http://www.airpower.maxwell/af.mil/airchronicles/cc/phillips.html; Internet; Accessed 31 March 2004.

Philpott, Don. "The Future of Terrorism Task Force." *Homeland Defense Journal.* April 2007, 16-20.

"Plague." *CDC Plague Home Page.* Available from http://www.cdc.gov/ncidod/dvbid/plague/index.htm; Internet; Accessed 9 July 2004.

Popenker, Max R. *Modern Firearms and Ammunition.* [Encyclopedia online]. N.p., n.d. Available from http://world.guns.ru/main-e.htm#md; Internet; Accessed 31 October 2002.

Prados, Alfred B. Congressional Research Service (CRS) Issue Brief for Congress. *Saudi Arabia: Current Issues and U.S. Relations*, 15 September 2003. Order Code IB93113.

Presley, Steven. *Rise of Domestic Terrorism and Its Relation to United States Armed Forces.* [Abstract] April 1996. Available from http://www.fas.org/irp/eprint/presley.htm; Internet; Accessed 12 may 2007.

"Preventing Terrorist Attacks on U.S. Soil." April 9, 2004. Available from http://www.fbi.gov/page2/april04/040904krar.htm; internet; Accessed 17 May 2007.

Rapoport, David C., ed. *Inside Terrorist Organizations*. New York: Columbia University Press, 1988.

Raufer, Xavier. "New World Disorder, New Terrorisms: New Threats for the Western World." In *The Future of Terrorism*, edited by Max. Taylor and John Horgan. Portland: Frank Cass Publishers, 2000.

Reid, Robert H. "Search for missing soldiers intensifies.' 15 May 2007. Available from http://news.yahoo.com/s/ap/20070515/ap_on_re_mi_ea/iraq&printer=1;_ylt+AujoSQGJ62...; Internet; Accessed 16 May 2007.

Reich, Walter, ed. *Origins of Terrorism: Psychologies, Ideologies, Theologies, States of Mind.* Rev. ed. Washington: Woodrow Wilson Center Press, 1998.

"Revolutionary Organization 17 November (17N)." CDI Terrorism Project, 5 August 2002. Available from http://www.cdi.org/terrorism/17N-pr.cfm; Internet; Accessed 24 September 2004.

Richardson, Michael. "A Time Bomb for Global Trade: Maritime-related Terrorism in an Age of Weapons of Mass Destruction." *Viewpoints* (25 February 2004): 8. Available from http://www.iseas.edu.sg/viewpoint/mricsumfeb04.pdf; Internet; Accessed 5 April 2004.

Robinson, Colin. *Military and Cyber-Defense: Reactions to the Threat* Washington: Center for Defense Information Terrorism Project, 2002. Available from http://www.cdi.org/terrorism/cyberdefense-pr.cfm; Internet; Accessed 24 June 2004.

Ross, Brian and Richard Esposito and Chris Isham. "U.S., Germans Fear Terror Attack." 11 May 2007. Available from http://blogs.abcnews.com/theblotter/2007/05/us_germans_fear.html; Internet; Accessed 17 May 2007.

"Saboteurs Disable Critical Iraqi Oil Pipeline." *HoustonChronicle.com.* 8 September 2003. Available from http://www.chron.com/cs/CDA/ssistory.mpl/special/iraq/2087438; Internet; Accessed 16 January 2004.

Schoomaker, Peter. Army Chief of Staff, "CSA Interview: Joint and Expeditionary Capabilities." (Washington, D.C.: Pentagon, 4 October, 2004). Available from http://www.army.mil/leaders/leaders/csa/interviews/04Oct04.html; Internet; Accessed 11 January 2005.

Schuurman, Jan. *Tourists or Terrorists?* Press review on-line. Radio Netherlands, 25 April 2002. Available from http://www.rnw.nl/hotspots/html/irel020425.html; Internet; Accessed 13 February 2004.

Schweitzer, Yoram. "Suicide Terrorism: Development and Main Characteristics." In *Countering Suicide Terrorism.* Herzilya, Israel: The International Policy Institute for Counter Terrorism, The Interdisciplinary Center, 2002.

Shanker, Thom. "Officials Reveal Threat to Troops Deploying to Gulf." *New York Times.* 13 January 2003. Available from http://www.nytimes.com/2003/01/13/politics/13INTE.html; Internet; Accessed 13 January 2003.

Sindlelar, Daisy. "Iraq: U.S. Military Investigating Deadly Mosul Blast." Available from http://www.rferl.org/featuresarticleprint/2004/12/17fac095-a36d-4a0e-abs9-635ee3e12ee3...; Internet; Accessed 17 May2007.

SITE Institute. "Abu Musab al-Suri Outlines Strategy for Attacks Against America, Britain, Russia, and NATO Countries." July , 13, 2005. Available from http://siteinstitute.org/bin/articles.cgi?ID=publications67905&Category=publications&Subcategory=0; Internet; Accessed 11 June 2007.

Small Wars Journal. "SWJ Blog: Luttwak's Lament."Available from http://smallwarsjournal.com/blog/2007/04/luttwaks-lament/; Internet; Accessed 12 May 2007.

Sprinzak, Ehud. "Rational Fanatics." *Foreign Policy,* no. 120 (September/October 2000): 66-73.

Stahl, Julie. "Palestinian Kindergarten Graduates Vow to Die for Allah." 1 June 2007. Available from http://www.memritv.org/search.asp?ACT=S9&P1=1468; Internet; Accessed 5 June 2007.

Statement Before the 107th [U.S.] Congress, Chairman of the Joint Chiefs of Staff, Senate Armed Services Committee. May 3, 2001.[database on-line] Available from http://www.dtic.mil/jcs/chairman/3MAY01_SASC_CJCS.htm; Internet; Accessed 18 February 2004.

"Suicide Terrorism." *The Economist* (January 2004): 3. Available from http://quicksitebuilder.cnet.com/supfacts/id396.html; Internet; Accessed 17 March 2004.

"Suicide Terrorism: a Global Threat." *Jane's Intelligence Review* (October 2000): 1, 4-5. Available from http://www.janes.com/security/international_security/news/usscole/jir001020_1_n.shtml; Internet; Accessed 20 January 2004.

"Terrorists Demand Extortion Cash in Euros." *TCM Breaking News* (September 2001): 1. Available from http://archives.tcm.ie/breakingnews/2001/09/04/story22584.asp; Internet; Accessed 31 March 2004.

Thachuck, Kimberly L. "Terrorism's Financial Lifeline: Can it Be Severed." *Strategic Forum* no. 191 (May 2002): 1-15. Available from http://www.ndu.edu/inss/strforum/sf191.htm; Internet; Accessed 29 August 2002.

"The Architect and Fifth Generation Warfare." June 4, 2006. Available from http://www.thestrategist.org/archives/2006/06/the_architect_o.html; Internet; Accessed 13 March 2007.

"The Asymmetric Threat From Maritime Terrorism." Available from http://jfs.janes.com/public/jfs/additional_info.shtml; Internet; Accessed 2 February 2004.

The Madrid Agenda, Club de Madrid. Available from http://www.clubmadrid.org/cmadrid; Internet; Accessed 26 April 2005.

"The Terrorism Maritime Threat." United Press International. 2 December 2003. [Militarycom database on-line]; Internet; Accessed 21 January 2004.

"The Unibomber Manifesto." Available from http://www.ed.brocku.ca/~rahul/Misc/unibomber.html; Internet; Accessed 30 May 2007.

The White House. *National Strategy for Combating Terrorism.* Washington, D.C. February 2003. Available from http://www.state.gov/s/ct/rls/rm/2003/17798.htm; Internet; Accessed 8 December 2003.

The White House, *The National Strategy for the Physical Protection of Critical Infrastructure and Key Assets.* Washington, D.C., February 2003. Preface by The President of the United States of America. Available from http://www.whitehouse.gov/pcipb/physical_strategy.pdf; Internet; Accessed 8 December 2003.

The White House. *The National Security Strategy of the United Sates of America,* 1, 17 September 2002. Available at http://www.whitehouse.gov/nsc/nss.html; Internet; Accessed 30 April 2004.

The White House. *The National Strategy to Secure Cyberspace.* Washington, D.C., February 2003. Preface by The President of the United States of America. Available from http://www.whitehouse.gov/pcipb/cyberspace_strategy.pdf; Internet; Accessed 8 December 2003.

Thompson, Don. "British Ecoterror Tactics Spread to U.S. Activists." *The Mercury News.* 10 May 2003. Available from http://www.mercurynews.com/mld/mercurynews/news/local/5832723.htm?1c; Internet; Accessed 21 April 2004.

Title 28. Code of Federal Regulations, Section 0.85. *Judicial Administration.* Washington, D.C. July 2001.

Truby, J. David. *How Terrorists Kill: The Complete Terrorist Arsenal.* Boulder: Paladin Press, 1978.

"Two soldiers die as another U.S. military helicopter goes down in Iraq." Available from http://www.today.com/news/world/iraq/2007-202-02-sectarian-violence_x.htm; Internet; Accessed 11 June 2007.

United Nations, Office on Drugs and Crime. "Definitions of Terrorism." Available from http://www.unodc.org/unodc/terrorism_definitions.html; Internet; Accessed 11 May 2007.

United Nations. "United Nations General Assembly Adopts Global Counter-Terrorism Strategy." Available from http://www.un.org/terrorism/strategy-counter-terrorism.html; Internet; Accessed 31 May 2007.

U.S. Air Force. *Independent Review of the Khobar Towers Bombing, Part A* (31 October 1996) by Lieutenant General James F. Record. Available from http://www.fas.org/irp/threat/khobar_af/recordf.htm; Internet; Accessed 9 February 2004.

U.S. Army Field Manual 3-06. *Urban Operations*, Washington, D.C.: Headquarters, Department of the Army. 1 June 2003.

U.S. Army Field Manual 3-24. *Counterinsurgency.* Washington, D.C.: Headquarters, Department of the Army. December 2006.

U.S. Army Training and Doctrine Command, TRADOC G2 TRADOC Intelligence Support Activity (TRISA) White Paper. *The Contemporary Operational Environment*, July 2007.

U.S. Army Field Manual FM 7-100, *Opposing Force Doctrinal Framework and Strategy,* May 2003, iv to xvi.

U.S. Congress. House. Armed Services Subcommittee on Terrorism, Unconventional Threats and Capabilities. *Cyber-Terrorism.* Statement by Major General James D. Bryan, U.S. Army Commander, Joint task Force-Computer Network Operations, U.S. Strategic Command and Vice Director, Defense Information Systems Agency. Washington, D.C., 24 July 2003. Available from http://www.defenselink.mil/search97/s97is.vts? Action=FilterSearch&Filter=dl.hts&query=cyber-terrorism; Internet; Accessed 6 April 2004.

U.S. Congress. House. Resources Subcommittee on Forests and Forest Health. *The Threat of Eco-Terrorism.* Statement by the FBI's Domestic Terrorism Section Chief, James Jarboe. Washington, D.C., 12 February 2002. Available from http://www.fbi.gov/ congress/congress02/jarboe021202.htm; Internet; Accessed 17 January 2003.

U.S. Congress. Senate. Armed Services Committee. *SASC Cole Commission Testimony: Hearing before the Armed Services Committee.* 107th Cong. 3 May 2001. Comments by Chairman of the Joint Chiefs of Staff.

U.S. Congress. Senate. Judiciary Subcommittee on Terrorism, Technology, and Homeland Security, Cyber *Terrorism.* Testimony of Keith Lourdeau, Deputy Assistant Director, Cyber Division, FBI, Washington, D.C., 24 February 2004, 3. Available from http://www.fbi.gov/congress/congress04/lourdeau022404.htm; Internet; Accessed 15 April 2004.

U.S. Department of Agriculture. "Final BSE Update – Monday, February 9, 2004." Newsroom Release Statement No. 0074.04. Available from http://www.usda.gov/Newsroom/0074.04.html; Internet; Accessed 12 July 2004.

U.S. Department of Commerce. National Institute of Standards and Technology, *Risk Management Guide for Information Technology Systems,* NIST Special Publication 800-30, by Gary Stoneburner, Alice Goguen, and Alexis Feringa. Washington, D.C., 2001: 22. Available from http://csrc.nist.gov/publications/nistpubs/800-30/sp800-30.pdf; Internet; Accessed 12 April 2004.

U.S. Department of Defense. "A Global Terror Group Primer," by Jim Garamone. *Defense Link* (14 February 2002): 1-7. Available from http://www.defenselink.mil/news/ Feb2002/n02142002_200202141.html; Internet; Accessed 29 August 2002.

U.S. Department of Defense, Defense Science Board, *Defense Science Board Task Force on The Role and Status of DoD Red Teaming Activities,* (Washington, D.C.: Office of the Under Secretary of Defense for Acquisition, Technology, and Logistics, September 2003).

U.S. Department of Defense. Defense Security Service, Technology Collection Trends in the U.S. Defense Industry 2002. Alexandria, VA, n.d. Available from http://www.wright.edu/rsp/Security/TechTrends.pdf; Internet; Accessed 19 April 2004.

U.S. Department of Defense. *DoD USS Cole Commission Report* (9 January 2001) by U.S. Army Gen. (Ret) William Crouch and U.S. Navy Adm. (Ret) Harold Gehman. Open-File Report, U.S. Department of Defense. 1 (Washington, D.C., 9 January 2001). Available at http://www.fas.org/irp/threat/cole.html; Internet; Accessed 16 February 2004.

U.S. Department of Defense. Naval Explosive Ordnance Disposal Technology Division. *ORDATA II - Enhanced Deminers' Guide to UXO Identification, Recovery, and Disposal,* Version 1.0, [CD-ROM]. Indian Head, MD: Naval Explosive Ordnance Disposal Technology Division, 1999.

U.S. Department of Defense. News Release Archive. "DoD News: Navy Announces Results of Its Investigation on USS Cole." Available from http://www.defenselink.mil/releases/2001/b011192001_bt031-01.html; Internet; Accessed 11 February 2004.

U.S. Department of Defense. *Report of the Assessment of the Khobar Towers Bombing* (30 August 1996) Letter by General (USA Retired) Wayne A. Downing. Available from http://www.fas.org/irp/threat/downing/downltr.html; Internet; Accessed 10 February 2004.

U.S. Department of Defense. *Report of the Assessment of the Khobar Towers Bombing* (30 August 1996) by General (USA Retired) Pre by Wayne A. Downing. Available from http://www.fas.org/irp/threat/downing/prefuncl.html; Internet; Accessed 10 February 2004.

U.S. Department of Defense. *Report of the Assessment of the Khobar Towers Bombing* (30 August 1996) by General (USA Retired) Rpt by Wayne A. Downing. Available from http://www.fas.org/irp/threat/downing/unclf913.html; Internet; Accessed 9 February 2004.

U.S. Department of Defense. *Report to Congress on The Role of the Department of Defense in Supporting Homeland Security.* Washington, D.C., September 2003.

U.S. Department of Defense. *Report on Personal Accountability for Force Protection at Khobar Towers*, by William S. Cohen. Washington, D.C., July 31, 1997.

U.S. Department of Defense. Report to the President. *The Protection of U.S. Forces Deployed Abroad* (15 September 1996) by Secretary of Defense William J. Perry. Available from http://www.fas.org/irp/threat/downing/report_f.html; Internet; Accessed 18 February 2004.

U.S. Department of Defense. *Special Briefing on the Unified Command Plan*, by Donald H. Rumsfeld. Department of Defense News Briefing Transcript presented at the Pentagon, Wednesday, 17 April 2002 – 11:30a.m. Available from http://www.defenselink.mil/ news/Apr2002/t04172002_t0417sd.html; Internet; Accessed 18 November 2002.

U.S. Department of Defense. *The National Defense Strategy of the United States of America.* (Washington, D.C.: GPO, 1 March 2005).

U.S. Department of Defense. Threat Support Directorate TRADOC DCSINT. *OPFOR Worldwide Equipment Guide.* Fort Leavenworth, KS, 24 September 2001.

U.S. Department of Defense. U.S. Marine Corps. Marine Corps University. Corporals Noncommissioned Officers Program. *Force Protection.* Quantico, VA, January 1999.

U.S. Department of Homeland Security, Homeland Security Advisory Council. *Report of the Future of Terrorism Task Force.* January 2007.

U.S. Department of Justice, Federal Bureau of Investigation, Counterterrorism Division. *Terrorism 2000/2001.* Report 0308, Washington, D.C. 2004.

U.S. Department of Justice. Federal Bureau of Investigation. Counterterrorism Threat Assessment and Warning Unit. Counterterrorism Division. *Terrorism in the United States 1999.* Report 0308. Washington, D.C., n.d.

U.S. Department of State, Bureau of Political-Military Affairs and Bureau of International Security and Nonproliferation. "The MANPADS Menace: Combating the Threat to Global Aviation from Man-Portable Air Defense Systems," September 20, 2005. Available from http://www.sate.gov/t/pm/rls/fs/53558.htm; Internet; Accessed 11 June 2007.

U.S. Department of State. *Country Reports on terrorism 2006.* April 2007. Available from http://www.terrorisminfo.mipt.org/Patterns-of-global-terrorism.asp; Internet; Accessed 2 May 2007.

U.S. Department of State. Office of the Coordinator for Counterterrorism. *Country Reports on Terrorism 2004,* Washington, D.C., April 2005.

U.S. Department of State. Office of the Coordinator for Counterterrorism. *Country Reports on Terrorism 2005,* Washington, D.C., April 2006.

U.S. Department of State. Office of the Coordinator for Counterterrorism. *Country Reports on Terrorism 2006,* Washington, D.C., April 2007.

U.S. Department of State. Office of the Coordinator for Counterterrorism. *Patterns of Global Terrorism 2001.* Washington, D.C., May 2002.

U.S. Department of State. Office of the Coordinator for Counterterrorism. *Patterns of Global Terrorism 2002.* Washington, D.C., 2003.

U.S. Department of State. Office of the Coordinator for Counterterrorism. *Patterns of Global Terrorism 2004.* Washington, D.C., 2004, revised 22 June 2004.

U.S. Department of State. U.S. Embassy, Jakarta, Indonesia. *Threats Involving Vehicle Borne Improvised Explosive Devices.* Jakarta, Indonesia, 2003, 2. Available from http://www.usembassyjakarta.org/vbied_vehicles.html; Internet; Accessed 14 January 2004.

U.S. Joint Chiefs of Staff, Joint Publication 3-07.2, *Antiterrorism,* 14 April 2006.

U.S. Joint Chiefs of Staff, J5 War on Terrorism, Strategic Planning Division. Briefing (U) *Countering Ideological Support for Terrorism.* Version 19Jan05, 5 April 2005.

U.S. Joint Chiefs of Staff, J5 War on Terrorism, Strategic Planning Division. Briefing (U) *The National Military Strategic Plan for the War on Terrorism (NMSP-WOT.* Version 18 April 2005.

U.S. Marine Corps, Marine Corps University, Corporals Noncommissioned Officers Program. Force Protection, Course CPL 0302. Quantico, VA, January 1999, Available from http://www.tecom.usmc.mil/utm/Force_Protection1_LP.PDF; Internet; Accessed 31 March 2004.

U.S. National Counterterrorism Center (NCTC), *Reports on Incidents of Terrorism 2005,* 11 April 2006.

U.S. Title 28. Code of Federal Regulations. Section 0.85. *Judicial Administration.* Washington, D.C., July 2001.

"Unraveling Al-Qaeda's Target Selection Calculus." April 17, 2007. Available from http://cns.miis.edu/pubs/week/070417.htm; Internet; Accessed 15 May 2007.

Van Creveld, Martin L. *The Transformation of War.* New York: The Free Press, 1991.

Venzke, Ben N. *Al-Qaeda Targeting Guidance – v1.0, Thursday 1 April 2004.* Alexandria: IntelCenter/Tempest Publishing, 2004.

_____. *The al-Qaeda Threat: An Analytical Guide to al-Qaeda's Tactics and Targets.* Alexandria: Tempest Publishing, LLC, 2003, 36, quoting Abu 'Ubeid al-Qurashi, "The Nightmares of America, 13 February 2002.

von Clausewitz, Karl. *War, Politics and Power.* Chicago: Regnery Gateway, 1962.

Vinocur, John. "Bomb Attempt on Gen. Haig's Life Not Tied to Major Terrorist Groups." *New York Times*, 27 June 1979.

_____. "U.S. General Safe in Raid in Germany." *New York Times*. 16 September 1981.

Wasielewski, Philip G. "Defining the War on Terror." *Joint Force Quarterly*. 44, 1st Quarter 2007,

Williscroft, Robert G. "The Economics of Demining Defines Success and Failure." *Defense Watch* February 13, 2002: 1-17. Available from http://www.sftt.org/ dw02132002.html; Internet; Accessed 13 December 2002.

Woolsey, R. James. "Intelligence and the War on Terrorism." *The Guardian.* 9, April 2007.

This Page Intentionally Blank

DCSINT Handbook No.1 *A Military Guide to Terrorism in the Twenty-First Century,* Version 5.0
U.S. Army Training and Doctrine Command, TRADOC G2
TRADOC Intelligence Support Activity (TRISA) - Threats, Fort Leavenworth, Kansas